INTERPERSONAL SKILLS AT WORK

Second edition

John Hayes

First published 2002
by Routledge
27 Church Road, Hove, East Sussex, BN3 2FA

Simultaneously published in the USA and Canada
by Routledge
29 West 35th Street, New York, NY 10001

Routledge is an imprint of the Taylor & Francis Group

© 2002 John Hayes

The author asserts the moral right to be identified as the author of this work

Typeset in Sabon by M Rules, London
Printed and bound in Great Britain by
TJ International Ltd, Padstow, Cornwall
Cover design by Jim Wilkie

British Library Cataloguing-in-Publication Data
A catalogue record for this book is available from the British Library

ISBNs 0-415-22775-5 (hbk)
0-415-22776-3 (pbk)

INTERPERSONAL SKILLS AT WORK

In this age of e-business, many of us over-rely on electronic communication and pay insufficient attention to the management of face-to-face relationships. John Hayes addresses this issue by examining the nature of interpersonal skills – the goal-directed behaviours that we use in face-to-face interactions in order to achieve desired outcomes. He argues that interpersonal competence is a key factor that distinguishes between successful and unsuccessful managers.

Interpersonal Skills At Work provides a clearly structured and comprehensive overview of the interpersonal skills that are essential for effective functioning at work. It presents a micro-skills approach to skill development that can be used to improve interpersonal competence, as well as explaining through the use of illustrations and practical examples how to read the actual or potential behaviour of others around us. This knowledge can then be used to guide the way in which we relate to others as we learn to manage our relationships more effectively.

This book will be ideal for practising managers and students of business and management studies and psychology. The skills it promotes ensure that it will also be of great value to a wide range of people including teachers, doctors, nurses, social workers and police officers in their everyday working environment.

John Hayes is Professor of Management, Associate Dean for Learning and Teaching and Director for the Centre for Organisational Behaviour Research and Analysis (COBRA) at Leeds University Business School. He has published nine books and over sixty papers on career development, interpersonal skills, processes of change in organisations and cognitive style.

TO SARAH
daughter, friend and mentor

CONTENTS

ILLUSTRATIONS

Figures

Tables

Exercises

PREFACE

In this age of e-business many of us over-rely on electronic communication, and pay insufficient attention to the management of face-to-face relationships. *Interpersonal Skills At Work* addresses this problem.

Interpersonal competence depends upon our ability to understand and manage the dynamics of social interaction. We require both diagnostic and action skills. We need to be able to read behaviour and act in ways that will bring about desired outcomes.

This book provides a clearly structured and comprehensive overview of the interpersonal skills required for effective functioning at work and presents a micro-skill approach to skill development. An important feature of the book is the inclusion of a wide range of exercises designed to help us monitor our own behaviour, identify areas for improvement and practise new ways of relating to others.

1

THE NATURE OF
INTERPERSONAL SKILLS
A historical perspective

Learning objective

To understand the nature of interpersonal skills from a historical perspective
and to develop a critical appreciation of the different approaches that have
been applied to the study of social interaction.

After reading this chapter you will:

- Be able to define interpersonal skill, and recognise that it involves the use
  of goal-directed behaviours to achieve desired outcomes.
- Be able to compare and contrast the behavioural and cognitive
  approaches to studying social interaction.
- Understand the difference between those behavioural approaches that
  restrict attention to observable behaviours and those behavioural
  approaches that pay attention to the intention that lies behind the behaviour.
- Be aware of how cognitive processes influence behaviour and how social
  interaction may be viewed as a transaction in which each interactor is
  seeking a satisfactory outcome.

Introduction

This chapter provides a review of the different theories and methodologies
that have been applied to the study of interpersonal interaction. Particular
attention is focused on cognitive models that view interpersonal interaction
as a transaction between parties who are each seeking satisfactory outcomes
for themselves. The importance of feedback for managing and improving
performance in response to the reactions of self and others is also
highlighted.

Chapter 2 outlines a hierarchical model of interpersonal skill and a micro-
skills approach to training that provides the conceptual framework for the
approach to skill development presented in this book.

The effect of behaviour on goal achievement

We spend a considerable part of our working day relating to others. One of the findings of the early work activity studies, echoed more recently by Oshagbemi (1988), is that we consistently underestimate the amount of time we spend in face-to-face interaction. There are also indications that we underestimate seriously the effect our behaviour has on the way others behave, and therefore on the achievement of personal and organisational goals.

Simple examples may serve to illustrate this point.

Selection interviewers need to obtain from applicants as much relevant information as possible in order to determine which applicant will be most suitable for the job. To achieve this end they need to manage the interaction in a way that encourages each applicant to provide the maximum amount of relevant and the minimum amount of irrelevant information. This objective is likely to be frustrated if the interviewers do most of the talking. It will also be frustrated if they prevent applicants from giving full answers by overusing the kinds of questions that limit their responses to yes or no, or if they ask questions in a way that prompts them into giving the answer which they think the interviewers want to hear.

In negotiations, there is evidence that negotiators' opening bids have an important influence on the expectations of opponents and that this can affect the outcome. There is also evidence that, in competitive negotiations, concessions are more likely to be reciprocated when the person offering the concession is perceived by opponents to be in a relatively strong position. It is possible for a negotiator to create this impression by behaving in certain ways.

In decision-making groups, one of the factors which can influence the quality of a decision is the extent to which the knowledge and skills of group members are applied to the task. Some of this task-relevant knowledge may not be available to the group because some knowledgeable but non-assertive members of the group lack the confidence to make their views known, or because some members fail to pay attention or give appropriate weight to the views of others. The person who is able to recognise what is happening, and who can use this awareness to intervene, to act consciously in ways that make it more likely that relevant knowledge will be applied to the task, can make an important contribution to improving group performance.

The importance of interpersonal skills

One of the most widely used definitions of management is getting things done through people. Mangham (1986) argues that a person's success as a manager depends upon the ability to conduct oneself in the complexity of the organisation as a subtle, insightful, incisive performer. He goes on to suggest that successful managers appear to have a natural and/or highly developed ability to read the actual and potential behaviour of others around them and to construct their own conduct in accordance with this reading. This is an ability we all have but, according to Mangham, 'the most successful among us appear to do social life with a higher degree of skill than the rest of us manage'.

Interpersonal skills as goal-directed behaviours

'Interpersonal skill' is one of a number of broadly similar terms that are sometimes used interchangeably. Other such terms include interactive skills, people skills, face-to-face skills, social skills and social competence.

Argyle (1984) defines socially competent people as those who possess the skills necessary to produce desired effects on other people in social situations. These desired effects may include persuading somebody to work harder, make a purchase, make a concession in a negotiation, be impressed by one's expertise or support one in a crisis.

Honey (1988) offers a similar definition. He refers to interactive skills as the skills people use in face-to-face encounters to arrange their behaviour so that it is in step with their objectives. He emphasises the point that interactive skills have very little to do with being nice or winning friends unless these sorts of outcomes are encapsulated in the individual's objectives.

A common theme in these definitions is the ability to behave in ways that increase the probability of achieving desired outcomes. It therefore seems appropriate to define interpersonal skills as goal-directed behaviours used in face-to-face interactions in order to bring about a desired state of affairs.

Approaches to the study of interpersonal interaction

The study of interpersonal skills and interpersonal relationships is multidisciplinary and, at one level, each discipline has tended to focus attention on different contexts and different kinds of relationship. In the management literature, relationships with bosses, subordinates, peers, customers and suppliers receive considerable attention whereas in the education literature, the focus is on the teacher–pupil relationship and in the social work literature, marital, family and similar relationships tend to be the focus of attention. Berscheid (1994) observes that this has led to a situation where the matrix of interpersonal relationship knowledge is fractured along the lines of relationship type. Even within the context of a particular relationship type, the study of interpersonal skills has been influenced by a rich array of conceptual approaches.

Behavioural approaches

One approach to the study of interpersonal interaction restricts attention to observable behaviour, but there are differences even within this broad approach.

At one end of the scale there are investigators (e.g. Chapple 1940), who believe that the most important characteristic of an individual's interaction may be measured along a dimension of action–silence. Using a machine which he called an interaction chornograph, Chapple conducted many studies that were based largely on recordings of the frequency and duration of speeches and silences. Social scientists and trainers who have followed in Chapple's footsteps have concentrated on observing the pattern of interaction (for example, who communicates, how often, how long and with whom) without reference to verbal or emotional content. Others have adopted a similar approach but have also attended to the basic elements of verbal and/or non-verbal behaviour. Duncan and Fiske (1977), for example, focus their attention on specific, immediately observable behaviours, such as head nods and eyebrow flashes, of which the larger actions are composed. They argue that when human conduct is characterised at this relatively low level of abstraction there is the advantage that observers are required to use only the minimum of inferring.

This contrasts with an alternative behavioural approach that pays attention to the intention that lies behind the behaviour and therefore requires more interpretation on the part of the observer. Advocates of this approach include Deutsch (1949), Bales (1950), Honey (1988) and Belbin (1993).

Deutsch was one of the first to develop a system for categorising role functions. He argued that members of an effective group must perform two kinds of function: one concerned with completing the task, and the other with strengthening and maintaining the group. Bales presents his approach to interaction process analysis as both a procedure for recording interaction and as a basis for assessing the characteristic ways in which different individuals participate in social interactions, for example, their approach to problem solving.

Honey argues that since any aspect of overt behaviour may be observed, it follows that all behaviour can be categorised. However, he is critical of those who restrict their attention to the most basic elements of observable behaviour. He believes that while we can monitor all non-verbal behaviour such as eyelid movements, eyebrow twitches and finger strumming, and all verbal behaviours including how frequently somebody says 'you know', swears and so on, this might be less useful than categorising behaviour at a higher level. One of the highest levels of categorisation is style. A widely accepted definition of style is an accumulation of micro behaviours that add up to a macro judgement about a person's typical way of communicating. Wright and Taylor (1994) refer to it as a person's overall approach, while Honey defines style as the conclusions we reach about the way others operate (for example, whether somebody is autocratic or participative).

Recognising the need for both careful analysis and synthesis, Honey illustrates his approach to the study of interpersonal interaction with the analogy of a broken cup. If the cup were broken into only six pieces it would be relatively easy to synthesise from the pieces to the whole cup. If, however, the cup were pulverised into powder it would be difficult to conclude that it was ever a cup. His approach to behaviour analysis is one which he believes facilitates both analysis and synthesis. It is based on a limited number (nine) of broad categories which may be used to monitor behaviour and also to provide a practical basis for planning how best to behave in the light of the situation and the actor's objectives. The nine categories are: seeking ideas, proposing, suggesting, building, disagreeing, supporting, difficulty stating, seeking clarification, and classifying/explaining/informing.

Cognitive approaches

All of the approaches presented so far fail to pay attention to what is going on in the actors' heads, to what they are thinking. They restrict attention to what people do. An alternative approach is based on the assumption that if we are to better understand the conduct of people in organisations we need to address what they appear to think and feel about themselves and others. Symbolic interactionists such as Mangham focus attention on the way situations are defined and the actors' ability to think through (rehearse) how the interaction might unfold before deciding what to do. This theme is developed in Chapter 6, when the interviewer and interviewee are presented as actors seeking to put on a skilled performance. Cognitive approaches to the study of social interaction place heavy emphasis on cognition as a guide to behaviour.

Exercise 1.1, presented at the end of this chapter, is designed to help you explore the link between cognition and behaviour. It illustrates how each actor's intention, and the way the other actor interprets this intention, influences how the parties to an interaction behave towards each other as the interaction unfolds.

A transactional approach to social interaction

Social interaction may be viewed as a transaction in which each interactor is seeking a satisfactory outcome.

The performance appraisal interview offers an example of a complex but typical social encounter in which the behaviour of each party is influenced by the other. The person being appraised is aware that his boss/appraiser is observing what he is saying and doing and that on the basis of these observations she (the appraiser) is making inferences about him. These inferences might affect the decisions she makes about the appraisee's pay, promotion and so on. Consequently the appraisee may not openly and honestly answer all the questions he is asked, and may attempt to manage the way he responds in order to maximise his personal benefit from the interaction rather than to help the appraiser achieve her objectives.

This brief description not only draws attention to the interactive nature of social encounters but also to the possibility of conceptualising any interpersonal interaction as a performance which is influenced by the actors' motives and goals.

Leary (1957) argues that people are motivated to behave towards others in ways that elicit from them desirable kinds of behaviour that are complementary to their own. His model of interpersonal behaviour suggests that interpersonal acts may be categorised according to eight broad varieties which are related to the two factors of dominance vs. submission and hate vs. love. While we might expect any individual to be capable of displaying behaviour across all eight categories, Leary suggests that in practice most people favour some categories more than others (reflecting their personality). He also suggests that they behave in ways which elicit complementary behaviours from others. When others respond with the desired complementary behaviour the interaction is perceived to be rewarding, whereas if they respond with non-complementary behaviour it is experienced as unpleasant and costly. For example, those who favour managerial-autocratic behaviours interact with others in ways that invite them to be obedient and respectful. When others respond towards them in this way they experience the interaction as rewarding.

Thibaut and Kelley (1959) also advance the notion of reward and cost. They conceptualise interpersonal interaction as a process of social exchange, and their basic assumption is that people voluntarily enter and stay in a relationship only so long as it is adequately satisfactory in terms of reward and cost. They evaluate the outcome of a relationship by referring to two kinds of comparison level: CL and CL-alt.

The first of these comparison levels (CL) is an average of the entire population of outcomes known to a person, including those they perceive as accruing to others as well as those they have personally experienced. This represents the neutral point on a scale of goodness vs. badness of outcome. If a relationship produces outcomes (rewards less costs) that are above this level, the relationship will be experienced as satisfactory.

The second kind of comparison level (CL-alt) compares the outcome from the current relationship with the outcomes available from alternative relationships. People may attempt to terminate or change a relationship where the perceived outcomes from alternative relationships exceed the outcomes available from the current relationship. However, if the outcome from the current relationship is greater than the perceived outcomes available from alternative relationships the interactor experiencing this outcome will be motivated to continue the relationship. This said, there will also be involuntary relationships where the outcome from the current relationship is less than both the comparison level (CL) and the potential outcome from alternative relationships (CL-alt), but where the individual has no option but to continue with the current (unsatisfactory) relationship. For example, a prisoner may be locked into an unsatisfactory relationship with a cell-mate. Carson (1970) also offers an example which illustrates this possibility in everyday life. A person may decide to remain in an unhappy marriage because, given the personal, social and economic problems that may be associated with separation or divorce, the available alternatives are perceived to be less rewarding or more costly than the present situation.

For each member of a voluntary relationship to be motivated to interact, they must each experience outcomes from their encounters that are greater than their CL, and where the outcomes are greater than those they perceive to be available through alternative relationships the existing relationship is likely to continue. All involved must see the relationship as a rewarding transaction. Mead is reputed to have said that the secret of human exchange is to give to the other person behaviour that is more valuable to him than it is costly to you, and to get from the other behaviour that is more valuable to you than it is costly to him.

Argyle's social skill model

One of the most frequently cited models of social interaction is Argyle's (1994) social skill model (Figure 1.1). Originally developed more than thirty years ago, it posits that in any social encounter individuals have plans or goals that they attempt to realise through the continuous correction of their social performance in the light of the reactions of others.

The sequences of behaviour that occur in social interaction are viewed as a kind of motor skill, and social performance is presented as a set of motor responses. Just as a yachtsman can take corrective action by moving the rudder, the interviewer can take corrective action when the respondent is talking too much by interrupting, asking closed questions or looking less

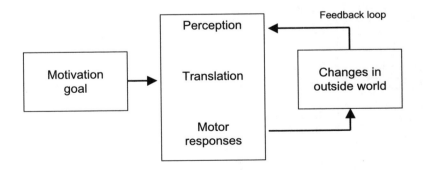

Figure 1.1 Argyle's motor skill model (from Argyle, 1994, reproduced with permission from The Penguin Group).

7

interested in what the respondent is saying. This model draws attention to the importance of feedback and the perception of appropriate cues, and to the ability to identify an effective correction routine (referred to as 'translation' in the model). The effectiveness of social performances may vary because, for example, not everyone knows that open-ended questions make people talk more and that closed questions make them talk less. Although this is presented as a motor skill model, Argyle recognises that there are some aspects of social behaviour that have no immediate parallel in motor skills such as seeing the other person's point of view and projecting a self-image.

Argyle reports that one of the criticisms levelled against his social skills model is that when people are engaged in relaxed informal 'chat' they do not appear to be motivated to influence or control the behaviour of others. His response to this criticism is that even in this kind of situation those concerned are trying to maintain a certain kind of interaction, and that this involves the control of others' behaviour. For example, it might involve keeping them relaxed and happy, preventing them from leaving or from getting too serious or keeping the intimacy at the right level.

Hargie (1997) has extended Argyle's model to take more explicit account of some of the features of social interactions, including their transactional nature (Figure 1.2). Attention is given to:

- the reciprocal nature of interactions and the goals of both interactors;
- the fact that feedback comes from one's own as well as the other person's responses;
- the influence of both emotions and cognitions on perception, interpretation and the planning of responses (what Argyle refers to as

PERSON-SITUATION CONTEXT

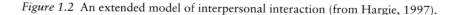

Figure 1.2 An extended model of interpersonal interaction (from Hargie, 1997).

'translation' in the original model is replaced by 'mediating factors' in Hargie's reformulation);

- the reciprocal relationship between goals and mediating factors;
- the influence of the person–situation context: while both people and situations are important, it is the interaction between the two that has greatest impact.

This transactional approach to social interaction presents interpersonal skill in a way that draws attention to our ability to shape the behaviour of others so that the rewards of interacting with them are greater than the costs. It is wholly consistent with the definition of interpersonal skills presented above, namely as goal-directed behaviours that a person uses in face-to-face interactions in order to bring about a desired state of affairs.

We attempt to realise satisfactory outcomes from our interactions with others by attending to feedback, assessing the effectiveness of our performance and continually correcting it in the light of our own assessment and the reaction of others. Perceiving, interpreting and acting on the basis of feedback are key elements of the process of skill development. This point will be elaborated in the next chapter.

Exercise 1.1 Cognition and behaviour

The aim of this exercise is to explore the link between cognition (what people are thinking) and behaviour. It involves deciding, on a step-by-step basis, how each party may react to how the other person behaves.

The interactive nature of relationships is illustrated in Figure 1.3. This diagram illustrates how each actor's intention, and the way the other actor interprets this intention, influences how the parties behave towards each other as the interaction unfolds.

The questions listed in the cognition 'bubbles' in Figure 1.3 suggest the kinds of things the actors might be thinking about during the interaction. This process is elaborated on in the following pages, but you may need to refer to Figure 1.3 as you work through the exercise.

Method

You can complete the exercise working alone or with another person.

The exercise format presented here is for use by two people working together. However, it can be easily adapted for use by one person. Simply assume the role of A and B in turn and reflect on how each party might interpret the behaviour of the other and what effect this is likely to have on

---

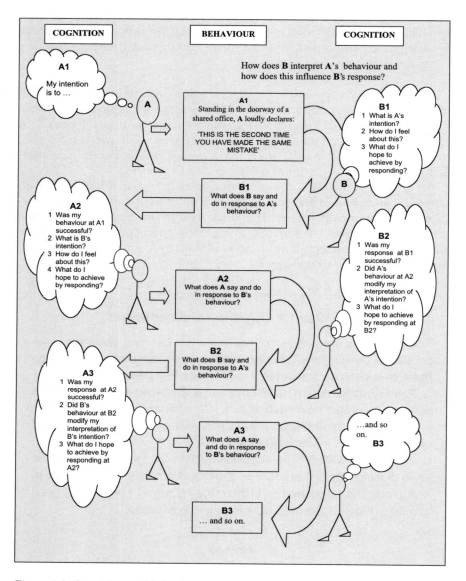

Figure 1.3 Cognition and behaviour.

how the relationship develops. Fill out the cognition 'bubbles' and behaviour boxes for both parties (A and B). After you have completed several exchanges, reflect on how interpretation of intent can influence behaviour.

If you decide to complete this exercise by working with another person, decide who will be A and who will be B.

Context

The context is a financial services organisation. A is B's supervisor. Part of B's role involves interviewing clients when they apply for a mortgage. B has been in post for three months. The supervisor (A) has discovered B has failed to collect all the required information from a client. This is the second time that B has made the same mistake. It is important because it means that there will be a serious delay in the company's ability to process the client's mortgage application, and it could result in the loss of the client's business.

Place a copy of Figure 1.3 somewhere where both A and B can see it.

The exercise begins with A (the supervisor) standing in the doorway of an office that B shares with others, loudly declaring that this is the second time B has made the same mistake.

1 **The person who is assuming the role of A starts by filling out the cognition 'bubble' at A1 indicating A's purpose in pointing out B's second mistake.**

   A *should* not *pass this information on to* B.

11

2   **While A is completing the above task, the person who is assuming the role of B (who is aware of how A behaved at the start of this interaction – box A1) can also start the exercise.**

- B should fill in the cognition 'bubble' at B1 on his or her own sheet, answering the questions listed in Figure 1.3. (What is A's intention? How do I feel about this? What do I hope to achieve by responding?)

  B should not share this information with A.

- B should then decide how to respond to A's behaviour at A1 and write this down in the behaviour box at B1.

Inform A how you decided to behave so that s/he can record this in box B1 on their copy of the exercise.

Note: A should make a note of B's behaviour in box B1 on his or her own copy of the exercise. B should *not* tell A what s/he has written down in the cognition 'bubble' B1.

A is now in a position to reflect on B's behaviour.

3 A reflects on B's behaviour at B1.

- A should fill in the cognition 'bubble' at A2, answering the questions listed in Figure 1.3.

  Do not share this information with B.

- A should then decide how to respond to B's behaviour at B1 and write this down in the behaviour box at A2.

  Inform B how you behaved.

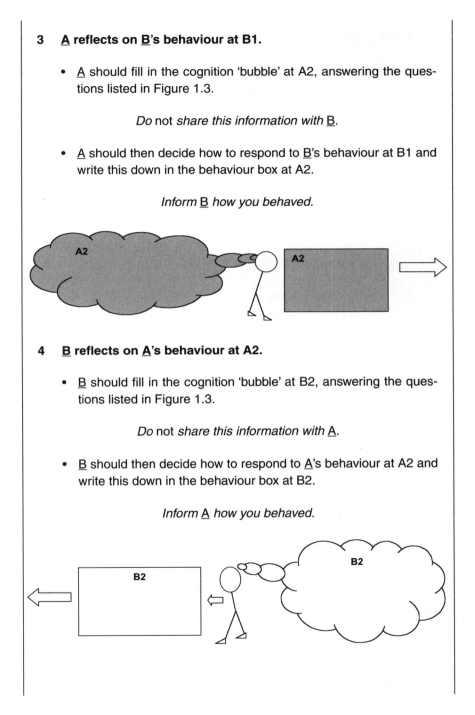

4 B reflects on A's behaviour at A2.

- B should fill in the cognition 'bubble' at B2, answering the questions listed in Figure 1.3.

  Do not share this information with A.

- B should then decide how to respond to A's behaviour at A2 and write this down in the behaviour box at B2.

  Inform A how you behaved.

5   <u>A</u> reflects on <u>B</u>'s behaviour at B2.

- <u>A</u> should fill in the cognition 'bubble' at A3, answering the questions listed in Figure 1.3.

    Do not share this information with <u>B</u>.

- <u>A</u> should then decide how to respond to <u>B</u>'s behaviour at B2 and write this down in the behaviour box at A3.

    Inform <u>B</u> how you behaved.

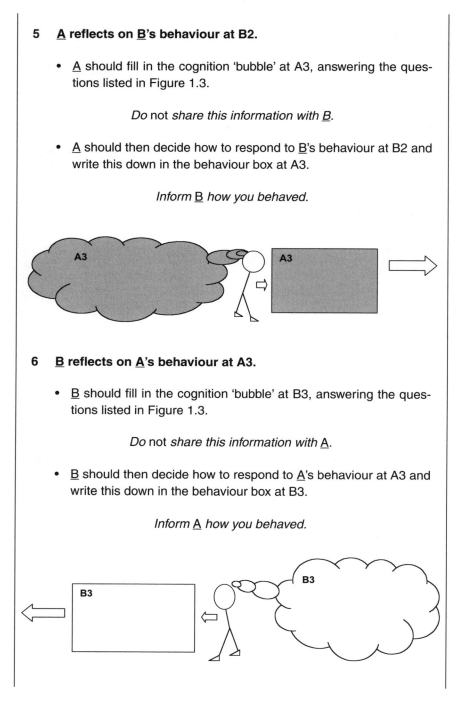

6   <u>B</u> reflects on <u>A</u>'s behaviour at A3.

- <u>B</u> should fill in the cognition 'bubble' at B3, answering the questions listed in Figure 1.3.

    Do not share this information with <u>A</u>.

- <u>B</u> should then decide how to respond to <u>A</u>'s behaviour at A3 and write this down in the behaviour box at B3.

    Inform <u>A</u> how you behaved.

7   Continue this process through as many steps as possible in the permitted time.

The next step involves A and B sharing what each wrote down in the cognition 'bubbles'. When you have shared the content of your cognition 'bubbles':

1   Note how accurate B's understanding of A's intention was at each stage of the interaction.
2   Repeat this process noting how accurate A's understanding of B's intention was at each stage.

- Were you surprised by how the other person had interpreted your behaviour?
- How did the way you interpreted the other's intent influence what you did next?
- Could the outcome of this interaction have been more rewarding/satisfying if either of you had behaved differently?
- Identify the behaviours which may have been more effective.

When interacting with others we need to consider how they are likely to interpret our behaviour and, when deciding how to respond to their behaviour, we need to be aware of the factors which might have influenced how they behaved towards us.

Be prepared to share what you have discussed in a plenary session.

Plenary discussion

When you share with others the accounts of your interactions it may be useful to begin by focusing on the first exchange between A and B. Everybody knew how A behaved in the first instance. A stood in the doorway of the office that B shared with others and loudly declared that this was the second time B had made the same mistake.

1   How did the people who assumed the role of A describe A's intent in behaving in this way? Possible examples include:

- To provide B with feedback that would help him improve his performance.

- To shame <u>B</u> in front of his colleagues and to jolt him into taking more care when completing mortgage applications in the future.
- To signal to <u>B</u>'s colleagues that <u>B</u> is an unreliable worker.
- To signal to <u>B</u> that his performance is unacceptable.

2 Did the people who assumed the role of <u>B</u> accurately interpret <u>A</u>'s intention?

3 How did the people who assumed the role of <u>B</u> respond to what <u>A</u> said in the office doorway? Possible examples include:

- Bursting into tears and leaving the room.
- Engaging in a public argument and blaming <u>A</u> for not providing adequate guidance about what <u>B</u> was required to do.
- Promising to work more carefully in the future.
- Telling <u>A</u> that she had an unhelpful attitude and indicating that he intended to seek a transfer or look for a job elsewhere.

4 Were any of the people who assumed the role of <u>A</u> surprised by how 'their <u>B</u>' responded?

Sharing this kind of information usually demonstrates how often one party (<u>B</u>) can misinterpret the intent of the other (<u>A</u>). The result can be that <u>B</u> responds to <u>A</u>'s behaviour in a way that <u>A</u> failed to anticipate. When this happens <u>A</u> has to take corrective action to steer the relationship back onto the course s/he intended it to take in the first place. This involves paying attention to what is going on in <u>B</u>'s head. <u>A</u> needs to consider the factors that may influence the way <u>B</u> is thinking and how these may influence how he interprets <u>A</u>'s intent and how he chooses to respond to <u>A</u>'s verbal and non-verbal behaviour.

In order to manage interactions effectively, it is not enough to restrict attention to what people say and do (to their behaviour). It is also necessary to attend to the cognitions that guide our own and others' behaviour, and to rehearse in our mind the possible consequences of behaviours before deciding what to do.

Summary

In this chapter, interpersonal skills have been defined as goal-directed behaviours used in face-to-face interactions to bring about a desired state of affairs. Different approaches to studying social interaction have been discussed and particular attention has been given to theories that view interpersonal relations in terms of a transaction in which each interactor is seeking a satisfactory outcome. The use of feedback and correction routines for managing performance in the light of the reactions of others has also been highlighted.

The model that underpins the content of this book is cognitive. It assumes that people are purposeful, and interact with others in order to secure desired outcomes. The interactive nature of this model is elaborated in Exercise 1.1 and in Chapter 6.

While the cognitive model provides the context for the micro-skill approach to skill development outlined in the next chapter, some of the exercises presented in later chapters also draw on the techniques developed by those usually associated with the behavioural approach to the study of interpersonal interaction. These exercises involve observing, modifying and practising behaviours in order to acquire or improve specific micro skills as a step towards improving overall performance.

References

Argyle, M. (1984) 'Social behaviour', in C.L. Cooper and P. Makin (eds) *Psychology for Managers*, London: British Psychological Society and Macmillan.

Argyle, M. (1994) *The Psychology of Interpersonal Behaviour* (5th edn), London: Penguin.

Bales, F.G. (1950) *Interaction Process Analysis: A Method for the Study of Small Groups*, Reading, Mass: Addison-Wesley. (The reader is also referred to a useful summary in D.S. Sills (ed.) (1968) *International Encyclopaedia of the Social Sciences*, Vol. 8, New York: Crowell Collier and Macmillan, pp. 465–471.)

Belbin, R.M. (1993) *Team Roles at Work*, London: Heinemann.

Berscheid, E. (1994) 'Interpersonal relationships', *Annual Review of Psychology* 45: 79–129.

Carson, R.C. (1970) *Interaction Concepts of Psychology*, London: George Allen & Unwin.

Chapple, E.D. (1940) 'Measuring human relations: an introduction to the study of interaction of individuals', *Genetic Psychology Monographs* 22: 3–147.

Deutsch, M. (1949) 'A theory of co-operation and competition', *Human Relations* 2 (2): 129–159.

Duncan, S. and Fiske, D.W. (1977) *Face to Face Interaction: Research, Methods and Theory*, Hillsdale, NJ: Lawrence Erlbaum.

Hargie, O.D.W. (1997) *The Handbook of Interpersonal Skills* (2nd edn), London: Routledge.

Honey, P. (1988) *Face to Face Skills*, Aldershot: Gower (presents a practical approach to shaping the behaviour of others.)

Leary, T. (1957) *Interpersonal Diagnosis of Personality*, New York: Ronald. (The essentials of Leary's model are presented in Chapter 4 of Carson's book.)

Mangham, I.L. (1978) *Interactions and Interventions in Organizations*, Chichester: Wiley.

Mangham, I.L. (1986) *Power and Performance in Organisations: An Exploration of Executive Process*, Oxford: Blackwell. (Mangham takes the stage as his organising metaphor and offers a good insight into the interactionist perspective.)

Oshagbemi, T. (1988) *Leadership and Management in Universities*, New York: Walter de Gruyter.

Thibaut, J.W. and Kelley, H.H. (1959) *The Social Psychology of Groups*, Chicester: Wiley.

Wright, P.L. and Taylor, D.S. (1994) *Improving Leadership Performance: Interpersonal Skills for Effective Leaders* (2nd edn), Hemel Hempstead: Prentice-Hall.

2

DEVELOPING INTERPERSONAL SKILLS

A micro-skills approach

Learning objective

To understand how the hierarchical model of interpersonal skills can facilitate a micro-skills approach to the development of interpersonal competence.
  After reading this chapter you will:

- Be aware of how the hierarchical model of interpersonal skills can be used to help individuals to critically assess the effectiveness of their social skills at every level.
- Be able to describe the hierarchical structure of interpersonal skills and explain how this offers the possibility of breaking down complex interpersonal skills into their component parts.
- Understand how isolating and practising these component parts (micro skills) can aid the development of more complex interpersonal skills.
- Understand the contribution that conceptual models and theories can make by sensitising you to the elements of your behaviour that might be the focus of micro-skills training.
- Recognise the importance of an individual's own subjective theory of social interaction and the role it plays in guiding behaviour.
- Understand the difference between cueing and learning.
- Understand how the experiential learning model can help people learn from their experience and refine their subjective theories of social interaction.

Interpersonal skills can be learned

This chapter explores what we can do to improve our ability to relate to others. Most people learn how to relate on the basis of experience, through unstructured and unintentional processes of trial and error. Sometimes this approach is successful but it can be unreliable and ineffective. It is not unusual for people to develop habitual modes of relating to others that consistently yield unsatisfactory results. For example, some managers may find it difficult to get job applicants to talk about themselves and, even though they may have come across this problem many times before, they may be unaware of how their own behaviour contributes to the problem. Furthermore, they may have little awareness of alternative ways of behaving that might improve matters.

Interpersonal competence involves diagnosing what is going on in social situations, identifying the action required to bring about a desired state of affairs and translating this requirement into an effective performance. This book offers a series of conceptual frameworks that may be used for developing these diagnostic and action skills.

The hierarchical nature of interpersonal skills

Social skill, according to Argyle (1994) and others, has a hierarchical structure in which the larger, higher level units consist of integrated sequences and groupings of lower level units. Wright and Taylor (1994) focus attention on three levels in this hierarchy.

At the lowest level are *primary components*. These are what we actually say and do, our verbal and non-verbal behaviour. Interpersonally skilled people are those who, at this level, have a wide range of verbal components (for example, questions and statement types) at their disposal and are able to select the one most appropriate to the situation and purpose at hand. They are also able to perform it well with the appropriate non-verbal cues.

The next level up is *structure*. This is concerned with the way in which we sequence the primary components of behaviour. At this level interpersonally skilled people are those who can organise and integrate the primary components into purposeful sequences which steer the interaction towards their objective. For example, in a problem-solving interview this might involve adopting a funnel sequence of questions which begins with very open questions and then progresses towards more closed questions. In an interrogation, however, a completely different sequence might be more effective.

The highest level in Wright and Taylor's hierarchy is the *overall approach*, or what Honey (1988) refers to as 'style'. The primary components people use in an interaction and the way in which these are structured will depend, at least in part, on the type of interaction they intend to have. At the stylistic or overall approach level interpersonally skilled people are those who are able to develop an approach to the interaction that is congruent with both their objectives and with the probable reactions of the others involved. For example, managers who want to help members of their team become more effective may decide to adopt a helping style that involves helping them to help themselves. They might place a high priority on empowering them to experiment and learn from their own mistakes, and they might deliberately resist the temptation to 'take them by the hand' and tell them precisely what they need to do to improve their performance. Managers may behave this way because they believe that a more prescriptive approach to helping would encourage others to become too dependent on their guidance and advice and would inhibit their learning.

Exercise 2.1, presented at the end of this chapter, is designed to help you identify different interpersonal styles and the patterns or structures of primary components that are associated with different styles.

Choice based on critical assessment

The hierarchical model may be used to help us step back and critically assess the effectiveness of our social skills at every level. Many writers adopt a prescriptive approach to the development of interpersonal skills and tell readers how they *ought* to behave when leading (for example, always adopt a consultative style), negotiating (always adopt a collaborative, win-win approach), and helping (always be supportive and avoid confrontation).

The hierarchical model highlights the possibility of adopting a range of different styles and component behaviours and focuses attention on the value of identifying ways of relating, in particular situations, that will contribute to the achievement of desired outcomes. Being supportive and avoiding confrontation or consulting and collaborating might be effective in some circumstances but not in others. For example, in those situations where people do not share a common goal or, because of a crisis, where there is insufficient time for consultation, the most effective leadership style might be directive and involve telling other people what to do.

The micro-skills approach to developing interpersonal competence

The hierarchical model of interpersonal skills offers the possibility of breaking down complex skills into their component parts. An example will illustrate this.

- *Accenting*, which is the term used to describe a one- or two-word restatement that focuses attention on what somebody has just said, is one of several behaviours that may be grouped together under the broad heading of following skills.
- *Following skills* are behaviours that help one person encourage somebody else to talk and help the first person concentrate on what the speaker has to say. Following skills are one of a number of sets of behaviours which, at another level, are referred to collectively as *listening skills*.
- *Listening skills*, which involve an active search for a full and accurate understanding of the meaning of another's message, are, in their turn,

just one of the sets of behaviour which comprise one of a number of *higher level skills*.

- *Helping and negotiating* are examples of such higher level skills. A person's style of helping or negotiating will be reflected in the way in which these various micro skills are sequenced and structured.

Micro-skills training is based on the assumption that an effective approach to developing interpersonal competence is to isolate and practise important sub or micro skills before bringing the components together and synthesising them into larger units of behaviour.

This reductionist approach to the development of interpersonal skills has a number of clear advantages, but Hargie (1997) highlights two potential disadvantages which merit consideration.

A central tenant of Gestalt psychology is that the whole is greater than the sum of its parts; thus once an overall structure is broken down into smaller units the original meaning or form can be changed. Studying a number of small units of behaviour in isolation may not be equivalent to studying the whole. This argument has some validity, but it does not apply to the treatment of interpersonal skills offered in this book. The approach adopted here analyses social interaction in terms of clearly identifiable behaviours while at the same time highlighting the way these behaviours relate to one another. The advantage offered by this approach is that information is presented and discussed in a way that can help people develop their skills by focusing their attention on selected aspects of social interaction. Hargie (1997: 476) describes this approach as one of:

> *homing in and honing up*, where one aspect of social interaction is focused upon at a time and trainees are encouraged to refine their use of this particular aspect. Once the trainee has acquired a working knowledge of a number of skills of social interaction, the ultimate goal is to encourage the appropriate use of these skills in an integrated fashion.

A second danger identified by Hargie is that by adopting a micro-training approach to skills development, social interaction will lose its natural beauty and become artificial and stilted. While it is true that in the short term focusing attention on particular skills can make people more conscious of their behaviour, thus making it more stilted, this is a transitory stage. A similar pattern may be observed in the process of learning other skills. For example, learning to drive a car requires the driver to become proficient in a number of perceptual–motor skills involved in such tasks as steering, changing gear and (if one has a manual gearbox) slipping the clutch on hill starts. Before allowing a learner to negotiate rush hour traffic the driving instructor might focus attention on each of these skills in turn. The first lesson may only involve stopping, starting and steering the car on quiet, level roads. Later the learner may be introduced to moving up and down the gearbox. Later still these skills may be practised on different roads and in different traffic conditions. While the learner driver is concentrating on perfecting each of these skills the overall effect may well be a jerky, uncoordinated drive. However, with practice, the skills become second nature and the driver develops an integrated and smooth approach to driving. Much the same happens when people are developing their interpersonal skills. At times the process may seem artificial and stilted, but this is only a transitory stage in the learning process. Eventually learners reach a point where they unconsciously exercise these skills when relating to others.

Using micro-skills training to develop behavioural mastery

Some of the first advocates of a micro-skills approach to developing interpersonal competence worked in the field of counselling and psychotherapy (Carkhuff 1971; Kagan 1973). Kagan's approach begins with a presentation of concepts followed by the practice of skills in simulated exercises. The next step involves studying self while working with real clients. Finally, trainees move on to develop an 'understanding of and skill at dealing with the complex bilateral impacts which occur when two people are in a relationship with one another'. The micro-skills training model presented here has many similarities to Kagan's model. There are two main stages: conceptual understanding and behavioural mastery (Kagan 1973: 44).

The first stage involves developing a *conceptual understanding* of the process of social interaction and the hierarchical nature of interpersonal skills, including the main elements of the hierarchy and the ways in which these elements may be sequenced and structured.

The second stage is concerned with using this conceptual understanding as a basis for developing *skilled practice*. This involves taking action in everyday or simulated situations, attending to feedback and reflecting on the consequences of the action and, where appropriate, modifying future action to achieve desired outcomes.

Conceptual understanding

Models and theories provide us with a conceptual map that we can use to alert us to those aspects of social interaction which deserve our attention. They facilitate diagnosis. They also supply an agenda for action by offering a vision of what might be possible, providing a sense of direction and indicating how we might need to act in order to steer a relationship in a particular way. For example, in the opening paragraph of this chapter reference was made to managers who experienced difficulty getting interviewees to talk about themselves. This problem might have been resolved if they had known more about how their own behaviour contributed to the problem, and if they had been aware of alternative ways of behaving that might have encouraged the interviewees to say more about themselves.

Models and theories of social interaction do not guarantee skilled performance, but they can facilitate it by alerting us to more effective ways of behaving. The content of this book is designed to help you develop this conceptual understanding and to sensitise you to the elements of behaviour that might be the focus of a micro-training approach to skills development. Chapters 4 to 6 are concerned with skills that are important in their own right (listening, listening to non-verbal messages, information getting, and presenting information to others). Each of these core skills involves many elements (micro skills) but they also form an important element of more complex skills. Some of these more complex skills (helping, influencing, negotiating and working with groups) are considered in Chapters 8 to 11. Chapter 12 presents some conceptual models that provide a more macro view of social interaction and suggest a range of diagnostic questions and action strategies that point to ways of managing relationships more effectively.

Developing behavioural mastery through experiential learning

Our behaviour towards others is not made up of random acts. It is purposeful, and is guided by our values, beliefs and attitudes, and by the assumptions we make about our self, others and the situation, and by the assumptions we make about the way all these elements relate to each other. This conceptual framework, our subjective theory of social interaction, provides the lens through which we view and interpret new information about the way other people react to what we do and say. It also provides a basis for determining how stored information about past interactions will be applied to facilitate our understanding of current situations. We use our subjective theories to guide everything we say and do.

Cueing and learning

When events do not go according to plan, when others do not respond as we anticipate, we use our subjective theory to determine what to do next. The theory suggests correction routines. It cues us to behave in certain ways that will lead to the achievement of desired outcomes. For example, if interviewees fail to provide sufficient information about themselves, the correction routine might be for the interviewer to start using more open-ended questions.

It is possible, however, to encounter problems for which our subjective theory of social interaction does not provide an effective correction routine. The feedback signals a problem but the theory fails to offer a ready solution. It may be that we are faced with a situation we have never encountered before (for example, interviewees say more when asked open-ended questions but are still evasive in their answers), or it may be that we have revised our standards and are no longer prepared to accept the level of outcome that the existing correction routines deliver. In these circumstances the feedback triggers a learning rather than a cueing activity. This process involves reflecting on the feedback, searching for more information to provide a better understanding of the problem, and adopting a trial-and-error approach to testing the effectiveness of new routines.

The experiential learning model

The experiential learning model developed by Lewin offers a four-stage process which we can use for refining the subjective theory that guides our interpersonal interactions (see Figure 2.1).

Kolb (1984: 21) highlights two important aspects of Lewin's theory:

1 The first is the emphasis it places on here-and-now concrete experience to validate and test abstract concepts. While we may draw on explicit

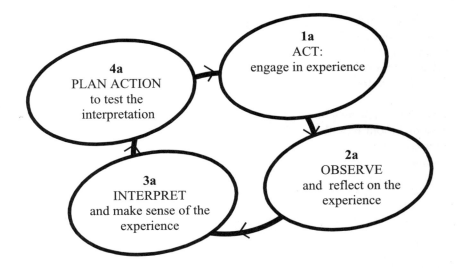

Figure 2.1 The experiential learning model.

conceptual models, such as those presented in this book, to alert us to new possibilities and to provide a guide for action, it is the immediate personal experience that is the focal point of learning.

2   The second is the importance attributed to feedback, the process that generates valid information to assess deviations from intended goals. This feedback provides the basis for the continuous process of goal-directed action and the evaluation of the consequences of that action.

The process of refining our subjective theories begins at Stage 1 (the first cycle is indicated here by the suffix 'a').

Stages in the learning process	*Illustrated in the context of a selection interview*
1(a) The actor/learner engaging in a here-and-now experience takes action in a social situation.	*In this case the action involves interviewing a job applicant.*
2(a) Action is followed, at Stage 2, by the interviewer observing and reflecting on what happened. • How did the interviewee react? • How does the interviewer feel about what happened?	*The interviewer is unhappy with the way the interview is progressing because the interviewee fails to provide the kind of information required to determine whether he or she is qualified for the job.*
3(a) The third stage involves the interviewer interpreting and making sense of this experience and, if (as in this case) it is not satisfactory, searching for an appropriate correction routine.	*The correction routine applied by the interviewer is to make greater use of open-ended questions.*
4(a) The fourth stage involves thinking about how to test the effectiveness of this correction routine.	*The interviewer:* • *searches for opportunities to introduce more open-ended questions into the interview;* • *thinks about how to monitor the consequences of this new behaviour in order to determine whether it produces the desired outcome.*

The cycle then starts again at 1(b), as illustrated in Figure 2.2.

1(b) At 1b the interviewer engages in a new here-and-now experience that provides the opportunity for generating feedback to test the effectiveness of the correction routine.

The interviewer intentionally makes greater use of more open-ended questions.

2(b) At stage 2b the interviewer once again observes and reflects on what has happened, in this case when greater use is made of open-ended questions.

The interviewer notes that while the interviewee says more, the answers are still vague and evasive.

3(b) Faced by the failure of the existing correction routine to deliver a satisfactory outcome, the interviewer begins to reflect on the meaning of the feedback and on the possible nature of the problem. At stage 3(b) this involves interpreting and making sense of this experience and assimilating any new understanding into the interviewer's conceptual framework. The outcome of this stage is a *tentative* revision of the subjective theory. This usually manifests itself as a new generalisation about an effective way to behave or a revised hypothesis about cause and effect.

In this case the interviewer hypothesises that a greater use of directive probes such as 'What exactly do you mean?' or 'Are you saying that . . .' will elicit more information from the interviewee and will provide clarification of vague or unsubstantiated claims about his or her qualifications and competencies.

4(b) The fourth stage involves thinking about how to test this new hypothesis.

In this case the interviewer thinks about ways of making use of directive probes later in the same interview, and decides how to monitor the consequences of this new behaviour in order to determine whether it produces the desired outcome.

The third cycle then starts (at 1(c)) with the interviewer engaging in a new here-and-now experience (*intentionally employing directive probes*). This provides feedback for testing the revised theory, and so the process continues (see Figure 2.2).

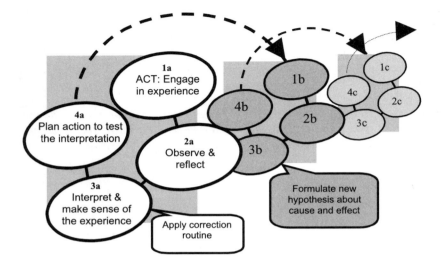

Figure 2.2 How learning occurs.

At various points in this book you will be presented with exercises that will require you to engage in and reflect on a here-and-now experience and to use this as a basis for identifying and practising new possibilities for interacting more effectively. Sometimes these exercises will be based on everyday encounters and sometimes they will involve participating in simulations. However, there will also be occasions when you will be invited to reflect on your past experience.

Cunningham (1999: 157) in his book *The Wisdom of Strategic Learning* refers to the value that may be gained from exploring one's own history. It often leads to the identification of deeply ingrained patterns of behaviour (such as correction routines) that tend to be repeated time after time. These patterns or habits may be effective, but they may sometimes be self-defeating. Reflecting on past experience can be a useful source of insights into, for example, correction routines that might not be as effective as we believe. These may be tested in the here-and-now of experiential learning. Exercise 2.1 is designed to help you to think about the hierarchical nature of interpersonal skills and some of the key components of behaviour.

Exercise 2.1 What's in a style?

The aim of this exercise is to help you identify different interpersonal styles and the patterns or structures of primary components that are associated with different styles.

Think about a type of relationship you have had on more than one occasion. It may have involved someone trying to sell you something, negotiating an agreement, supervising your work, teaching you, helping you with a problem, or even trying to seduce you!

Identify *two* different people who have occupied one of these roles (selling; negotiations). They should be people who have managed the particular relationship in very different ways.

> For example, in the context of the selling relationship, one may have adopted a 'soft-sell' approach whereas the other adopted a 'hard-sell' approach. (These are just two examples of a wide range of different styles of selling.)

When you have identified two different examples of the same relationship:

1   Give each of them a *label* that describes the *overall approach or style of the role occupant.* Describe, in a few words, what each of these labels means. The descriptions may refer to the role holders' purpose or objectives, their beliefs, the assumptions they appeared to make about themselves and others, and so on.

> For example, if one label used to describe a supervisor is 'charismatic' the description may refer to the fact that s/he appeared to exude self-confidence, had a very clear sense of purpose, involved others in what s/he was doing and was prepared to take personal risks to achieve his or her objectives.

2   Now, think about some of the details of how each of them behaved when 'acting out' their style. Add this as a second paragraph to your description.

    Were there identifiable differences in the way they behaved?

For example, at a basic level, did one of them spend more time in one-to-one relationships than the other? Did one say a lot more than the other? Did one of them spend more time making statements – giving you facts or opinions – whereas the other made relatively few statements but asked lots of questions? Did one shout or make a lot of use of body language, for example, eye contact? In other words, were there clear *differences in the type of 'primary components' of behaviour* that they used? Did they structure or sequence them in different ways?

It will be much easier to complete this exercise when you are more familiar with the wide range of micro skills that will be discussed in this book and with the way they can be integrated into different structures and styles. However, this exercise has been introduced at this stage to sensitise you to the different ways in which people can behave when occupying the same role and engaging in the same type of relationship.

3   Review your descriptions and consider:

- Whether you feel that one style or overall approach is more effective than the other. Why is this? Is it because this style is superior and will always be more effective, or is it because it is the best approach for a particular situation or set of circumstances? If so, what is it about the 'circumstances' that makes one style more effective than the other?
- How different are the two styles in terms of the use of the detail elements or components of behaviour? Does this analysis highlight ways of behaving that are especially effective or ineffective?

4   Share your observations with a partner or small group. Even though you might have focused on different types of relationships, are there any common themes in the conclusions you reached?

Summary

This chapter has examined how the hierarchical model of interpersonal skills can facilitate a micro-skills approach to training. Attention has been given to ways in which complex skills may be broken down into their component parts. These components or micro skills may then be isolated and practised before they are reintegrated with other micro skills, that have also been practised in isolation, to facilitate the competent performance of complex skills. The contribution of conceptual models to skill development has also been discussed, particularly in the context of diagnosis and action planning. Finally, Lewin's model of experiential learning has been discussed in the context of developing behavioural mastery. This model informs the design of many of the exercises presented later in this book.

References

Argyle, M. (1994) *The Psychology of Interpersonal Behaviour* (5th edn), London: Penguin.

Carkhuff, R.R. (1971) *The Development of Human Resources,* New York: Holt, Rinehart & Winston.

Cunningham, I. (1999) *The Wisdom of Strategic Learning: The Self Managed Learning Solution* (2nd edn), Aldershot: Gower.

Hargie, O.D.W. (1997) 'Training in communication skills: research, theory and practice', in Owen Hargie (ed.) *The Handbook of Communication Skills* (2nd edn), London: Routledge, pp. 473–482.

Honey, P. (1988) *Face to Face Skills*, Aldershot: Gower.

Kagan, N. (1973) 'Can technology help us towards reliability in influencing human interaction?' *Educational Technology* 13: 44–51.

Kolb, D.A. (1984) *Experiential Learning*, Englewood Cliffs, NJ: Prentice-Hall.

Wright, P.L. and Taylor, D.S. (1994) *Improving Leadership Performance: Interpersonal Skills for Effective Leaders* (2nd edn), Hemel Hempstead: Prentice-Hall.

3

AWARENESS OF SELF AND OTHERS AND THE DEVELOPMENT OF INTERPERSONAL COMPETENCE

Learning objective

To understand how values, beliefs, assumptions and subjective theories of social interaction can influence interpersonal competence. This involves understanding how self-awareness affects a person's ability to read behaviour, identify the action required to bring about a desired outcome and translate this requirement into an effective performance.

After reading this chapter you will:

- Know the difference between espoused theories and theories in use.
- Understand why people are often unaware of their 'theory in use' and how this can affect the way they relate to others.
- Be aware of some of the factors that may distort a person's perception of others.
- Recognise the importance of the questions people ask themselves about others and how they interpret the information they obtain.
- Be aware of how beliefs about self can influence self-presentation and the quality of performance in social settings.
- Understand the difference between subjective and objective self-awareness.
- Be aware of some of the steps you can take to improve the level of your objective self-awareness.

Why self-awareness is important

Our awareness of self is closely linked to our ability to read the behaviour of others, construct courses of action and deliver an effective performance. People who have a high level of self-awareness understand how their own values, beliefs and subjective theories influence what they see and do. This awareness offers them the possibility of taking account of known biases to reappraise first impressions and rehearse alternative ways of behaving.

Espoused theory and theory in use

In practice, however, many of us are not as self-aware as we think. Argyris (1982) argues that people acquire, through socialisation, two kinds of theory for dealing with others.

Espoused theory

The first reflects the values and beliefs that are uppermost in our mind and that we espouse to others (our *espoused theory of action*). We may be especially conscious of our espoused theories because they are the kinds of theories we talk about on training courses or read about in books. They may also be the theories that reflect the values and beliefs of the people we respect. At the conscious level, therefore, they become the unquestioned and taken-for-granted basis for relating to others. For example, a counsellor who has had a long and rigorous professional training may espouse the importance of always adhering to the high standards of professional practice that were part of that training.

Theory in use

The second kind of theory, which we may be less aware of, reflects the values and beliefs that actually underpin our behaviour (our *theory in use*). Theories in use are the product of a prolonged period of social conditioning and we are often unaware of the extent to which this conditioning influences our behaviour. The counsellor, referred to above, may, over the course of her career, have modified her working methods to cope with the pressure of work and new types of problem. This process may have involved many small changes, incremental adjustments over a prolonged period of time – a short cut here and a new procedure there. The end result may be that her actual working practice, reflecting her theory in use, is different from the theory that underpinned her training and which she still espouses as the most effective way of working.

Awareness of 'theory in use'

We are more effective at reading behaviour and constructing courses of action when there is a high level of congruence between our espoused theory of social interaction and our theory in use. Problems arise when there is a significant difference between them. For example, a manager may espouse a consultative leadership style but in practice take decisions without reference to what others think and feel. She may think she has consulted, but in reality she may have failed to listen to what others have to say, and her behaviour may have clearly signalled this failure to everybody around her.

The outcome is a situation where others know things about her that she does not know about herself. Consequently she may fail to understand why others react as they do to her behaviour towards them.

Covey (1989) in his book *The Seven Habits of Highly Effective People* suggests that we are all products of our habits. He argues that habits are powerful factors in determining how effective we are because they can be both consistent and unconscious. His argument suggests that the more we are aware of our habits and our basic 'paradigms, maps and assumptions' (Argyris' theories in use) and the more we are aware of the extent to which these habits have been influenced by our experience, the more we take responsibility for them. We can examine them, test them against reality, listen to others and be open to their perceptions, and thereby gain a far more objective view of ourselves and our approach to others.

Mention has already been made of the need to be aware of any discrepancies between espoused theories and theories in use. It is our theory in use that underpins how we interact with others. In order to raise our awareness of how our theory in use influences the way we manage our interactions with others:

- We need to observe our self in action. We can do this by reflecting on patterns of past behaviour and monitoring how we behave in the here-and-now.
- We also need to be open and responsive to feedback from others.

However, before considering the kinds of things we can do to develop a greater sense of self-awareness we will briefly examine how factors such as our own values, beliefs, needs and attitudes can affect the way we read behaviour and construct courses of action.

Awareness of others

To be a skilled reader of the behaviour of others we need to be aware of 'who we are' (what we value and believe) and how this influences the way we look at the world around us, including the people whom we encounter. We also need to be aware of how other people perceive us, and how this influences how they behave towards us.

Reading the behaviour of others

The way we perceive others is influenced by the way we selectively attend to some aspects of the situation and ignore others. This selectivity is influenced by a range of factors (see Chapter 6). The focus of attention here is how internal factors influence the questions we ask ourselves about others. One of these internal factors is what we believe and value. For example, we may

34

believe that the people who matter are those who can make things happen. We may also believe that such people tend to be assertive, seek to take control of situations and adopt a task-centred approach to leadership. These beliefs will influence the kinds of questions we ask ourselves about others. We may pay attention only to information that helps us to assess the extent to which they manifest these qualities, and we may completely ignore information about, for example, whether they are warm and friendly and whether they can win the confidence of the people with whom they work.

We need to be aware that we adopt a blinkered approach to perceiving others and that the questions we ask ourselves about them are influenced by factors such as our values, beliefs, needs, attitudes and mood states. However, we also need to be aware that we often ask relatively few questions and that we use the limited information we obtain to infer much more about them than the evidence merits. We do this by making assumptions about how personal characteristics tend to be clustered. Thus if we observe certain characteristics we assume others will also apply. For example, we may assume that people who are well dressed, have neatly trimmed hair and manicured nails are also reliable, attend to detail, carefully monitor progress and adopt a conservative approach to assessing risks before making decisions. On the other hand, we may assume that people who pierce parts of their bodies and wear nose studs are unreliable, fail to pay proper attention to detail and are inclined to disregard risks when taking decisions. In other words, we often assign people to categories for which we already have stereotypes. These stereotypes are important because there is evidence which suggests that first impressions persist. Once we have stereotyped somebody we tend to be reluctant to revise this assessment.

Our approach to perceiving others affects both our reading of their behaviour and the way we behave towards them. For example, after being appointed to manage a new team of computer operators, we may ask ourselves whether our new subordinates are reliable. If we observe that one member of the team wears a nose stud we may gain the (false) impression that he is not as reliable as his colleagues. It is this impression (which we believe to be true) that influences how we behave towards him. We may decide that because he is the least reliable member of the team we will need to supervise closely everything he does. If, however, he is the kind of person who does not like to be watched over and controlled, he may respond to this close supervision by withdrawing his commitment and enthusiasm (which we failed to notice in the first place). This negative response is provoked by our behaviour towards him (which is based on the way we stereotyped him). If we had formed a more accurate impression of him, and if we had behaved differently towards him, he might have responded with enthusiasm and demonstrated his reliability and effectiveness.

In order to improve our ability to 'read' others, and to use these perceptions to construct effective courses of action, we need to be aware of the kinds of questions we typically ask ourselves about others. We also need to be aware of the implicit assumptions we make about how personal characteristics are related to each other and the categories we use to stereotype people.

Awareness of how others perceive us

We also need to be aware of the way other people perceive us. Different people use different frameworks for perceiving others, and the people with whom we are interacting may be asking themselves very different questions about us to the questions we are asking ourselves about them. Understanding more about their values, beliefs, needs, attitudes and mood states will help us understand more about how they perceive us, and how they are likely to respond to what we say and do.

Self-presentation

The quality of our performance in any social encounter is influenced by our beliefs about self.

Performance and beliefs about self as agent

An all too common self-defeating belief which can undermine our interpersonal competence is the conviction that there is nothing we can do to control the outcome of a social interaction. People who believe this may engage in what Ellis describes as disabling self-talk and tell themselves that they cannot cope. This can create a set of circumstances in which we fail to take any voluntary action to improve a relationship because we believe that there is nothing we can do to bring about a desired change.

Gahagan (1984: 148) also refers to this and argues that: 'People must *do* something in order to change their encounters and relationships, but they won't do so unless they believe that as agents they can be effective.' She notes that it is often our passivity which undermines our achievement of valued outcomes in social encounters. All too often we allow others to determine the occasions of interaction and the course that interaction will take.

The lack of a sense of agency and associated passivity can have many causes. It may be related to low self-esteem and negative beliefs about one's own value. This can undermine self-confidence and the motivation to act. It can also be learned, based on personal experience or the observation of what has happened to others. Seligman (1975) developed a theory of learned helplessness which asserts that our expectation about our ability to control outcomes is influenced by our past experience. The theory states that when we are subjected to events that are uncontrollable (that is, where the probability of an outcome is the same irrespective of how hard we try to influence what happens), we develop the *expectation* that whatever we do we will not be able to exercise much influence over the outcome. This expectation produces motivational and cognitive deficits. In social situations, motivational deficits can result in our failing to take any voluntary action to shape the outcome of an interpersonal interaction. Because we believe we cannot exercise any control over outcomes we are not motivated to even try.

Cognitive deficits, on the other hand, can lead to our failing to recognise situations where we can control what happens. Once we have learned that we are helpless, we fail to see opportunities to exercise influence, even after we have engaged in encounters where our own behaviour has actually had an important impact on outcomes. A consequence of cognitive deficits may be that we attribute any success to chance or good luck rather than to our own efforts. Changing this expectation requires us to change our attribution of success or failure from factors we cannot influence, such as luck, to factors we can control.

Re-examining our past experience to identify the extent to which we have actually managed to exercise control over outcomes can sometimes help us reinforce beliefs about self-agency. However, this may have the opposite effect if expectations of helplessness and motivational deficits have influenced our behaviour and encouraged us to adopt a passive role in recent encounters.

An alternative approach is to challenge the assumption of helplessness by deliberately taking action, behaving in new ways and reflecting on the outcome (both essential steps in the cycle of experiential learning). This can provide fresh evidence about our ability to influence outcomes, and this evidence may help us challenge any assumptions of helplessness that are part of our subjective theory of social interaction.

Developing greater self-awareness

The more aware we are of our values, beliefs and attitudes (and how these affect the assumptions we make about ourselves, others and the situations we encounter), the better equipped we will be to read the actual or potential behaviour of others and to construct effective courses of action in accordance with our reading. Two exercises that are designed to help you raise your level of self-awareness are presented at the end of this chapter.

Furnham (1990) notes that individuals who are high 'self-monitors' appear to be better able to regulate their presentation of self to fit with what they perceive to be a desirable and appropriate pattern of behaviour than people who are low self-monitors.

People differ in terms of the extent to which they are aware of themselves. Wicklund (1975) differentiates between subjective and objective self-awareness. Subjective self-awareness refers to our awareness of the sensations associated with doing a task. When trying to ride a bike for the first time we may be so involved in maintaining our balance that we give little thought to how we appear to others or to ourselves. If, however, we notice that there are other people observing us we may begin to think about what they are thinking about us and how they are evaluating our performance. This is an example of objective self-awareness. It is an awareness of ourselves as objects in our own eyes and the eyes of others. For the purpose of developing interpersonal skills it may be useful to work at improving the level of our objective self-awareness.

Monitoring how we behave in the here-and-now

One way of improving our objective self-awareness is to monitor how we behave in the here-and-now. We can do this by opening a 'second channel' and observing ourselves interacting with other people. This approach may be likened to an 'out-of-body' experience. Imagine yourself floating somewhere in a corner of the room looking down on the interaction as it unfolds. Observe how you are behaving and think about the reasons behind your actions.

You might open a second channel and observe what you are doing while you are trying to help somebody with a problem.

- *How do you attempt to help?* Do you listen until you are confident that both you and the other person have a clear understanding of the problem, or do you quickly move on to tell the other person what he 'should' do to manage his problem more effectively?
- *What makes you behave in this way?* Once you are aware of what you are doing, give some thought to why you are doing it. For example, if you have observed that you adopt a prescriptive approach to helping, consider why you adopt this approach. Is it because you believe that you know best, and therefore that you have a duty to solve the other person's problem for him?
- *Give some thought to outcomes.* If you suspect that this belief is what is motivating your behaviour, consider how it may affect the outcome of the interaction. Consider, also, how this belief may influence your behaviour and other people's response in different situations, such as team meetings or when discussing domestic affairs with your partner or flat mate.

Another example of where opening a second channel may be helpful is when you meet somebody for the first time. Monitor what you are thinking at the time and coach yourself to identify and test the assumptions you are making.

- What is your first impression of the other person?
- What information have you used to form this impression?
- Resist accepting this first impression as fact. Tell yourself to regard the image as a working hypothesis and actively seek out additional information that will test it.
- Monitor yourself to ensure that you not only seek out information that confirms your first impression but also that you pay particular attention to behaviour that does not fit.

Reflecting on patterns of past behaviour

Another way of improving our objective self-awareness is to reflect on our past experience in order to identify habitual, and possibly unconscious, ways of behaving (Exercise 3.1 will help you do this). Once we have identified patterns of past behaviour we will be able to recognise them as we monitor our behaviour in the here-and-now. We can reflect on whether these habitual patterns are functional. We can also consider whether they tell us anything about our values, beliefs and assumptions and how these are reflected in the outcomes that we seem to be seeking in our relationships with others.

Exercise 3.1 Reflecting on patterns of past behaviour

You could, for example, write down an account of the last three performance appraisal interviews you were involved in (identify interviews where you occupied the same role, either as appraiser or appraisee). Alternatively, you could reflect on three discussions with your supervisor or course tutor. Present each record in the form of a script:

What I said,

What he said, and so on.

It does not have to be a word-perfect record. If you cannot remember the precise details of what was said record how you think each of the interviews probably unfolded. When you have done this, review the scripts for clues about your overall approach. Are there any similarities between the interviews? If you were the appraiser or supervisor, what does the evidence tell you about your approach? For example, were you developmental or judgemental? If you were the appraisee or supervisee what does the evidence tell you about your interpersonal style? For example, were you assertive or submissive? How does this evidence of your 'theory in use' compare to the theory you espouse?

Audio- and video-recordings of our social encounters can be a useful source of information for identifying patterns of behaviour. However, when using this kind of data we need to remember that if we had been aware of the fact that we were being recorded this may have influenced how we behaved. We may have made a conscious effort to behave in accordance with our espoused theory, and therefore the evidence may not reflect how we *typically* behave. (This effect can, however, be a positive aid to skills development. When we are practising interpersonal skills, recordings can provide objective feedback on our ability to behave in new ways and break habitual patterns of interacting.)

Being open and responsive to feedback from others

Other people are often aware of things about us that we are not conscious of. For example, they may be aware that we never fail to communicate our preferences when relating to some colleagues but that we are not assertive when relating to others. They may also recognise that when we are being assertive it is usually when we are relating to younger, less experienced or junior colleagues, and that when we fail to be assertive it is usually when we are interacting with older, more experienced or senior colleagues.

It may be very helpful if we were aware of this information about ourselves, but others may be reluctant to give it to us. One reason has to do with 'face'. If we present ourselves as a confident and competent professional who is never afraid to tell others what we think, it can be humiliating if this positive self-image is challenged in public. A successful challenge may cause us to 'lose face'. This can also be an embarrassing experience for the person who gives the feedback that causes the loss of face, and for anyone else who is present. Consequently, people tend to be tactful in their behaviour towards others and are often reluctant to give them honest feedback. (A dentist noticed, as a patient was recovering from an anaesthetic, that she had been wearing a wig and that it had become dislodged during the treatment. He quickly replaced it. Just as the patient was leaving the surgery the dentist noticed that he had replaced the wig the wrong way round. He had known the patient for many years but had not known that she wore a wig. He assumed that it was important to her that this was her secret and, quickly thinking on his feet, he decided not to tell her that it was on back to front so as not to embarrass her. It was only when she had left the surgery that he realised she would find out anyway. She would realise that it must have fallen off in the surgery and that the dentist knew about it, and also that many of the people whom she had met on the way home would also have noticed. The dentist regretted that he had not told her, but he recognised that he had behaved this way in the mistaken belief that it would save his patient embarrassment and loss of face.)

Even when people are reluctant to give us feedback, it may be possible for us to pick up clues about what they are thinking and feeling. Their body language often gives off unintentional non-verbal signals that can indicate their true feelings. The kinds of signals that might indicate whether somebody is disgusted, angry or bored with another person's behaviour are considered in Chapter 5.

There may also be many occasions when other people are willing to give us honest feedback but we are reluctant to receive it. While we may have a need to know (did I do well?), we may also have a fear of finding out. We all like to receive feedback that reinforces our own positive self-image (for example, that we are a very competent negotiator, especially under pressure). We may be less happy to be told that we failed to get a good deal out of the negotiation because we gave away too much information when pressed by the other party.

There are many factors that prevent us from being truly open to feedback. Reference has already been made to our reluctance to admit to ourselves anything that might undermine our self-image. Accepting this kind of information when we have discovered it for ourselves is one thing. We may be willing to monitor our own behaviour in the here-and-now or to re-evaluate our past performance and search for dysfunctional patterns of behaviour. However, it is quite another thing to be given this kind of feedback by somebody else. It is not uncommon for the recipients of feedback to be defensive and to dismiss it as an invalid message from a single, unreliable source. We may also be reluctant to accept feedback from others, and especially to work with others to explore what its implications are, because we feel that this may in some way make us dependent on the provider of the feedback. However, while many of us find it difficult to accept feedback, it can be an invaluable source of information about the effectiveness of our performance when relating to others.

Developing interpersonal skills

Mention has already been made of the possibilities for monitoring our own behaviour in the here-and-now and for reflecting on previous episodes of behaviour. Both of these approaches can help us identify how our values, beliefs, attitudes and mood states influence how we behave. They can also be a source of valuable data for diagnosing what we may want to do differently and for obtaining feedback on how successful we are at changing and managing our performance.

The perception matrix (Exercise 3.2) is designed to help you identify the kinds of questions you ask yourself about others and provide you with feedback about how others see you.

Exercise 3.2 Perception matrix

The objectives of this exercise are to:

- Identify the kind of information we attend to when perceiving other people.
- Compare the kind of information we attend to (the questions we ask ourselves about others) with the information others attend to when we are looking at the same third party.
- Consider the complexity of our person perceptions. Do we ask ourselves only a limited number of questions about others or do we attend to a wide range of different kinds of information?
- Review the answers to the above and consider whether there are things we typically ignore but which, if attended to, could improve our understanding of others.

The exercise is designed to be used in small groups. The ideal group size is between four and six members. It involves two steps.

First, working alone, write down lists of words or statements that describe how you see yourself and every other member of the group. (It may be helpful to reproduce each of the following tables on sheets of A3 paper in landscape format.)

HOW I SEE:

HOW I SEE MYSELF	Jo	Bill	Anne	Steve	Mary

Note the kinds of things you attend to. Do you ask yourself the same questions when producing your descriptions of yourself and others? If not, why not? Speculate about why you ask yourself these questions. Is it to do with your values, beliefs, past experience or what?

Second, when everybody has completed this step, meet as a group and begin to share your lists with each other. An effective procedure is for one person to be the focus of attention in turn. When it is your turn, fill out the left-hand column of the second table with your own description of yourself. Then invite each member of the group to share with you their description of you and record what they say in the appropriate column.

HOW I AM SEEN BY:

HOW I SEE MYSELF	Jo	Bill	Anne	Steve	Mary

Compare the way you see yourself with the way others see you.

- Are there any common themes that others mention?
- If so, are they reflected in your description of yourself?

If different people see you in very different ways, why is this?

- Could it be because different people, with different values, beliefs, attitudes and so on, ask themselves different questions about you (and others)?
- Alternatively, could it be because they have different kinds of role relationship with you (boss, subordinate, colleagues, intimate friend or casual acquaintance)?

When it is somebody else's turn to receive feedback, pay attention to the kind of information people refer to when describing them.

- Does their feedback refer to things that you have noted and feel are important?
- Alternatively, does it refer to things you have not considered?

When everybody has had their 'turn' share your views about what you have learned from the experience.

The identity review (Exercise 3.3) is an exercise designed to help you learn more about yourself, and how your beliefs and the things you value affect the way you relate to others.

Exercise 3.3 Effect of our concept of self on our behaviour towards others

The aim of this exercise is to develop a greater sense of awareness of who you are and how this influences how you behave towards others.

You can do this exercise by yourself but there are advantages to be gained from doing it with somebody else. The need to present your thoughts to somebody else can help you clarify your thinking. The other person may also be able to offer an alternative way of viewing the information you present about yourself and may challenge some of your taken-for-granted assumptions.

In order to complete this exercise you will need ten filing cards, post-its or similar-sized pieces of paper. Number them 1 to 10.

1   *Working alone*, write on each card a different statement of how you see yourself.

There are no constraints on the form these statements might take. For example, some people see themselves in terms of:

*   Roles (student, sister, manager, carer).
*   Group membership (Australian, working class, Rotarian, member of first team).
*   Beliefs (Christian, pacifist, superior to others – for example, men superior to women).
*   Qualities (extrovert, honest, confident).
*   Styles or patterns of behaviour (passive, autocratic, demanding).
*   Needs (to be in control, win, belong, etc.).

Typically lists contain more than one type of statement.

Focus on those things which are really central to your sense of yourself – things that, if you lost them, would make a radical difference to your identity and to the meaning of life for you. Be honest, describe yourself as you think you really are, not as you think you should be.

---

2 Still working alone, consider each item on your list of 'Who you are' in turn. Try to imagine how it would be if that particular item were no longer true of you. For example, if 'student' or 'employee' is one of the items, what would the loss of this role mean to you? How would it feel? What would you do? What would your life be like then?

3 After you have gone through all ten statements reviewing them in this way, the next step is to arrange them in rank order. The first or highest ranked card should be the one which names the aspect of self (for example, role or pattern of behaviour) which you find is most essential to your sense of self – the one which, if lost, would require the greatest adjustment. The rest of the statements should be ranked in descending order of difficulty in adjusting to the loss. The end result should be a list ranked on grounds of what is essential to your sense of being yourself.

   Avoid the trap of using *desirability* as the basis for your ranking. Some of your statements may refer to aspects of yourself that do not fit with your concept of 'ideal self'. For example, you may describe yourself as shy and unassuming but have a preferred image of self as assertive and outgoing. This does *not* mean that this kind of less desired aspect of self automatically falls towards the lower end of the ranking. The rank ordering is to be based on how big an adjustment you would have to make if you lost it. Sometimes it is the aspects of our self that we most dislike (heavy smoker) that we find hardest to give up.

4 Still working alone, look at how you have sorted and ranked the cards. Do they fall into any groupings? What comes next to what? How do you feel about these groupings and the ranking?

5 *How does 'who you are' influence how you relate to others?*
   This is the final step in the exercise. It can be helpful to do it with somebody else. Take turns in sharing your identity review with each other. When it is your turn to share do not justify who you are. First of all, concentrate on explaining what the items you have generated mean for *you*. Then move on to speculate about how they may affect your relationships with others.

45

Some of the questions you might consider could include:

- *'Do your needs affect the quality of your relationships?'*
  You may, for example, have a high need to control others but work with others who do not wish to be controlled.

- *'Do you assume that what is important to you is also equally important to others?'*
  You may, for example, attach great importance to work and the achievement of work-related goals. This may be reflected in the way you behave towards others and the way you react to them when they do not seem to be as committed as you think they should be to the achievement of work goals.

- *'Do you assume that the roles you occupy (parent, spouse, child, subordinate, expert, boss) give you certain rights and obligations when relating to others?'*
  You may, for example, assume that when you are in a subordinate role you should only behave in certain ways.

Note: The first four sections of this exercise are based on Galvin Whittaker's abridged form of a life-planning exercise that was originally developed by Herbert A. Sheppard.

Summary

This chapter has considered how self-awareness can contribute to interpersonal competence. It has examined how it can affect our ability to read the behaviour of others, construct courses of action and deliver an effective performance. It has also discussed some of the ways in which we can improve our level of self-awareness by monitoring our behaviour in the here-and-now, reflecting on patterns of past behaviour and being more receptive to feedback from others. The chapter concluded with two exercises designed to raise self-awareness.

References

Argyris, C. (1982) 'The executive mind and double loop learning', *Organizational Dynamics*, autumn: 5–22.

Covey, S.R. (1989) *The Seven Habits of Highly Effective People*, London: Simon & Schuster.

Furnham, A. (1990) 'Language and personality', in H.Giles and W.P. Robinson (eds) *Handbook of Language and Social Psychology,* Chichester: Wiley.

Gahagan, J. (1984) *Social Interaction and its Management,* London: Methuen.

Seligman, M.E.P. (1975) *Helplessness,* San Francisco, CA: W.H. Freeman.

Wicklund, R. (1975) 'Objective self-awareness', in L. Berkowitz (ed.) *Advances in Social Psychology,* Vol. 8, New York: Academic Press.

4

LISTENING

Learning objective

To recognise the factors that can influence a person's ability to fully and accurately appreciate the messages others are trying to communicate to them and the steps they can take (and the skills they need to develop) to improve their capability to listen.

After reading this chapter you will:

- Be aware of four different types of listening.
- Recognise listening problems associated with the speaker, the listener, the message and the environment.
- Understand the nature of active listening.
- Be aware of steps listeners can take to prepare to listen.
- Recognise the importance of attending skills and communicating to others that the listener is 'with them'.
- Recognise the importance of following skills and encouraging the speaker to communicate effectively.
- Recognise the importance of reflecting skills and demonstrating understanding and acceptance.

Listening is a core competence

People who cannot listen cannot relate. Poor listening undermines our ability to communicate with others. Anyone who wants to be an effective negotiator, interviewer, coach, consultant, leader or group member needs to be a good listener. However, few of us ever receive any formal training in how to listen effectively.

Listening involves more than just hearing what somebody has said. It involves interpreting what has been heard, and searching for a full and accurate understanding of the meaning of the other's message. Listening also involves more than merely attending to verbal messages. To be a good listener we need to be able to 'read' both verbal and non-verbal messages. A

48

more detailed treatment of non-verbal communication is reserved for the next chapter.

We are all aware that different people can and do interpret the same message in different ways. Tannen (1991) illustrates this with the example of a patient who has just had a lump removed from her breast. The patient told her sister that it was upsetting to have been cut into, and that looking at the stitches was upsetting because they left a seam that had changed the contour of her breast. Her sister replied: 'I know. When I had my operation I felt the same way.' The patient made the same observation to her friend, who said: 'I know, it's like your body has been violated.' When she told her husband he said: 'You can have plastic surgery to cover up your scar and restore the shape of your breast.' Tannen argues that, when talking to her sister, friend and husband, the patient wanted them to understand how she was feeling. The husband failed to listen to this aspect of the message. She interpreted his response as suggesting yet more surgery, just at the time when she was trying to tell him how much this operation had upset her.

In the work context, poor listening can be the source of many damaging misunderstandings. This chapter examines some of the most common barriers to effective listening and explores what people can do to improve the quality of their listening.

Hargie et al. (1994), after reviewing the work of others, identified four main types of listening.

1   *Comprehension listening* is the kind of listening we engage in when conducting fact-finding interviews or attending lectures. It involves listening for facts, ideas and themes that may be of future use.
2   *Evaluative listening* is the kind of listening we engage in when trying to assess the merits of another's argument, especially where the argument is intended to persuade. Persuading involves motivating us to accept an argument by biasing the message to increase its appeal. Most advertisements are persuasive in nature, as are the arguments of sales persons and negotiators. Evaluative listening involves us in trying to detect bias, and to identify the strengths and weaknesses of the propositions the other is making.
3   *Empathic listening* is the kind of listening we engage in when we are trying to understand what another is trying to communicate from their perspective. It not only involves us in attending to and understanding the thoughts, beliefs and feelings of the speaker, but also in communicating this understanding to the speaker.
4   *Appreciative listening* is the kind of listening we engage in for pleasure. It may occur when listening to poetry or children playing. It involves us in seeking out signals or messages that we want to hear.

The content of this chapter is not concerned with appreciative listening.

Many of the concepts and techniques discussed here will apply equally to comprehension, evaluative and empathic listening; however, most attention will be focused on empathic listening because experience suggests that this is the kind of listening which managers find most difficult.

The first part of the chapter considers the factors that influence our ability to listen. Some of the ideas introduced in Chapter 3 are elaborated, and consideration is given to why certain kinds of information are attended to and others are ignored. Attention will also be given to some of the variables that determine how we interpret information and give meaning to messages. This discussion will be followed by a more detailed look at the process of communication, and some of the common listening problems associated with the speaker, the listener, the message and the environment.

The second part of the chapter considers the steps we can take and the skills we need to develop if we are to improve our capacity to listen effectively. Several exercises designed to promote skill development are presented at the end of each section of the discussion.

Factors influencing our ability to listen effectively

There are many competing demands for a listener's attention. For example, in a selection interview the total attention of all members of the appointing committee may not be focused on what the candidate is saying. One of the interviewers might be more interested in factors such as how the candidate is dressed, the mark on his collar and the smell of tobacco smoke that surrounds his person.

Being aware of our own filters can help us listen more effectively. Interviewers can prepare a check-list to help them make sure that proper attention is paid to all the relevant messages and that the effects of *selectivity* are minimised. An awareness of personal bias may also help with the *interpretation* of information. Empathic listening involves deliberately working to suppress our own biases. It involves thinking about the background and experience of the speakers and trying to understand what they are saying from within their own frames of reference.

Some of the factors that influence what we attend to and how we interpret what we hear will be considered in more detail in Chapter 6. In this chapter attention will be restricted to a brief consideration of some of the common barriers to effective communication. Following Hargie *et al.* (1994), these barriers may be grouped under four headings: the speaker, the listener, the message and the environment.

The speaker

Speaker characteristics can influence our ability to listen.

Who the speaker is can affect how the message is interpreted. Sometimes we hear who the other people are rather than what they are saying. Messages from high-status people may receive more attention than messages from low-status people. A common problem which detracts from the effectiveness of work groups is the inappropriate way in which members often weigh the contributions of others (see Chapter 9). A speaker's task-relevant expertise may be discounted because of his or her gender, age or lack of seniority.

Speech rate can also affect listening. The normal speech rate is about 140 words per minute. Tubbs and Moss (1994) refer to research that has involved the time compression of speech in which tape-recorded messages have been speeded up without changing pitch level (thereby avoiding the chipmunk-like effect). Findings suggest that, depending on the complexity of the message, subjects can maintain reasonable levels of understanding up to rates of between 400 and 500 words per minute. Others support this view but suggest that comprehension begins to deteriorate at rates less than 400 words per minute. Wolff *et al.* (1983) report that listeners 'prefer to listen, can comprehend better, and are more likely to believe a message that is presented at the rate of 190 words or more per minute.' They go on to suggest that listening can improve up to 280 words per minute but that it begins to deteriorate with higher rates. Although it appears that we can think at a rate considerably faster than 280 words per minute, we require a reasonable differential between speaking and thinking rates to process what we have heard. However, there is also evidence that slower rates of speech, especially when they drop much below 125 words per minute, can impair effective listening just as much as excessively fast rates. Our capacity to process information is under-utilised, so our attention begins to drift. Day-dreaming, thinking about a difficult situation at home or a challenging new assignment at work are the kinds of interference that can affect listening when the speaker is talking too slowly. Of course, the optimum speech rate in any situation will always be influenced by a number of factors such as the complexity of the message being communicated, its novelty and so on.

Emotionality can be an important barrier to effective listening. When a speaker expresses high levels of emotion – for example, anger or despair – we may be overwhelmed by the emotional content of the message and find it very difficult to listen to the words.

Hargie *et al.* (1994) suggest that one way of managing this kind of problem is to allow speakers time to ventilate emotions, to have their say. If we are to understand the speaker's message we cannot ignore the emotional content, since it is important. However, if we allow ourselves to be overpowered by it we may fail to pay proper attention to the factual content of the message and therefore may fail to fully and accurately understand what the speaker has to say.

Ostell *et al.* (1999) suggest several principles and tactics for managing others' emotions. These include:

- allowing speakers to ventilate their emotions by giving them permission to express the emotions they find difficult to control;
- calling 'time out' so that the speaker has the opportunity to go away and control his or her emotions before the discussion is resumed;
- using reflective statements (such as 'you seem annoyed that . . .');
- apologising if we feel that we have behaved inappropriately and provoked the other's emotional state;
- avoiding behaviours that might further heighten the other's emotional state (such as describing their behaviour as stupid or their work as worthless).

By sustaining the interaction and helping speakers to ventilate or control their emotions we can help them reach a point where, on the one hand, they are able to communicate a more balanced message and, on the other, they are more ready to listen to a reasoned response.

The listener

Several factors can interfere with our ability to listen.

Premature formulation of response. While someone is talking to us we listen and interpret what they are saying. However, we may sometimes begin to think about how to reply before the other person has finished speaking. This kind of premature response, even if only in the mind, can undermine our ability to listen. The effect of working out a reply before the other party has finished speaking may be illustrated by thinking about what you picture when you hear the words '*Woman, Table, Knife, Cloth*'.

Many people think of a domestic scene, possibly a mealtime or the preparation of food. For these people, if the words 'woman, table, knife, cloth' were to be followed by 'emergency, surgeon, blood, intestines' the message or picture in their mind would change dramatically. The person who had stopped listening after the first four words (in order to prepare a reply) would be unable to offer an appropriate response to the speaker's message. Effective listening requires that we give full attention to everything the speaker has to communicate.

Motivation can influence how well we will attend to what the speaker has to say. If we feel that others have something useful to say we are more likely to work harder at listening than if we expect their message to be boring or irrelevant.

Physical condition is another factor that can influence how well we attend. Listeners who are ill or tired may find it more difficult to concentrate than listeners who are well rested and alert. It is not unusual, for example, for us to find it easier to listen to a lecture in the morning than immediately after a heavy lunch when we are feeling sleepy, or late in the evening after a busy day.

Linguistic aptitude. People who can make sense of a message are more likely to listen attentively than those who cannot understand what is being said. One factor that can influence this is our ability to organise incoming information, to identify key elements of the message and to store these in appropriate conceptual compartments. Hargie *et al.* (1994) suggest that linguistic aptitude may be correlated positively with the ability to comprehend what is being said because those with a wider vocabulary can more readily understand and assimilate a wider range of concepts.

The message

The structure of the message can influence how easy or difficult it will be to comprehend. It is not unusual to hear critical comments about people who seem unable to 'stick to the point' or whose messages are 'as clear as mud'.

Background knowledge. Difficulties can arise if speakers assume, incorrectly, that we are in possession of important background information and/or know what it is that the speakers are attempting to achieve. If speakers make these kinds of assumptions they may only bother to communicate part of the message, thus leaving us with the problem of making sense of a message that is incomplete or ambiguous.

The amount of detail, either too much or too little, and the order in which information and arguments are presented can influence comprehension.

Significance and order of presentation. The significance that different parts of the message might have for listeners may also be linked to order of presentation in a way that can either help or hinder listening. If one part of the message is highly significant for some of the listeners, they may continue to think about its implications after the speaker moves on to talk about the next point. In this way listeners may miss important parts of the message. Elements of the message that some or all of the listeners might want to think about need to be taken into account when the speaker is formulating the structure of a communication. Listeners also need to be ready to store significant information for later processing or to signal to the speaker if parts of the message go unheard.

The environment

The environment is a variable which intervenes between the speaker and the listener in a way that can influence the quality of the message which the listener receives.

Auditory noise. The level of noise in a machine shop might make it very difficult for us to hear what the speaker is saying. If the message is important, those involved may decide to move to a quiet office to change the nature of the environment.

Other noise. Auditory noise is only one of many environmental problems.

The quality of ventilation can influence our ability to listen, as can the presence of anything which competes with the message for our attention, for example, a letter left where it can be read or an interesting view from a window.

Active listening

Effective listening involves more than simply hearing what the speaker has said; it involves the search for a full and accurate understanding of the meaning of another's verbal and non-verbal messages. Active listening offers an approach to understanding other people's messages in a way that deals with many of the problems identified so far.

The aim of this second part of the chapter is to identify and elaborate the skills we need in order to improve our ability to listen effectively. This involves developing the skills which:

- help speakers 'tell their stories' to the best of their ability;
- keep our attention focused on the speaker's message;
- help us give appropriate weight to what the speaker says;
- assist us in organising the information we receive so that we can make sense of even complex or badly structured messages;
- minimise the problems of personal bias.

Skilled listeners are able to attend to both the factual and effective content of a message. We should neither ignore nor be overwhelmed by the speaker's emotionally and we need to be able to interpret what is said in a way that reflects accurately what the speaker is thinking and feeling about the content of the message.

Listening skills

While different writers describe the behaviours that promote effective listening in different ways, there appears to be a large measure of agreement about what constitute the core listening skills.

Egan (1998) identifies four basic communication skills:

1 *attending*, which refers to the way listeners orient themselves to speakers, both physically and psychologically;
2 *listening*, which involves receiving and understanding the verbal and non-verbal messages transmitted by speakers;
3 *empathy*, which involves listeners understanding messages from within the speakers' frames of reference and communicating this to them;
4 *probing*, which involves encouraging and prompting speakers to talk about themselves and to define their concern in more concrete and specific terms.

54

Deetz and Stevenson (1986) discuss the importance of:

- *attending to others*, and
- *taking the perspective of others.*

Hargie *et al.* (1994) mention a range of responses required in active listening such as:

- *verbal following,*
- *reflecting,* and
- *probing.*

Bolton (1986) identifies twelve separate listening skills which he groups into three skill clusters:

1   *attending skills,*
2   *following skills,*
3   *reflecting skills.*

Listening skills will be discussed in this chapter under four headings. The first is preparation, and the following three are those labelled by Bolton as attending, following and reflecting.

Preparation

There are a number of things we can do to prepare for listening. Preparation is possible because many of the occasions when we need to listen (such as during a performance appraisal interview, project review or daily debrief with the children after school) may be anticipated. Deetz and Stevenson (1986) note that all too often the opportunity for preparation is lost because potential preparation time, if used at all, is spent worrying about what to say rather than how to listen. The kind of preparation we can engage in involves:

- Arranging important listening tasks for a time when we are least likely to be stressed or fatigued, or eating a light meal and avoiding alcohol immediately prior to an important meeting.
- Increasing receptivity by making a conscious effort to temporarily put aside preoccupying concerns, such as a recent row with a boss or the need to book a holiday flight as quickly as possible.
- Arranging an environment which contains as few distractions as possible, thereby encouraging all parties to concentrate on communicating.
- Reviewing background material, such as notes and reports, or issues to be discussed.

This kind of preparation can stimulate interest and help create the right mental set, which in turn can facilitate understanding by helping us identify key messages and organise incoming information into appropriate conceptual compartments.

Exercise 4.1 involves reflecting on the extent to which you prepare yourself for important listening tasks.

Exercise 4.1 Preparing to listen

Think about some recent occasions when it was important that you paid careful attention to what others had to say. Reflect on what you did to prepare yourself to listen.

Did you do all that you could to:

• Arrange an appropriate time to listen?	Yes		No
• Put aside other concerns?	Yes		No
• Arrange an environment free of distractions?	Yes		No
• Consult and review background material?	Yes		No

What else could you have done to prepare yourself to listen?

Attending

The second set of listening skills involves us in letting others know that we are 'with them'. Most of us have been told, at some time or other, that we are not listening, and we have leapt to our own defence by repeating most of what had been said. We had heard, we could repeat the message like a tape-recorder, but if the truth were known we had not been listening, and this fact was apparent to the speaker.

People want to feel that listeners are genuinely interested in what they have to say and that they will work hard to understand their message. It will be more difficult to develop rapport, and speakers will be much less likely to give a full account of themselves, if they feel that the listener is preoccupied and disinterested.

You may find that Exercise 4.2 will help you identify the effects of not attending and raise your awareness of some of the behaviours that signal to others whether or not you are attending to them and listening to what they say.

Exercise 4.2 Not attending to others

Divide into pairs. Identify one person as <u>A</u> and the other as <u>B</u>.

<u>A</u> talks to <u>B</u> *for at least two minutes* about any topic that comes to mind.

> For example, the ingredients of an ideal holiday, the person you find it most difficult to get on with, or the most pressing problem facing the world community today.

<u>B</u> tries <u>not</u> to listen to what <u>A</u> is saying (without leaving the room!).

At the end of the two minutes <u>A</u> and <u>B</u> reflect on the experience and:

*   Identify what <u>B</u> did which signalled to <u>A</u> that <u>B</u> was not listening.
*   Identify how <u>A</u> felt when trying to talk to somebody who appeared not to be listening and what effect this had on <u>A</u>. (Sometimes the people who assume the role of <u>A</u> find it very difficult to continue talking for the full two minutes.)
*   Relate this experience to the way you typically attend to others. Consider whether you tend to be an 'active' or a 'passive' listener. Active listeners use appropriate non-verbal behaviours to signal to others that they are attending to them and listening to what they have to say. Passive listeners may pay very careful attention to what others are saying but they fail to signal this to the others concerned.

Listeners, all of the time, give out cues and messages with their bodies. Egan (1998) argues that by being mindful of the cues and messages we are sending, listeners can deliberately develop and project an image that tells speakers that we are 'with them'. Egan offers the mnemonic *SOLER* as an aid to remembering ways in which we can project a sense of presence.

S: Face the speaker *Squarely*. This is a basic posture of involvement that tells speakers we are with them. Sitting 'squarely' need not be taken too literally. In some situations anxious speakers may be overpowered by too much attention, so a slight angling of the position may be called for, but if we turn too far away the message we communicate might be one of indifference or rejection. We have all heard the expression 'he gave me the cold shoulder'.

O: Adopt an *Open posture*. Tightly crossed arms or legs may communicate to the speaker that we are in a defensive mood and/or not open to influence. Uncrossed or loosely crossed limbs communicate a sense of openness and approachability.

L: *Lean* the upper part of your body towards the speaker. A slight inclination of the listener's body towards the speaker communicates interest and attention. An enthralled audience may sometimes be described as 'sitting on the edge of their seats'. Leaning backwards or slouching can be taken to mean that we are not in tune with the speaker or are bored by the message we are hearing. As with facing the speaker squarely, leaning too far forward can be overpowering in some circumstances. Good listeners are alert to feedback which tells them whether to lean more towards the speaker or to back off slightly at different points in the interaction.

E: Maintain good *Eye contact*. Maintaining good eye contact with speakers is one of the most powerful ways of communicating that we are with them and want to hear what they have to say. Good eye contact does not mean maintaining a hard, fixed stare. This can project an image of hostile confrontation. To communicate involvement the eyes should be focused softly on the speaker's face and, rather than maintaining uninterrupted contact, the gaze should shift occasionally, to a gesturing hand or to the notes the speaker might be consulting, and then returning to the speaker's face. Looking away, especially if this happens too frequently, signals that we are not involved. Consider how you feel when talking to somebody who keeps glancing over your shoulder to look at other people in the room or who keeps looking at their watch or the clock on the wall. Taken to an extreme, the almost total absence of eye contact usually signals indifference or boredom. However, many people are passive listeners. They pay close attention to what is being said but they doodle on their pad or look out of the window while the speaker is talking. Although they are listening, the message the speaker receives is that they 'don't want to know'. This can be very inhibiting for the speaker and is one of the reasons why this part of the chapter is headed 'Active listening'. The communication process can be considerably more effective if we engage *actively* in the process of listening.

R: Try to be relatively *Relaxed* while engaging in these behaviours. If we are too tense or nervous the speaker will not feel at ease. The aim is neither to be so relaxed and laid back that the speaker feels that we are not prepared to work at understanding what they have to say, nor so tense that they are frightened off and disinclined to talk. What is required is the projection of a relaxed but alert posture that suggests both a comfortable relationship and a genuine interest in what the speaker has to say. Listeners who are too tense are likely to hold their body too still and create an impression of being very controlled and aloof. Smooth movement, especially if it responds to and reflects what the speaker is saying, suggests listening with empathic understanding.

The *SOLER* mnemonic offers a set of pointers to the kinds of behaviour that communicate a sense of presence to the speaker. These need not always be adhered to strictly. They are not rules; rather they are reminders of the importance of non-verbal behaviour. The listener's body is a vehicle for communication. We need to be constantly aware of all the cues and messages that we are sending.

DEVELOPING ATTENDING SKILLS

A three-step process can help you develop many of the listening skills referred to in this chapter.

1   The first step involves observing what others do, and thinking about what they could do differently to listen more effectively. Observing others in this way can help you develop your observation skills and focus your attention on what people actually do when they are listening. Relating what you observe to the ideas and concepts presented in this chapter may also help you identify a standard or benchmark of good practice.
2   The second step involves using these observation skills to monitor and assess how *you* listen and to identify what you could do differently to improve your listening skills.
3   The third step involves experimenting with new behaviours, taking action to improve the way you listen and monitoring the effect this has.

Exercise 4.3 focuses on observing others, the first of these three steps. You can observe people listening almost anywhere. For example, you may have the opportunity to observe diners in a restaurant, a parent listening to what a child has to say or a shop assistant trying to understand the nature of a customer's complaint. You may also observe video-recordings of people interacting with each other or trainees engaged in a role-play exercise. However, it will be helpful if wherever possible, you can, observe at least two people, one whom you believe is a poor listener, and another whom you believe is a good listener.

Exercise 4.3 Attending to others

Observe at least two people listening to others. Did the people whom you observed communicate to others that they were interested in what they had to say? Use the SOLER mnemonic as a check-list to record how much of the time they attended to the other person.

Time spent:

S Facing speaker **S**quarely	Most of the time			Little of the time
O Adopting **O**pen posture	Most of the time			Little of the time
L Leaning towards speaker	Most of the time			Little of the time
E Maintaining **E**ye contact	Most of the time			Little of the time
R Appearing **R**elaxed	Most of the time			Little of the time

What could they have done to improve their attending behaviour?

After completing this exercise you may find it useful to seek opportunities to monitor and reflect on your own attending behaviour and identify what you can do to improve the way you attend to others.

Following

Bolton (1986) argues that one of the primary tasks of the listener is to stay out of the speaker's way so that the listener can discover how speakers view their situation. However, this objective is often frustrated because the 'listener' interrupts and diverts the speaker by asking too many questions or making too many statements. All too often, when we think we are listening, we do too much of the talking.

We can encourage the speaker to talk, can better concentrate on the task of listening and can gently seek out more information to help promote a better understanding of the speaker's message by using door openers, minimal prompts, accents, statements, questions, attentive silences and a number of special concentration techniques.

DOOR OPENERS

Careful attention to non-verbal clues can often signal when somebody is preoccupied or worried and may want to talk. In these circumstances the listener may be able to help the other by offering what Bolton (1986) describes as a non-coercive invitation to talk. This may be either an invitation to begin a conversation or an encouragement to continue if the speaker shows signs that he is unsure about saying more. Bolton suggests that door openers typically have four elements:

1   A description of the other person's body language, for example, 'You are not looking yourself today'; 'You sound a bit low'.
2   An invitation to talk or continue talking, for example, 'Feel like talking?'; 'Do you want to tell me about it?'
3   Silence – not rushing the other person but giving them time to decide.
4   Attending – engaging in the attending behaviours already discussed, especially eye contact and a positive involvement that demonstrates the listener's interest in and concern for the other person.

Door openers will not always receive a positive response. The other person may be reluctant to talk. However, it may sometimes be helpful to encourage a reluctant speaker with more than one *non-coercive* invitation to talk, but remember that door openers should be perceived as non-coercive, and the reluctant speaker must not be pushed too hard. There is a marked distinction between gentle seduction and a coercive assault. A relationship may be seriously damaged if the over-eager listener attempts to coerce a reluctant speaker.

MINIMAL PROMPTS

In conversation minimal prompts such as:

'uh-huh'	'right'
'mmm'	'really'
'yes'	'and . . .'
'tell me more'	'wow'

can signal to speakers that we are listening and encourage them to continue. Sometimes, on the telephone, if the listener has remained silent for too long, the speaker feels the need to ask 'are you still there?' In face-to-face conversation a minimal prompt need not be a verbal prompt. It can take the form of a gesture, a nod of the head or a slight inclination of the body.

Bolton makes the point that minimal prompts do not imply agreement or disagreement. 'Yes' means 'yes, I hear what you are saying, go on' rather than 'yes, I agree with what you are saying'. The purpose of the minimal prompt is to let speakers know that they have been heard and that we would be interested to hear more. It is not used to offer a judgement on what the speaker is saying.

ACCENTING

Another response that may help uncover relevant information is a type of minimal prompt that involves emphasising a point made by the speaker. Accenting typically involves using a few words to draw attention to something the speaker has said. For example:

MANAGER: Most of the customer reports seemed OK.
COLLEAGUE: Seemed OK?
MANAGER: Well, I suppose I'd hoped for better. What I had expected
     was . . .

Accenting can be used to encourage others to express more fully what they have implied or only half said.

LIMITED USE OF QUESTIONS

Bolton (1986) believes that when we are 'listening' we often make an excessive and inappropriate use of questions. The main reason for this is that we tend to use questions to yield information related to our concerns rather than those of the speaker. This kind of self-centred questioning may be helpful when our aim is to better comprehend information that we might want to use later, or to evaluate the worth of another's persuasive argument. However, it is less appropriate when we are attempting to accurately understand the thoughts and feelings of the speaker. The different kinds of questions the listener can ask are dealt with elsewhere (Chapter 6).

With empathic listening, questions may be used to good effect when we have not followed what the speaker has been saying or when we feel a need for more information in order to develop a better understanding of the speaker's point of view. Questions may also be used to provide a useful prompt to encourage speakers to think a little more deeply about what they have been saying. For example: 'Could you say a little more about why you felt the negotiations broke down?' Egan (1998) even suggests that speakers can be helped to sort out their own thoughts by being encouraged to ask relevant questions of themselves. For example: 'What are some of the important questions you need to ask yourself regarding the breakdown in negotiations?'

Some of the dangers associated with the over-use of questions are well stated by Benjamin (1981: 71), cited by Egan (1998):

> I feel certain that we ask too many questions, often meaningless ones. We ask questions that confuse the interviewee, that interrupt him. We ask questions the interviewee cannot possibly answer. We even ask questions we don't want the answers to and, consequently, we do not hear the answer when forthcoming.

STATEMENTS

Egan (1998) suggests that if listeners ask too many questions speakers may end up feeling they are being grilled. An alternative to some questions might be the kind of statement that makes a demand on the speaker to say more, to elaborate or clarify. For example, the statement: 'What you have been saying seems to have made you very angry' might encourage the speakers to talk about their anger without feeling that they are being quizzed.

ATTENTIVE SILENCES

We sometimes ask too many questions because we cannot cope with even a short silence. We use questions to fill the gap.

Learning the art of silent responsiveness has been described as the key to good listening. Bolton (1986) suggests that a silence can give speakers time to consider what to say. It enables them to go deeper into themselves and examine their thoughts. Whether or not speakers are using the silence for this purpose can often be detected by the direction of their gaze. If, when they stop talking, the speaker fails to make any eye contact with the listener, this is likely to be a sign that they are thinking, and that in time they will continue talking. If, on the other hand, they stop talking and look towards the listener, they are probably signalling that they have finished and now it is the other person's turn to speak. The listener might respond to this cue with a statement or a question, or might allow the silence to continue in order to gently nudge the speaker into saying more. A silence used in this way can be a powerful prompt, especially if it is accompanied by any of the non-verbal behaviours which indicate to the speaker that they have our full attention and that we are waiting to hear more.

63

We can improve our ability to follow what speakers are saying by using one of a number of techniques which aid concentration.

- Hargie *et al.* (1994) discuss the use of intrapersonal dialogue. Listeners concentrate on what speakers are saying and heighten their receptivity by asking themselves questions such as 'Why are they telling me this now?' or engaging in covert coaching and telling themselves whenever they are not paying enough attention.
- Memory devices (see Smith 1986) such as using rhymes to remember names, or visualisation, whereby listeners create a mental picture of what the speaker is saying, can help listeners concentrate on the message and remember it later.
- Listeners may also find the kind of listening framework proposed by Egan (1998), which focuses attention on experiences, behaviours and feelings, a helpful aid to concentration. This kind of framework provides a useful structure for organising incoming information and suggesting areas that might be explored with speakers. Egan (ibid.: 82) suggests people should talk about:

> *Experiences* – that is, what happens to them. If a colleague tells you he has been fired from his job, he is talking about his problem situation in terms of an experience.
> *Behaviours* – that is, what they do or fail to do. If your colleague tells you he is drinking too much, he is talking about his problem situation in terms of his behaviour.
> *Affect* – that is, the feelings and emotions that arise from or are associated with either experiences or behaviour. If your colleague tells you how depressed he becomes after drinking bouts, he is talking about the affect associated with the problem situation.

Egan advocates the use of this framework to help people clarify their problem situation or explore their unused opportunities. If the listening task involves a personal problem Egan believes that it will be clear to both speaker and listener when it is seen and understood in terms of specific experiences, specific behaviours, and specific feelings and emotions.

- Note taking may also aid concentration but, because it interrupts eye contact, it can inhibit free communication. In some circumstances the speaker may also feel less free to talk if notes are being taken that might be shown to others later.

Exercise 4.4 provides an opportunity to observe how others use following skills. Observe others when they are listening and search for evidence that indicates how good they are at getting others to tell their stories. After completing this exercise you may find it useful to seek opportunities to monitor and reflect on your own following behaviour and identify what you might do to improve the way you listen to others.

Exercise 4.4 Following skills

Observe at least two people listening to others. How good were they at getting others to tell their story? Did they respond to cues offered by the speaker or use appropriate 'door openers' to get them talking? Did they manage to keep out of the speakers' way by using minimal prompts or accents to show the speakers that they were following what they were saying? Did they interrupt too often and/or ask too many of the kinds of questions that divert speakers away from the story they want to tell?

Check (✓) number of times used

• Non-coercive invitations to talk (door openers)	
• Minimal prompts ('uh-huh, and . . .?, tell me more')	
• Accents (one- or two-word restatements)	
• Short statements	
• Questions for clarification	
• Attentive silences	

What could the listeners have done differently that would have communicated to the speakers that they had been following what they were saying without, at the same time, interrupting their flow and getting in the way?

Reflecting

A reflective response, according to Bolton (1986), is when the listener restates the feeling and/or content of what the speaker has communicated and does so in a way that demonstrates understanding and acceptance. This kind of restatement not only provides speakers with an opportunity to check that they have been understood, but it can also help them clarify their own thoughts.

Understanding is not easily achieved, especially if it is to include an awareness of what messages mean to the speakers. Defined in this way, understanding involves us taking the speakers' perspective into account. Deetz and Stevenson (1986) suggest that this calls for an imaginative reconstruction of what speakers think, feel and see in a situation. They go on to argue that this is not accomplished by magic, luck or feeling good about a speaker; it is based on knowledge. This knowledge is gained by listening to the messages speakers send, while at the same time being constantly aware of the things which influence how they see the world: their values, culture, attitudes and so on. Information gained in this way may be used to formulate hypotheses about what a message means to a speaker. These hypotheses may then be tested against new information or they may be checked out by reflecting them back to the speaker.

Acceptance must not be confused with sympathy or agreement. Egan (1998) makes the point that sympathy, when aroused in listeners, can distort the stories we hear by blinding us to important nuances. Acceptance means withholding judgement, especially in the early part of a conversation, neither agreeing nor disagreeing with what the speaker has said. It involves a readiness to understand the messages from the other's point of view, and communicating this readiness to the speaker by letting them know that what they have said has been both received and understood.

There are basically two types of reflective response: content responses and affect responses.

PARAPHRASING

Paraphrasing deals with facts and ideas rather than with emotions. Bolton defines a paraphrase as a concise response to speakers which states the essence of their content in the listener's own words. The paraphrase may be distinguished from a detailed word-for-word summary (sometimes referred to as parroting), because it is brief, focused and is presented in the listener's own words, reflecting our understanding of the speaker's message.

REFLECTING BACK FEELINGS

We often ignore the emotional dimension of a conversation and focus attention on the factual content of the message. Consider what this might mean in the context of a performance appraisal interview. By listening to the 'facts', a manager may build up an accurate picture about the quality of the work done by a subordinate but, by filtering out the affective component of the message, may fail to appreciate that the subordinate finds the current work very enjoyable and would be very unhappy with any change the manager might propose.

Bolton suggests a number of techniques we can use to become more aware of the affective component of a message.

- We can listen for feeling words such as happy, sad, afraid, angry, surprised, disgusted;
- we can pay attention to the general content of the message and ask ourselves what we would be feeling;
- we can observe body language.

People often express their feelings without talking about them. Two newly promoted employees who talk listlessly about their work, avoid eye contact and stare at the floor may not actually say that they are unhappy, but their non-verbal behaviour might suggest that this is the case. Skilled listeners check out their understanding (their hypothesis that the newly promoted employees might be unhappy) by reflecting back to them the emotions they appear to be communicating.

Feeling and content may be reflected back together. The reflective responses offered by a listener who has used a listening framework similar to that proposed by Egan (see above) may involve the expression of core messages in terms of feelings, and the experiences and behaviours that underlie these feelings. After listening to the newly promoted employee the manager may reflect that 'You feel unhappy about your promotion because you used to enjoy what you were doing and because you miss your friends'. Carkhuff (1973) suggest that using a 'You feel . . . because . . .' format for reflective responses offers an easy and useful way of combining both feelings and fact.

SUMMATIVE REFLECTIONS

Bolton (1986) defines a summative reflection as a brief statement of the main themes and feelings that have been expressed by the speaker over a longer period of conversation than would be covered by the other two reflecting skills. In addition to providing listeners with an opportunity to check out their understanding of the overall message, summative reflections can help both listeners and speakers develop a greater awareness of themes by tying together a number of separate comments. They offer an especially useful way of helping speakers appreciate the bigger picture. If, after listening for some time to what a speaker has to say, the listener summarises, and reflects back their understanding of the speaker's predicament by making a statement along the lines of:

> 'The problem doesn't just seem to be that you are unhappy about giving up the old job and losing contact with the people you used to work with. You also appear to be anxious and insecure in the new job because you think that you don't have what it takes to successfully supervise other "professionals".'

The speaker may begin to appreciate that there may be links which had not been previously considered, and, as a result, may begin to think differently about the problem.

Summative reflections are also useful because they can reinforce positively the speaker's effort to communicate by providing direction to the conversation, creating a sense of movement and confirming that we are working hard to understand the speaker's message. Summative reflections also offer a very useful way of restarting interrupted conversations.

Research indicates that reflecting can have positive effects. Dickson (1997) summarises the findings of several studies. He notes that empathic understanding and positive regard tend to be related to a reflective style of interviewing. He also reports evidence which suggests that reflecting produces an increase in the amount and intimacy of information interviewees reveal about themselves.

Exercise 4.5 Reflecting skills

Observe at least two people listening to others. Did the listeners whom you observed reflect back what they had heard in order to:

- Check that they had understood what had been said?
- Help speakers clarify their thoughts or develop a better understanding of the bigger picture?

Record the use of reflecting behaviours below:

Check (✓) number of times used

- Paraphrasing
- Reflecting back feelings
- Summarising

What could they have done to improve their attending behaviour?

After completing Exercise 4.5 you may find it useful to seek opportunities to monitor your own reflecting behaviour and identify what you might do to improve the way you listen to others.

Developing effective listening skills

It was noted above that an effective approach to developing listening skills is to follow a three-step process that involves observing others, monitoring self and experimenting with new behaviours. The exercises presented in this chapter have focused on observing others. The hard part involves opening a second channel and observing yourself and, on the basis of these observations, identifying priority targets for improvement and then experimenting with new behaviours.

Summary

Listening has been defined as the active search for a full and accurate understanding of the meaning of another's message.

The first part of this chapter considered those factors which influence our ability to listen. The reasons why some kinds of information are attended to and others are ignored were examined, together with some of the variables that determine how information is interpreted and messages given meaning. This was followed by a more detailed look at the process of communication, and some of the barriers to effective communication associated with the speaker, the listener, the message and the environment were examined.

The second part of the chapter identified and elaborated some of the key skills we can deploy to improve the quality of our listening. These skills were grouped under four headings:

1 *preparation skills* which include what we need to do to prepare to listen;
2 *attending skills* which include the behaviours we need to engage in to let speakers know that we are paying careful attention to what they are saying;
3 *following skills* which include keeping the focus of attention on what speakers have to say and encouraging them to tell their story;
4 *reflecting skills* which provide us with the opportunity to check out our understanding and communicate this to speakers and to help speakers clarify their own thoughts.

The next chapter is concerned with listening to non-verbal messages, a rich source of information about people's feelings.

References

Benjamin, A. (1981) *The Helping Interview* (3rd edn), Boston, MA: Houghton Mifflin.

Bolton, R. (1986) *People Skills,* Sydney: Prentice Hall of Australia.

Carkhuff, R.R. (1973) *The Art of Helping: An Introduction to Life Skills*, Amherst, MA: Human Resource Development Press.

Deetz, S.A. and Stevenson, S.L. (1986) *Managing Interpersonal Communication*, New York: Harper and Row.

Dickson, D.A. (1997) 'Reflecting', in O.D.W. Hargie (ed.) *The Handbook of Communication Skills* (2nd edn), London: Routledge, pp. 159–182.

Egan, G. (1998) *The Skilled Helper* (6th edn), Belmont, CA: Brooks/Cole.

Hargie, O., Saunders, C. and Dickson, D. (1994) *Social Skills in Interpersonal Communication* (2nd edn), London: Croom Helm.

Ostell, A., Baverstock, S. and Wright, P. (1999) 'Interpersonal skills of managing emotion at work', *The Psychologist* 12 (1): 30–34.

Smith, V. (1986) 'Listening', in O. Hargie (ed.) *A Handbook of Communication Skills*, London: Croom Helm.

Tannen, D. (1991) *You Just Don't Understand: Women and Men in Conversation,* New York: Ballantine Books.

Tubbs, S.L. and Moss, S. (1994) *Human Communication* (7th edn), New York: McGraw-Hill.

Wolff, F., Marnik, N., Tracey, W. and Nichols, R. (1983) *Perceptive Listening*, New York: Holt, Rinehart & Winston.

5

LISTENING TO NON-VERBAL MESSAGES

Learning objective

To understand how attention to non-verbal behaviour can affect the ability to diagnose emotional states and understand other people's intentions.
  After reading this chapter you will:

- Understand the relationship between verbal and non-verbal signals.
- Be aware of how emotions are reflected by body language.
- Recognise how to determine the meaning of non-verbal signals.
- Understand how the face, looking behaviour, gestures, touching, posture, the use of furniture, spatial behaviour, appearance and vocal cues can convey meaning.
- Understand how to decipher the meaning of contradictory signals.

There is more to listening than meets the ears

The spoken word is not the only way people present information. The rate at which words are spoken, the tone of voice used, and its pitch and volume can all convey meaning, as can the way speakers are dressed, their gestures, eye contact and body movements. If we hear their words in isolation and ignore the accompanying non-verbal signals, audio-vocal and visual gesturals, we will miss important information, and our understanding of the message we receive will be incomplete.

The relationship between verbal and non-verbal signals

Argyle and Kendon (1967) make the point that verbal utterances are closely dependent on non-verbal signals, which keep the speaker and listener attending properly to each other, sustain the smooth alternation of speaker and listener and add further information to the literal messages transmitted. The link between verbal and non-verbal signals is further elaborated by Knapp (1978). He identifies six different ways in which non-verbal behaviour can be related to verbal behaviour. These are:

1   *Repeating*: The non-verbal signal simply repeats what was said verbally; for example, while telling somebody the way to the railway station the speaker points in the proper direction.

2   *Contradicting*: Non-verbal behaviour contradicts verbal behaviour; for example, banging the table and shouting 'I'm not angry'. (See below for a discussion about which of these contradictory signals should be believed.)

3   *Substituting*: Non-verbal behaviour substitutes for the verbal message. In response to the question, 'How did the interview go?' the other offers a thumbs-down gesture. Sometimes when the substitute non-verbal behaviour fails, the communicator may resort back to the verbal level. For example, a woman who wants her date to stop making sexual advances may stiffen, stare straight ahead, and act unresponsive and cool. If this does not deter her date she might say something like 'Look Jo, please don't ruin a nice friendship.'

4   *Complementing*: Non-verbal behaviour can elaborate or modify a verbal message; for example, a slight forward inclination of the body and a smile might signal that you are satisfied with the verbal report you are giving and that you expect it to be received with enthusiasm by your boss. If his reaction is cold and critical your annoyance at his response might be signalled, as you continue with the report, by a change of posture and facial expression. A verbatim transcript of the interaction may totally fail to capture and record these affective aspects of the message.

5   *Accenting*: Non-verbal behaviours such as a nod of the head or a gesture of the hand may be used to emphasise or accent part of the spoken message.

6   *Regulating*: Non-verbal behaviours may also be used to regulate the communicative flow between people. The importance of a person's regulatory skills is reflected by the evaluative statements we often make about others such as 'talking to him is like talking to a brick wall', 'you can't get a word in edgeways' or 'she keeps butting in'. A number of non-verbal signals may be used to synchronise the sequence of utterances. Argyle (1975), summarising the experimental work of others, lists many of these. They include behaviours that signal when:

- the listener wants to take the floor (for example, interrupting or making impatient non-verbal signals like triple head nods);
- the speaker wants to keep the floor (for example, speaking more loudly when interrupted or keeping a hand in mid-gesture at the end of a sentence);
- the speaker wants to yield the floor (for example, gazing at the other at the end of a speech or by ending a sentence by trailing off saying 'you know' etc.);
- the listener wants to decline an offer of the floor (such as merely offering a nod or a grunt when the other pauses).

The expression of feelings

While Bolton (1986) acknowledges that there is considerable overlap between the type of information that is transmitted verbally and non-verbally, he maintains that words tend to be best for communicating factual information and non-verbal signals are best for communicating emotions. Sometimes we deliberately signal our emotions in order to influence others (for example, anger or suffering), but people often work hard to camouflage what they are feeling. This is especially the case when they fear that the open expression of emotion will involve some sanction; for example, that the quick-tempered candidate will be passed over for promotion.

The majority of us find it easier to control the words we utter than to control the way we behave and the non-verbal signals we transmit. Non-verbal signals offer a rich source of data about emotional states (such as anger) and interpersonal attitudes (such as being angry with a particular person). The most difficult non-verbal signals to control are autonomic displays such as perspiration and skin colour, but leakages may occur in many areas.

The observation of body language is an important element in effective listening because it can provide us with many useful clues to what the speaker is really feeling. DePaulo (1992) makes an obvious but important point: people can decide to stay silent and say nothing but they cannot 'not act' non-verbally. Non-verbal behaviour is always a rich source of data. However, great care needs to be exercised when interpreting non-verbal signals, otherwise their true meaning may not be understood.

Determining meaning

Verbal and non-verbal signals need to be listened to together if we are to properly understand the messages being presented by the speaker. Taken in isolation, it is difficult to be sure what any one signal means. Knapp (1978) maintains that non-verbal signals can have multiple meanings and multiple uses. For example, a smile can be part of an emotional expression (I am happy), an attitudinal message (I like you), part of a self-presentation (I'm the kind of person your customer will like), or a listener response to manage the interaction (I'm interested in what you're saying).

Patterson (1988, 1995) argues that when interpreting the meaning of non-verbal signals we need to give attention to the relational nature of behaviours and the perceived function of the exchange. He also cautions against adopting a reductionist view and stresses the importance of a multi-channel approach that involves attending to the interdependent and coordinated relationship between, for example, facial expression, non-verbal vocal expressions and other channels.

Non-verbal signals have little or no meaning in themselves: they acquire meaning in particular contexts. Argyle (1975) illustrates this well. He argues that the significance of touching another person will vary depending upon whether the other person is '(a) one's spouse, (b) someone else's spouse, (c) a complete stranger, (d) a patient, (e) another person in a crowded lift'. The meaning of a non-verbal signal can depend on its position in time and its relation to other signals. For example, two men kissing on the football field immediately after one has scored a winning goal may have a completely different meaning to the same kiss in the privacy of a hotel bedroom.

Rozelle *et al.* (1997) draw attention to how the physical and social setting can affect how people will behave. For example, in terms of physical setting, the layout of furniture in an office and whether people are sitting behind desks or in open chairs can influence body movements. In terms of social setting, the level of perceived stress can also affect behaviour.

Eisenberg and Smith (1971) have identified two factors that have important implications for the way we determine the meaning of non-verbal messages:

- *Discrimination*, the recognition of a non-verbal element that has potential message value.
- *Pattern recognition*, the process whereby discriminated elements are sorted into meaningful patterns.

For example, a colleague may fail to reply when spoken to. You recognise this as unusual (you discriminate), because normally you spend a lot of time in conversation with this person and you both get on well together. This may prompt you to search for other signals that will help you determine whether the colleague just did not hear you or whether there is some other reason for the failure to reply. If you notice that the colleague goes on to break the lead of a pencil, slams a drawer shut and marches out of the room without saying goodbye, you may begin to build up a more complete picture that will help you determine what the failure to reply means (pattern recognition). You may conclude that it is more likely that the colleague is upset about something (that the colleague attributes to you), rather than a failure to hear what you said.

The next section of this chapter offers a brief review of some of the non-verbal signals which can convey important information, signals that can be helpful when attempting to develop a full and accurate understanding of the meaning of another's message.

The face

We often pay a lot of attention to other people's faces because they are a rich source of both emotional expressions and interaction signals. A number of studies have attempted to identify those emotions that can be most readily distinguished from facial expression. In practice it would appear that this is more difficult than many people imagine. A major problem is that the subject may be expressing more than one emotion at the same time (e.g. disappointment and anger), thus presenting a confusing expression. None the less, there is evidence that we are able to identify the six primary emotional states (surprise, fear, anger, disgust, happiness and sadness) without too much difficulty.

In an attempt to determine how accurately emotions can be recognised from facial expressions Ekman *et al.* (1971) developed a scoring system. It involved dividing the face into three areas: (1) the brows and forehead; (2) the eyes, lids and bridge of the nose; and (3) the lower face including the cheek, nose, mouth, chin and jaw. They presented coders with photographs of each facial area giving examples of the six emotions. The coders were then asked to score a range of photographs by matching them against the examples provided. It was found that after being given six hours' training the coders were able to identify emotional expressions with high levels of accuracy. On the basis of the evidence from this and other studies, Ekman *et al.* (1972) concluded:

> Contrary to the impression conveyed by previous reviews of the literature that the evidence in the field is contradictory and confusing, our analysis showed consistent evidence of accurate judgement of emotions from facial behaviour.

This conclusion is based on evidence derived from studies that used posed rather than spontaneous expressions. There is a danger that these may be caricatures of natural expression which both simplify and exaggerate what occurs spontaneously. Some researchers have tried to base their studies on actual emotions. One of the earliest such attempts was by Dunlap (1927). The way he tried to elicit emotions is illustrated by the following quotation. It makes entertaining reading:

Exercise 5.1 Facial expressions

Identify which emotional states are portrayed by each of the six faces presented below. There is one face for each of the following six emotions:

surprise	sadness	fear
disgust	happiness	anger

Match each of the six emotions to one of the six faces and make some brief notes alongside each face to identify which elements of the expression enabled you to recognise the emotional state.

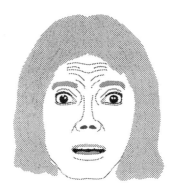

Figure 5.1

Figure 5.2

Figure 5.3

Figure 5.4

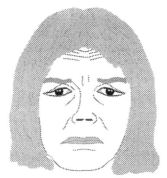

Figure 5.5

Figure 5.6

Figures 5.1–5.6 The six emotions.

Compare your answers with those provided later in this chapter.

- Amusement. This was readily evoked by the use of a carefully selected stock of jokes, casually introduced as if suggested by the details of the work . . .
- Startle: A pistol was fired, unexpectedly behind the sitter . . .
- Expectation: After the pistol had been fired, it was brought into the sitter's view and, after time had been given for the sitter to become composed, he was told that the next pistol would be deliberately fired to the slow count of one-two-three . . .
- Pain . . . The stimulation consisted in bending a finger joint backwards forcibly.
- Disgust. (The sitter was asked to smell) . . . a test tube in which tissues dissected from a rat had reposed, corked, for several months.

More recent experiments have been less contrived and have, for example, made use of newspaper photographs to capture spontaneous behaviour. Argyle (1975) reports that such studies achieved levels of accuracy of identification comparable with those derived from studies using posed photographs, approximately 70 per cent in both cases.

A number of studies undertaken in the late 1980s and the early 1990s offer further support for the view that facial expression is a good indicator of emotional state. They also suggest that there is a considerable measure of agreement in the way people from different cultures judge primary emotions from facial expression, although norms about acceptable behaviour may mask the display of emotions in different cultures (see Ekman 1992, 1994; Matsumoto and Ekman 1989).

It would therefore appear that it is possible to identify emotional states from facial expressions. Accuracy is likely to be greater when a simple or 'pure' emotional state is being experienced. When the face conveys multiple emotions it may be considerably more difficult to interpret these 'affect blends'. In such circumstances it is especially important to pay attention to pattern recognition. Knapp (1978) refers to several studies which show that additional knowledge concerning the context within which a particular facial expression occurred can positively affect the accuracy of judgement.

At this point let us return to Exercise 5.1 and consider how many of the faces you correctly matched to the corresponding emotional states. When trying to identify emotional states it is useful to divide the face into three parts: (1) the brows and forehead; (2) the eyes, eyelids and bridge of the nose; and (3) the lower face including the cheek, nose, mouth, chin and jaw.

Surprise. The emotional state of the first face is surprise. It tends to be signalled by curved and raised brows, a wrinkled forehead, clearly visible whites of the eye (the sclera often being visible below as well as above the iris), dropped jaw and loosely opened mouth (Figure 5.7).

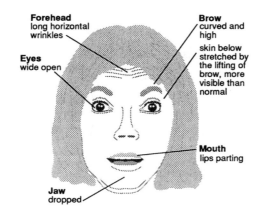

Forehead
long horizontal
wrinkles

Brow
curved and
high

skin below
stretched by
the lifting of
brow, more
visible than
normal

Eyes
wide open

Mouth
lips parting

Jaw
dropped

Figure 5.7 Surprise.

Fear is expressed through raised brows that are drawn together, a wrinkled forehead (but, unlike surprise where the wrinkles tend to go across the entire forehead, the wrinkles are concentrated in the centre), tensed lower eyelids but with the whites of the eye showing above the iris, and the mouth open with lips that are tensed and drawn back (Figure 5.8).

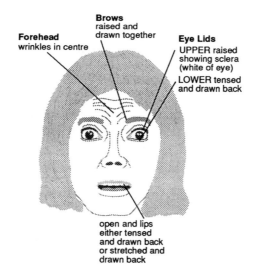

Brows
raised and
drawn together

Forehead
wrinkles in centre

Eye Lids
UPPER raised
showing sclera
(white of eye)

LOWER tensed
and drawn back

open and lips
either tensed
and drawn back
or stretched and
drawn back

Figure 5.8 Fear.

Anger is portrayed by brows that are lowered and drawn together, with vertical creases visible between the brows. The upper and lower eyelids are tensed and the eyes have a hard stare. The lips may either be pressed firmly together or open in a tense square shape, as if shouting (Figure 5.9).

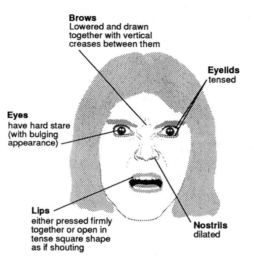

Brows
Lowered and drawn together with vertical creases between them

Eyelids
tensed

Eyes
have hard stare (with bulging appearance)

Lips
either pressed firmly together or open in tense square shape as if shouting

Nostrils
dilated

Figure 5.9 Anger.

Disgust is signalled by a lowering of the brow which in turn pushes down the upper eyelid. The cheeks are raised and, importantly, the nose is wrinkled. The upper lip is raised but the lower lip may be either pushed up to meet the raised upper lip or lowered and pushed out (Figure 5.10).

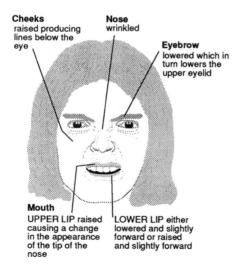

Cheeks
raised producing lines below the eye

Nose
wrinkled

Eyebrow
lowered which in turn lowers the upper eyelid

Mouth
UPPER LIP raised causing a change in the appearance of the tip of the nose

LOWER LIP either lowered and slightly forward or raised and slightly forward

Figure 5.10 Disgust.

Happiness is associated with an unwrinkled forehead, crow's feet creases radiating from the outer corner of the eyes, raised cheeks and folds which run from the nose to just beyond the outer edges of the lip corners, which are drawn back and up to produce a smile (Figure 5.11).

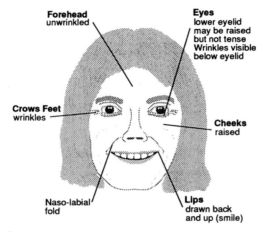

Figure 5.11 Happiness.

Sadness is expressed through eyebrows that are drawn up at the inner corner, revealing a triangle of skin (with the apex pointing inward and slightly upward below the brows and above the upper eyelids whose inner corners are raised). The corners of the lips are turned down and the lip may be trembling (Figure 5.12).

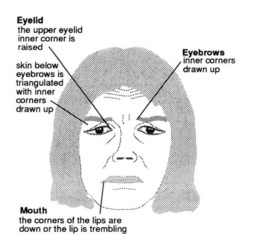

Figure 5.12 Sadness.

Facial expressions may also be used to regulate an interaction. A greeting signal, which has been observed across a wide range of cultures, is the eyebrow flash (Morris 1977). At the moment of recognition the head tilts back, the eyebrows arch up and the face breaks into a smile. Head nods and smiles, as mentioned in the previous chapter, may also play an important role in the synchronising of conversations and in listening behaviour. A person's looking behaviour may also be important in this respect.

Gaze

Looking behaviour can signal a desire to communicate. A glance across the room at a manager engaged in conversation with others can tell her that you would like a word when she has finished. At a party a similar glance may signal to a member of the opposite sex that you would like to initiate some contact, and a glance towards a waiter or a barman might be used to signal that you desire some attention.

In Chapter 11 it is suggested that by paying attention to the direction of gaze we can identify important relationships during meetings. Speakers often look to leaders for permission to speak or for feedback on what has been said. They may also look towards possible opponents for their reactions. Observing the pattern of such glances over a period may reveal alliances because people are likely to glance most at the person who is championing their cause.

Looking behaviour can provide a lot of information about the nature of relationships. Argyle (1975) reports that we tend to look most at those whom we like. This conclusion is well supported by experimental evidence. It has also been found that gaze is perceived by others as a signal that they are liked. Mehrabian (1972) found that when two subjects were interviewed it was the ones who were looked at most who inferred that they were preferred.

Status also affects gaze. In a small group we tend to look most at the person with highest status. Efran (1968) found that, in triads where a freshman addressed a senior freshman pair, he or she tended to look most at the senior. There is also evidence that those people who are looked at most see themselves as the most influential members of the group.

Hostility and aggression can be conveyed via looking behaviour. It has been found that a gaze of longer than ten seconds is likely to induce irritation and discomfort in many situations. The long, hard stare is often used to threaten others.

Looking behaviour can signal a desire to influence. Another study by Mehrabian (Mehrabian and Williams 1969) showed that when people are trying to be more persuasive they tend to look more. Knapp (1978) also reports that listeners seem to judge speakers who gaze most as the most persuasive, truthful, sincere and credible.

Looking behaviour can also signal a desire to cooperate, to be included and an interest in what the other is saying. A change in the pattern of eye contact can provide the 'listener' with useful information. Cutting off gaze is a powerful signal that, for example, a flirtatious glance has been recognised and the implied invitation rejected or, in response to a threatening stare, that the person cutting off the gaze is willing to submit or seek appeasement.

Less eye contact can also signal that people are ashamed or embarrassed about something, or that they are too sad or preoccupied to engage the other in conversation. The wish to avoid involvement also tends to result in limited eye contact. When the chairman of a meeting is seeking a volunteer for some undesirable task it is not unusual to observe a marked reduction in eye contact – people look away. The same thing happens when a teacher asks a question to which no one knows the answer. Lack of confidence also tends to result in limited eye contact, as does lack of interest, a point that received attention in the previous chapter on listening.

Gestures

It is possible to distinguish between gestures that are intended to communicate something and those that signal private reactions to what is going on.

Intentional gestures

Ekman and Friesen (1969) offer three categories of gestures that are intentionally used to communicate a message to others.

1   *Emblems* are gestures that have a specific verbal translation and are used as a substitute for words. They are often employed when the verbal channel is blocked, for example, by divers working under water or by the floor staff in a television studio who need to inform the participants of a chat show that they must draw their conversation to a close. They may also be used in everyday interactions, for example, rubbing hands for coldness, thumbs up for approval or the nose-thumb for mockery. There are, however, many emblems that are specific to one group of communicators, for example, tick-tack men on a race course. Ekman *et al.* (1984) have also found important regional and cultural differences in emblems. An implication of this is that outsiders may not always be able to translate the meaning of emblems or may interpret them in a way that was unintended by the communicator. 'The ring' is an example of a gesture that means different things in different cultures. It is formed by holding the hand up, palm facing away, with the thumb and forefinger touching to form a circle. In Britain this is the A-OK gesture signifying that something is good. In some parts of France it can mean that something is worthless and in Sardinia it is a sexual insult. A number of

studies have examined how members of different cultures interpret emblems (Payrato 1993; Pooringa *et al.* 1993; Safadi and Valentine 1988).

Most emblem gestures are formed by the hands, but this need not always be the case: the nose can be wrinkled as a sign that something smells or is in some other way undesirable.

2 *Illustrators* are non-verbal acts that are directly tied to speech. They are used to repeat, complement or accent the verbal content of the message. Illustrative gestures may be used in many ways: for example, to point to objects or people, to sketch a train of thought, to demonstrate a rhythm or to depict spatial relationships. Bull (1983) summarises a number of studies which provide evidence that some illustrators do assist the process of communication. One of the studies he cites tested the hypothesis that visual information is communicated more easily through hand gestures (Graham and Argyle 1975). English students were asked to communicate information about some two-dimensional shapes to others without the use of hand gestures. The decoders were asked to draw what they thought the shapes were and the results were rated in terms of their similarity to the original. The experiment was repeated with a group of Italian students. It was found that when gestures were permitted the results were significantly more accurate. It was also found that this effect was more pronounced for the Italian students; a result which suggests that gestures make a more important contribution to accurate communication in some cultures.

Illustrative gestures can also facilitate the comprehension of speech by enabling the speaker to stress certain words or phrases. Desmond Morris, in his popular book *Manwatching* (1977), provides a wealth of examples of such signals. These include the 'hand chop', a straight hand slashed downward through the air, possibly indicating that the speaker wants their ideas to cut through the confusion that may exist, and the 'vacuum precision grip' where the tips of the thumb and forefinger are brought together as though holding some small, delicate object, suggesting that the speakers want to express themselves with great exactness.

Illustrators can also communicate the speakers' enthusiasm for their subject and can help increase the listeners' level of attention by providing greater stimulation. It is important to note, however, that inappropriate gestures, such as picking one's nose or rubbing one's crutch, can be very distracting for the listener, but these are *not* illustrative gestures and will be considered later.

3 *Regulators* have been defined as those non-verbal acts that maintain and regulate an interaction. They tend to be associated with greetings, turn-taking and partings, and include gestures such as the eyebrow flash, waving and nodding which have already been discussed above.

Unintentional gestures

These are gestures that can provide others with a rich source of information about what a person is really thinking and feeling. They can take several forms. They may manifest themselves as 'unintentional' illustrators that either complement or modify the verbal content of a message. Peter Mayle, in his book *A Year in Provence* (1989: 41), offers an interesting example.

> We learned also to interpret the hand language that accompanies any discussion of deadlines. When a Provençal looks you in the eyes and tells you that he will be hammering on your door ready to start work next Tuesday for certain, the behaviour of the hands is all important. If they are still or patting you reassuringly on the arm, you can expect him on Tuesday. If one hand is held out at waist height, palm downwards, and begins to rock from side to side, adjust the timetable to Wednesday or Thursday. If the rocking develops into an agitated waggle, he's really talking about next week or God knows when, depending on circumstances beyond his control. These unspoken disclaimers . . . seem to be instinctive and therefore more revealing than speech.

They can also include gestures that may not be directly related to a spoken message. Such unintentional gestures often involve touching self, objects or others.

1   *Touching self.* Morris (1977) suggests that the most common form of self-touching is self-intimacy: movements which provide self-comfort because they are unconsciously mimed acts of being touched by somebody else. People stroke their own face, clasp their hands, gently press their knuckles against their lips, caress their own hair, cross their legs so that one limb feels the comforting pressure of the other, rock their bodies and so on. In order of frequency, the most common self-intimacies appear to be the jaw support, the chin support, the hair clasp, the cheek support, the mouth touch and the temple support.

   In addition to indicating a need for comfort and reassurance, self-touching may signal that a person is experiencing negative attitudes towards the self. Ekman and Friesen (1969; see also Ekman *et al.* 1972) found that when people experienced shame they tended to cover their eyes. Others have suggested that a hand over the mouth can also be associated with shame or self-blame, and that picking fingers, nose, ears and teeth can also be linked to feelings of self-blame.

   Attitudes towards others may be signalled through self-touching. Experimental results suggest that the hand-to-nose gesture is associated with fear or anxiety, and that anxiety is also signalled by tightly clenched hands. The clenched fist gesture implies aggression. The exposure of parts of the body can be a sexual invitation, whereas covering up the body may signal a wish not to get involved, as can the gesture of folding one's arms across the chest. Flight behaviour, reflecting a wish to get away from others, may be signalled by restless movements of the hands and legs.

2   *Touching objects.* Unintentional gestures that serve the function of relieving tension can also involve the touching of objects other than self. Morris (1977) describes these gestures as displacement activities, agitated fill-in actions performed during periods of acute tension. He offers the example of a girl waiting for an interview. She wants very much to attend the interview, but at the same time is very scared and would like to flee the waiting room. This inner conflict makes it extremely difficult for her to wait calmly to be called. She reacts by filling the behaviour void with displacement activities. These can take many forms: fiddling with the clasp on her bracelet, polishing her glasses, smoking and so on.

3   *Touching others.* Bodily contact and touching behaviour is the most basic way in which people express such interpersonal attitudes as aggression and affiliation. Children pat, slap, punch, pinch, stroke, lick, suck, kiss, hold, kick and tickle others much more than adults do. Maturity tends to bring with it a considerable reduction in touching behaviour, many of the functions normally served by such behaviours being fulfilled by facial and gestural expressions. None the less, adults touch others to offer encouragement, express tenderness and show emotional support. They also touch others, but in different ways (slapping, punching, kicking) to express aggressive interpersonal relationships. Sexual intimacy is another area of social interaction that inevitably involves bodily contact.

Many factors influence the meaning of touching behaviour. Context can be important, as illustrated by the kissing example cited above. Intensity and duration can also be important. Handshakes may be formal and polite or they can express real warmth. Warm handshakes tend to involve a firm grip, and are sustained for a longer period than the merely formal greeting. Knapp (1978) suggests the possibility of plotting touch behaviour along an intimacy continuum ranging from touch and release (least intimate), through touch and hold, to touch and stroke (most intimate). The meaning can also be influenced by the kind of touch. A pat is usually interpreted in terms of encouragement or play, whereas a stoke suggests comfort and/or intimacy.

The importance of touch is well illustrated by a number of studies. Agulera (1967) found that the touch behaviour of nurses increased the verbal output of patients and improved patients' attitudes towards nurses. Fisher *et al.* (1976) found that in those situations where library clerks touched some students when returning their library cards, those who were touched evaluated the clerk and the library more favourably than those who were not touched.

It is possible to gain some clues about differences in status by observing touching behaviour. It is usually the high-status person who touches first. This often occurs within the context of managing an interaction. People touch others when guiding them. They may also hold or squeeze the other when accenting part of the message. Touch may also be used as a means of attracting attention.

Posture

It has been found that when people are presented with drawings of stick figures they tend to attribute similar meanings to different postures (see Exercise 5.2).

A number of factors influence the posture a person will adopt. They include context, culture and attitudes towards others. Mehrabian (1968) found that subjects adopted different postures towards those whom they liked and disliked. One example is that with people who were disliked there was an increased tendency to adopt an arms-akimbo posture. In a later study (Mehrabian 1972), it was found that people adopted a more relaxed posture (consisting of asymmetrical arm positions, sideways lean, asymmetrical leg positions, hand relaxation and backwards lean) with others of lower status. Argyle (1975) cites a report by Goffman (1961) which supports this finding. Goffman noticed that at meetings in mental hospitals it was the most important people who sat in the most relaxed postures. Posture can be a good indicator of feelings. At a team meeting a person who is sitting slumped in a chair is likely to be feeling very different to somebody who is sitting on the edge of a chair and leaning towards the team leader. Similarly, if a colleague who normally 'explodes' into your office with an easy stride and an erect posture shuffles in with stooped posture and eyes downcast, you may safely assume that the colleague is not feeling their usual self. Changes in a person's posture in the course of a conversation are also worth observing. If the slumped team member suddenly straightens up and sits forward in the chair it might be worth considering what it was that prompted the change.

Observe the different postures people adopt in different situations. The manager conducting a disciplinary interview is much more likely to sit upright and appear more tense than when she is reading a bedtime story to her young daughter later the same day. The affection she has for her daughter is likely to manifest itself in a much more relaxed and open posture. The mother is also much less likely to position herself so that there is a piece of furniture between herself and her daughter, whereas at work she may well have conducted the disciplinary interview across her desk.

Exercise 5.2 Interpreting the meaning of different postures

Look at the stick figures presented in Figure 5.13 and decide how each of them may be feeling. An answer key is provided below.

Figure 5.13 Posture: interpretations of stick-figure diagrams.

Source: Based on an experiment by Sarbin and Hardyck (1953).

The feelings portrayed by the stick figures in Exercise 5.2 are:

(a) determined (b) puzzled
(c) indifferent (d) rejecting
(e) violent anger (f) shy

How did your answers compare?

The use of furniture

It has long been recognised that the shape of a table in a meeting room, the layout of chairs in a lecture room and the arrangement of furniture in a sitting-room can have an important effect on the flow of communication. For example, people sitting along the same side of a long boardroom table may experience problems communicating with each other because eye contact, apart from with immediate neighbours, is difficult.

The way people arrange or use the furniture in their office or home can provide valuable clues to how they are feeling. Managers who feel insecure in a meeting may prefer to keep a desk between themselves and the person or persons with whom they are interacting. Managers may also prefer to stay behind their desk as a way of signalling that the meeting is formal, for example, in a disciplinary interview. However, on those occasions when they want to encourage a more informal relationship (for example, when counselling a colleague), they may decide to move from behind their desk to a more informal seating arrangement. They may also prefer this kind of setting when meeting people they like and/or when they are under less time pressure. An interesting study of doctor–patient relationships suggests that the presence or absence of a desk can alter the patient's 'at ease' state (White 1953). It was found that when the doctor sat behind a desk only 10 per cent of the patients were perceived to be at ease, whereas when the desk was removed the proportion increased to 55 per cent.

Furniture may be used to key the climate for an interaction. Sitting behind a desk with your back to a window so that a visitor can see only a silhouette of your face deprives the other person of the opportunity to observe your facial expression. Experiments suggest that the silhouetted person is likely to be perceived as being more dominant, especially so if the visitor is seated in a lower chair.

Spatial behaviour

The distance between people signals something about the nature of their relationship. Four proximity zones have been suggested for different kinds of relationship (Hall 1959).

- *Intimate: up to 18 inches.* At this distance bodily contact is easy. Each person can smell the other and feel their body heat. They can see, if not very well, and they can talk in a low whisper.
- *Personal: 18 inches to 4 feet.* At this distance people can touch each other, but they are sufficiently far apart to see better and not smell the other's breath.
- *Social-consultative: 9 to 12 feet.* This is the distance at which important relationships are conducted, for example, talking to somebody across a desk. A louder voice is needed.
- *Public: 12 feet and above.* This is the distance associated with public figures and public occasions. Public figures addressing an audience often do so from a stage. Even where there is no stage the public figure usually stands apart when speaking to a large group.

In the UK, friends or colleagues when talking about agreeable matters tend to stand about 24 inches apart. Problems sometimes arise when people from different cultures, with different concepts of personal space, engage each other in conversation. Some of the parties may feel comfortable standing close to others, whereas others may experience discomfort because they feel that their personal space has been invaded. It is not unusual in such circumstances to see the latter turning away or taking a step backwards to restore a comfortable distance.

There is evidence that in interactions between people of different status the more junior persons may require more personal space than senior persons. Senior people may inadvertently make juniors feel uncomfortable because they approach too close and invade their personal space. I have observed inexperienced drilling teams on oil rigs lose their rhythm of working together when a senior manager visiting the rig has approached too close in order to observe their work. During certain operations this loss of rhythm has been known to be the cause of accidents.

Experiments have shown that when a person's personal space is invaded, measures of emotional arousal, such as skin resistance, increase.

Appearance

Appearance is included here as an important element of non-verbal communication because it is something that can be manipulated. People can choose what clothes to wear and how they will wear them; they can choose the kind of jewellery, badges and accessories they will adorn themselves with; they can choose how to dress their hair or care for their skin. They can even choose how they will smell and, to a lesser extent, what kind of physique they will have.

When people deliberately exercise this kind of choice they will usually be making decisions which reflect the impact they wish to have on others, decisions concerned with impression management. 'Power-dressing' is a modern term which has come to mean choosing what to wear in order to create an influential/dominant image.

This chapter has not adopted the perspective of social actors attempting to manage the image they project. The theme has been interpretation, and the focus has been those clues which may help listeners to better understand the messages they are receiving. A person's appearance can provide the listener or observer with messages about personality, status and interpersonal attitudes. Argyle (1975) suggests that people with certain kinds of personality prefer certain colours and other features. For example, people who are sociable and extroverted prefer brighter and more saturated colours, and conformists also conform in the clothes they wear. Uniforms signal rank, as in the army, or disguise rank as in some (e.g. Japanese) work organisations. Status differences and social class are often communicated by the cost and 'cut' of the clothes people wear and by the condition of their body, especially their hands and finger-nails.

Appearance can also convey messages about one person's attitude towards others. Certain kinds of clothes worn within a certain context may signal a person's sexual availability. Respect for another may also be communicated through appearance. Arriving at a business meeting in worn, dirty, casual clothes may give others, especially customers, the impression that they are not highly regarded. Skinheads and rockers may also be seen as aggressive and threatening by some people because of the clothes they wear and their general appearance.

Vocal cues

This chapter opened with a statement that the rate at which words are spoken, the tone of voice used and its pitch and volume can convey meaning. Research in this area has been fraught with difficulties, largely because of the problem of separating the meaning of the words spoken from the vocal expression. Various approaches have been tried to eliminate verbal information. Some researchers have experimented with meaningless content, speakers being asked to express emotions by reciting numbers or nonsense syllables; others have used a standard passage which has been spoken in different ways, and others have filtered the statement electronically to eliminate verbal information. The results of all these experiments have been encouraging, and seem to provide clear evidence that people are able to make reasonably accurate judgements from audio-vocal messages about another's emotions and feelings as well as about many personal characteristics such as age, sex and status.

Davitz (1964) has summarised many of the research findings in the area of emotional sensitivity in an attempt to produce an emotion-vocal cue dictionary. The key variables identified by Davitz are loudness, pitch, timbre, rate, inflection, rhythm and enunciation. Figure 5.14 presents the different patterns of vocal expression for two emotional states: affection and anger.

Feeling	Loudness	Pitch	Timbre	Rate	Inflection	Rhythm	Enunciation
Affection	Soft	Low	Resonant	Slow	Steady and slight upward	Regular	Slurred
Anger	Loud	High	Blaring	Fast	Irregular up and down	Irregular	Clipped

Figure 5.14 Characteristics of vocal expression.

Mention has already been made of the way in which vocal cues may help to regulate the interaction between people. Change in pitch (for example, raising the pitch at the end of an utterance) is just one vocal cue which can influence how the other will behave. The change in pitch signals a question that demands an answer.

The audible inspiration of breath, changes in volume, changes in the frequency and duration of silences and interrupting are just some of the many vocal cues that can be used to regulate turn-taking in conversations.

Vocal cues are also used by people to make a judgement about another's personality. For example, breathiness suggests females who are more feminine, prettier, more petite, more effervescent, more highly strung and shallower than others, and nasality in both males and females suggests a wide array of socially undesirable characteristics (see Addington 1969). Research evidence, however, suggests that while 'listeners' do tend to agree on the judgements they make, many of these stereotypes do not correlate with the scores achieved by speakers on personality tests. None the less these stereotypes, even though they are often inaccurate, may well have an important influence on the way we interpret what others say and how they behave.

Deciphering contradictory signals

This chapter has looked at the ways in which attending to non-verbal behaviour can contribute to effective listening. It has been argued that it is important that we 'listen' to both verbal and non-verbal signals because, while there is overlap, words tend to emphasise the factual, whereas non-verbal signals emphasise the affective content of messages. However, problems may arise when the words and the non-verbal signals appear to be sending contradictory messages.

Returning to the exchanges cited earlier in this chapter; what is the true meaning of the message if a red-faced man bangs the table with a clenched fist and declares that he is not angry? Research evidence suggests that non-verbal behaviours generally offer the most reliable clues to what a person is really feeling, in spite of his denial that he is not angry.

It appears that people are less likely to inhibit or manipulate certain signals. These tend to be the signals they are least aware of, believe others pay little attention to or are beyond their control. Morris (1977) has proposed a 'Believability Scale' for different kinds of action. He suggests that autonomic signals are the most believable and verbalisations are the least believable. The seven elements in his scale are:

1   *Autonomic signals.* These include sweating, skin colour, respiratory patterns, etc. They are almost impossible to control because they result from physiological changes within the body. However, while they offer a very reliable indication of a person's emotional state, their occurrence tends to be limited to relatively few dramatic situations. The body actions listed below tend to occur more frequently and therefore deserve attention.

2   *Leg and foot signals.* People tend to focus most attention on the face, possibly because it is a highly expressive area. Even when it is possible to observe the whole body it is the face that receives the most attention. It would appear that we normally pay least attention to those parts of the body which are furthest away from the face and, probably for the same reasons, we exert least deliberate control over these same parts of our own body. Since the feet are as far away from the face as one can get, it is not unreasonable to assume that they will provide valuable clues to a person's true mood. Foot actions that might be observed include aggressive toe jabs that may be at variance with friendly words and a smiling face, or restless and repetitive foot movements which suggest that the person is anxious to discontinue the interaction and get away. Moving on to consider the leg as a whole, it may be possible to observe the soothing leg squeezing, mentioned above, which suggests that a seemingly confident person is seeking some self-assurance or flirtatious leg displays which conflict with upper body primness.

3   *Trunk signals.* Posture can reflect the general muscular tonus of the whole body and therefore can be a useful guide to mood states. Somebody who is keyed up and excited will find it much more difficult to adopt a slumped posture than someone who is bored, unhappy or depressed.

4 *Unidentified gesticulations*. People tend to be more aware of hands – their own and others – than they are of feet. However, their awareness still tends to be relatively low, especially when the hands are used to make the vague and indefinite actions which accompany speech. Assertive finger wagging, imploring palm-up hand gestures or hand chops are some of the signals which can indicate what a person is really feeling. These 'illustrative gestures' are a better guide to the truth than the 'emblems' which are included in the next category.

5 *Identified hand gestures*. We tend to be more aware of those hand gestures which are precise units of communication and which are deliberately performed. For this reason, emblems such as the A-OK or the victory V signs cannot be trusted if they appear as part of a contradictory signal. People may deliberately signal A-OK or thumbs up when they are feeling less than satisfied with their state of affairs. Consequently, such signals merit less weight than those discussed above.

6 *Facial expressions*. It is relatively easy to lie with the face. Most of us can fake anger or surprise with relative ease, and therefore when contradictory signals are observed it may be best to ignore facial expressions. However, the careful observer may be able to see through many faked facial expressions and observe frozen smiles or other minute facial movements which provide clues to what the other is really feeling.

7 *Verbalisations*. As mentioned above, people are able to exercise most control over the verbal messages they give out. For this reason they are the least reliable guide to true feelings when contradictory signals are observed.

Exercise 5.3 will help raise your awareness of the non-verbal behaviours that you typically attend to and those that you tend to neglect.

Exercise 5.3 Listening to non-verbal signals

Observe other people in conversation and ask yourself what they really feel about each other, about the issues being discussed and about themselves. Ask yourself who has the highest status and who is taking the lead in managing the interaction.

Think about the non-verbal behaviours you attended to when making your assessment. The check-list presented below offers examples of some non-verbal signals that have been organised under the headings discussed in this chapter. Using this as a framework, keep a record of the signals you attend to. After you have observed and recorded a number of interactions between people, you will be able to develop a profile of the signals you attend to most and least.

Which non-verbal behaviours do you attend to?

FACE	Brows and forehead	☐
	Eyes, lids, bridge of nose	☐
	Cheek, nose, mouth, jaw	☐
	Other, specify:	☐
GAZE	Direction	☐
	Frequency	☐
	Length	☐
	Soft/hard	☐
	Cut off	☐
	Lack of	☐
	Other, specify:	☐
GESTURES	Emblems (A-OK, thumbs up, etc.)	☐
	Illustrators (finger wagging, vacuum precision grip, etc.)	☐
	Regulators (nodding, eyebrow flash, etc.)	☐
	Self touching: self-comfort – stroking face, hair caress, rocking	☐
	Self touching: negative attitudes to self – picking, hand over eyes	☐
	Self touching: attitudes to others – fist gesture, clenched hands	☐
	Object touching: polishing glasses, smoking, filling pipe	☐
	Touching others: kind, target and duration of touch	☐
POSTURE	Upright	☐
	Slumped	☐
	Tense	☐
	Relaxed	☐
	Other, specify:	☐
FURNITURE	As barrier	☐
	As status symbol	☐
	Other, specify:	☐
PERSONAL SPACE	Proximity zones	☐
APPEARANCE	Clothes	☐
	Hair	☐
	Skin	☐
	Smell	☐
	Other, specify:	☐
VOCAL CUES	Loudness, pitch, timbre, rate, inflection, rhythm, enunciation	☐

Note whether you attend to a wide or a narrow range of non-verbal behaviours. Bearing in mind Morris' 'Believability Scale', ask yourself whether you are paying sufficient attention to the most reliable signals.

You may find it useful to start observing those signals which you tend to neglect and to monitor how your new pattern of observation improves your ability to better understand the meaning of the messages you receive from other people.

One final point. Remember that it can be dangerous to over-interpret the meaning of an isolated behaviour. The art of effective listening to non-verbal messages is to recognise behaviours that may have potential message value and then to search for other behaviours that suggest a pattern. It is these patterns of behaviour, interpreted within context, that will enable you to determine the meaning of what you have seen and heard with a greater degree of confidence.

Summary

This chapter has considered how attention to non-verbal behaviour can affect the ability to diagnose emotional states and understand other people's intentions. The relationship between non-verbal and verbal behaviour has been examined and the ways in which the face, gestures, touching, posture, the use of furniture and space, personal proximity, appearance and vocal cues can convey meaning have been discussed. Attention has also been given to a range of issues concerned with the accurate interpretation of the meaning of non-verbal signals and the deciphering of contradictory signals.

References

Addington, D.W. (1969) 'The relationship of selected vocal characteristics to personality perception', *Speech Monographs* 35: 492–503.
Agulera, D.C. (1967) 'Relationships between physical contact and verbal interaction between nurses and patients', *Journal of Psychiatric Nursing* 5: 5–21.
Argyle, M. (1975) *Bodily Communication*, New York: International Universities Press.
Argyle, M. and Kendon, A. (1967) 'The experimental analysis of social performance', *Advances in Experimental Social Psychology* 3, 55–98.
Bolton, R. (1986) *People Skills*, Sydney: Prentice Hall of Australia.
Bull, P. (1983) *Body Movement and Interpersonal Communication*, New York: John Wiley.
Davitz, J.R. (1964) *The Communication of Emotional Meaning*, New York: McGraw-Hill.

DePaulo, B. (1992) 'Nonverbal behavior as self-presentation', *Psychological Bulletin* 111: 203–223.

Dunlap, K. (1927) 'The role of eye-muscles and mouth muscles in the expression of emotions', *Genetic Psychology Monographs* 2: 199–233.

Efran, J.S. (1968) 'Looking for approval: effect on visual behavior of approbation from persons differing in importance', *Journal of Personality and Social Psychology* 10: 21–25.

Eisenberg, A. and Smith, R. (1971) *No Communication*, Indianapolis: Babbs-Merrill.

Ekman, P. (1992) 'Facial expression of emotions: new findings, new questions', *Psychological Science* 3: 34–38.

Ekman, P. (1994) 'Strong evidence for universals in facial expression: a reply to Russell's mistaken critique', *Psychological Bulletin* 115: 268–287.

Ekman, P. and Friesen, W.V. (1969) 'The repertoire of non-verbal behaviour: categories, origins, usage and coding', *Semiotica* 1: 49–98.

Ekman, P., Friesen, W.V. and Beat, J. (1984) 'The international language of gestures', *Psychology Today* May: 64–69.

Ekman, P., Friesen, W.V. and Ellsworth, P. (1972) *Emotion in the Human Face: Guidelines for Research and Integration of Findings*, Elmsford, NY: Pergamon Press.

Ekman, P., Friesen, W.V. and Tomkins, S.S. (1971) 'Facial affect scoring technique: a first validity study', *Semiotica* 3: 37–58.

Fisher, J.D., Rytting, M. and Heslin, R. (1976) 'Hands touching hands: affective and evaluative effects of an interpersonal touch', *Sociometry* 39: 416–421.

Graham, J.A. and Argyle, M. (1975) 'A cross cultural study of the communication of extra-verbal meaning by gestures', *International Journal of Psychology* 10: 57–69.

Hall, E.T. (1959) *The Silent Language*, Garden City, NY: Doubleday.

Knapp, M.L. (1978) *Non-verbal Communication in Human Interaction*, New York: Holt, Rinehart & Winston.

Matsumoto, D. and Ekman, P. (1989) 'American–Japanese cultural differences in intensity ratings of facial expressions of emotion, *Motivation and Emotion* 13: 143–157.

Mayle, P. (1989) *A Year in Provence*, London: Hamish Hamilton.

Mehrabian, A. (1968) 'The inference of attitude from the posture, orientation and distance of a communication', *Journal of Consulting Psychology* 32: 296–308.

Mehrabian, A. (1972) *Non-verbal Communication*, Chicago, IL: Aldine-Atherton.

Mehrabian, A. and Williams, M. (1969) 'Non-verbal concomitants of perceived and intended persuasiveness', *Journal of Personality and Social Psychology* 13: 37–58.

Morris, D. (1977) *Manwatching: A Field Guide to Human Behaviour*, London: Jonathan Cape.

Patterson M.L. (1988) 'Functions of non-verbal behaviour in close relationships', in S. Duck (ed.) *Handbook of Personal Relationships: Theory, Research and Interventions*, New York: Wiley.

Patterson, M.L. (1995) 'A parallel process model of non-verbal communication', *Journal of Nonverbal Behavior* 19: 3–29.

Payrato, L. (1993) 'A pragmatic view of autonomous gestures: a first repertoire of Catalan emblems', *Journal of Pragmatics* 20: 193–216.

Pooringa, Y.H., Schoots, N.H. and Van de Koppel, J.M. (1993) 'The understanding of Chinese and Kurdish emblematic gestures by Dutch subjects', *International Journal of Psychology* 28: 31–44.

Rozelle, R.M., Druckman, D. and Baxter, J.C. (1997) 'Non-verbal behaviour as communication', in O.D.W. Hargie (ed.) *Handbook of Communication Skills* (2nd edn), London: Routledge.

Sabin, T.R. and Hardyk, C.D. (1953) 'Contributions to role taking theory: role perception on the basis of postural cues', unpublished study cited by T.S. Sabin (1954), in G.Lindzey (ed.) *Handbook of Social Psychology*, Cambridge, MA: Addison-Wesley.

Safadi, M. and Valentine, C.A. (1988) 'Emblems and gestures among Hebrew speakers in Israel', *International Journal of Intercultural Relations* 12: 327–361.

White, A.G. (1953) 'The patient sits down: a clinical note', *Psychiatric Medicine* 15: 256–257, cited in M. Argyle (1975) *Bodily Communication*.

6

QUESTIONING AND THE INFORMATION-GETTING INTERVIEW

Learning objective

To understand how the interactive nature of social encounters affects the quantity and quality of information that individuals can obtain from others, and recognise the steps that individuals can take to improve their ability to obtain information.

After reading this chapter you will:

- Understand the importance of defining the purpose of any information-getting activity.
- Recognise that effective information getting involves structuring and managing social interactions in ways that minimise the communication of irrelevant information and maximise the full and accurate communication of information that is relevant to the purpose of the interaction.
- Be aware that effective information getting involves much more than the application of a standard set of 'techniques', and that the interviewers' purpose and the context of the information-getting activity will have an important influence on the way the activity needs to be managed.
- Be aware of the main sources of bias in interviews.
- Understand the importance of building rapport.
- Be aware of how the phrasing of questions can signal to others a preferred response, and be able to differentiate between the different types of leading question.
- Be aware of how the phrasing of questions can affect the respondents' freedom to answer, and be able to explain the advantages and disadvantages of open and closed questions.
- Be able to explain how the use of directive and non-directive probes can affect the information available to interviewers.
- Recognise how the organisation of topics and the sequencing of questions can affect understanding, condition respondents to answer in particular ways and affect the motivation of respondents to provide information.

Information getting

This chapter examines information getting in the context of the interview. One of the most common definitions of the interview is 'a conversation with a purpose' (Bingham *et al.* 1941). This is a wide-ranging umbrella-like definition which encompasses many kinds of purposeful conversations ranging from disciplinary interviews to counselling sessions, and possibly even including negotiations. In this chapter a much narrower definition has been adopted and the interview is defined as a face-to-face interaction in which one person seeks information from another. For example, we may want information that will help us:

- assess a person's suitability for a job;
- determine why customers are unhappy with a product;
- anticipate people's reactions to the introduction of some new arrangement such as flexi-time;
- decide whether an insurance claim is justified.

When we engage in these kinds of interaction with others we may have little interest in much of the information they may be prepared to divulge, nor may we have time to listen to it.

The effective interviewer is someone who is able to structure and manage the encounter in such a way that information irrelevant to the purpose of the interaction is largely eliminated, and relevant information is fully and accurately communicated in a relatively brief period of time. Many of us have engaged in interactions that are very different to this. We may fail to manage the interaction and allow, maybe even encourage, the respondent to spend much of the time talking about things that are irrelevant to the purpose of the interview. The aim of this chapter is to identify and discuss many of the skills that can help you conduct an effective information-getting interview.

The information-getting interview is not restricted to objective fact finding. Nadler (1977) argues that the interview is an effective instrument for obtaining several kinds of information. These include: (1) descriptive accounts (a systems analyst, for example, might interview members of a department in order to discover how some system or procedure works); (2) diagnostic evaluations (the analyst may not only want to know how the system or procedure operates but also how effective it is, and therefore may ask respondents for their assessment of whether or not it is fulfilling its purpose); (3) affective reactions (even if the system is working effectively, people may or may not like it. Affective reactions are the positive or negative feelings people have, they may feel satisfied or dissatisfied, challenged or frustrated). In other words, information getting can involve gathering many different kinds of information, including other people's attitudes, values, hopes and fears. It is not restricted to obtaining 'objective facts' and often

99

involves asking people to talk about private thoughts they may not normally share with others, or about partially formed attitudes or personal feelings they may never have articulated before.

The interview as a social encounter

Obtaining full and frank answers from another person is not an easy task. The interview is a complex social encounter in which the behaviour of each party is influenced by the other. An often used but over-simplified model of the interview presents the process solely in terms of the interviewer getting information from the respondent, and fails to take full account of the inter-active nature of the encounter. Respondents are aware that when we are seeking information from them (interviewing) we are observing what they say and do, and that on the basis of these observations we are making infer-ences about them. Consequently they may not answer all the questions we ask openly and honestly. They may attempt to manage the way they respond so as to maximise their personal benefit from the interaction rather than help us achieve our purpose.

Goffman (1959), Mangham (1978) and others have used drama as a metaphor for describing and explaining a wide range of interactions, and this metaphor may usefully be applied to the interview. Goffman talks about putting on a performance for an audience, and argues that people's portrayal of action will be determined by their assessment of the audience. He also notes that actors use mirrors so that they can practise and become an object to themselves backstage, before going 'on-stage' and becoming an object to others. Similarly, interviewees may anticipate the nature of their audience, namely the interviewers, and rehearse the way they want to present them-selves. Problems may arise, especially in selection interviews, if interviewers (the audience) interpret what they observe as being a true reflection of stable personal dispositions of the interviewees. In reality the interviewees' behav-iour may well be a performance, a reaction to the situation as they perceive it, and consequently may not be a good predictor of how they will behave in different situations.

The problem can be further complicated because in the interview situation the respondents' ability to manage their behaviour, 'to put on a perfor-mance', may be impaired. Farr (1984) argues that if respondents are too sensitive to the fact that others are evaluating them they may become appre-hensive, and this may cause them to perform poorly. This could be an important problem for the chronically shy and may help to explain why those who lack confidence may fail to do well in selection interviews.

The nature of the social encounter involved in an interview is illustrated in Figure 6.1. Let us assume that we are looking at a situation in which one or more consultants are interviewing organisational members to determine the need for change.

Stage 1

The consultants are likely to structure the situation and behave in ways that they feel will best project their definition of the purpose of the encounter and the role they want to assume in the interaction. This behaviour not only says a lot about who the consultants wish to be taken for, but also about who they take the other organisational members to be and the role they are expected to play. The consultants (A) attempt to influence the others' interpretation of the situation and to focus their attention on those issues which they (the consultants) regard as important. Much of what takes place at this stage involves cognitive scene setting.

Stage 2

At Stage 2, in Figure 6.1, the organisational members (B) seek to understand what it is that the consultants (A) are projecting and what implications this has for them. Do the consultants, for example, appear to see the encounter as an information-gathering exercise designed to provide *them* with the information they need to determine what has to be changed? Alternatively, do they see it as the first step towards *involving organisational members* in the management of the change process?

Organisational members may detect a difference between the performance the consultants (A) consciously and deliberately give, and what Mangham refers to as the information they 'give off'. The consultants (A) may attempt to perform in a way that gives the impression to others (B) that they are committed to a shared approach to the management of change; however, they may actually 'give off' signals, verbal and non-verbal, that contradict this intended impression. Thus, as the interaction progresses through stages 3 and 4, the organisational members (B) may decide to cooperate and give the consultants (A) the information they are seeking. Alternatively, they may decide not to be completely open and to distort or withhold information until they are more confident about the consultants' intentions.

Stage 3

Reference has already been made to rehearsal of action. At Stage 3, organisational members have to decide, on the basis of their interpretation of the situation, how to respond to the consultants. Farr (1984), discussing the work of Mead, notes that people not only act but also react to their own actions. They react to their own behaviour on the basis of the actual or *anticipated* reactions of others. They can anticipate their reactions through simulation or rehearsal. They can try out, in their own mind, a few pieces of behaviour and test them for fit. Mangham even suggests that people can simulate several stages into alternative futures for an interaction, a form of mental chess in which various moves and their consequences are tested.

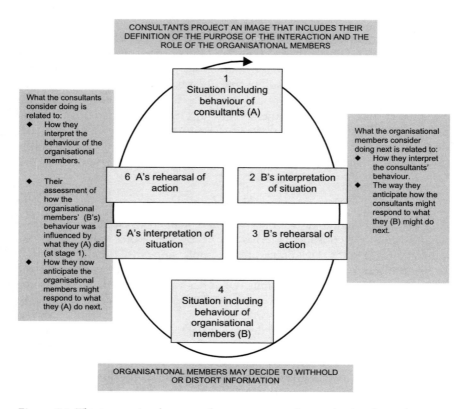

Figure 6.1 The interaction between change agents and organisational members.

Stage 4

Once the organisational members (B) have decided what to do and have responded to the consultants' (A) initial behaviour, the situation changes. Both A and B, at Stage 4 of the cycle, are faced with a situation that includes the most recent behaviour of B. If the consultants failed to make their purpose explicit (at Stage 1), organisational members may misinterpret their behaviour and act in ways that the consultants either did not anticipate or feel is inappropriate to the situation.

Stage 5

The consultants have to assess this situation (Stage 5) and attempt to understand the meaning of the organisational members' behaviour. Their interpretation of the organisational members' response offers a basis for assessing the relevance and validity of any information communicated by them. Good interviewers/information gatherers have the ability to empathise with the other party. They can assume the others' role in the interaction, and they can put themselves in the others' shoes and replay in their mind the situation the respondents/organisational members face. They can also interpret the others' behaviour from this perspective, including their answers to questions.

Stage 6

On the basis of their interpretation of the situation, including the organisational members' (B) behaviour, the consultants (A) can rehearse the next move (Stage 6) before deciding what to do and/or say. This then forms part of the unfolding scene to which the organisational members (B) will have to respond, and so the process continues.

The point of this example is that the nature of the encounter will influence how both parties will interpret what they see and hear. It will also influence the quantity and quality of the information each is prepared to offer.

Error and bias in interviews

Interviews may be used to acquire information for a number of purposes. For example:

- to determine whether things are going according to plan and, if not, why not;
- to ascertain people's attitudes and feelings regarding something or somebody;
- to predict future performance (as in the selection interview).

The extent to which the interview can be an effective instrument in helping us to achieve such purposes will be determined, at least in part, by the accuracy of the information we acquire.

Kahn and Cannell (1957) in their seminal book, *The Dynamics of Interviewing*, review some of the early evidence which points to the prevalence of error and bias in the interview. They found:

1   *Persistent and important differences between interview data and data obtained from other sources.* For example, it was found, in one study, that one out of every nine families receiving city relief *failed to report this* when asked a specific question in the course of an interview. People may not have wanted to admit to the interviewer that they were receiving relief payments because this was incongruent with the image they wished to project. One might have expected more accurate answers if the question had enquired about something less sensitive, such as the respondent's gender.

2   *Differences between two sets of interview data when respondents were reinterviewed.* Kinsey, in his study of sexual behaviour, reinterviewed 150 respondents and found that while the answers to some questions showed close agreement, the answers to others evidenced considerable variability. Many factors may have accounted for these differences including the possibility that the answers to some of the questions in the first interview were less accurate than others (perhaps for the kinds of reasons discussed above). Where answers in the first interview represented deliberate distortions of the truth, the respondents may have experienced more difficulty recalling the answers they gave, whereas they may have experienced less difficulty recalling and repeating accurate (truthful) answers.

3   *Differences between the results obtained when two interviewers interviewed the same individuals.* Two selection interviewers questioned independently twenty-three job applicants regarding their work experience, family history, and social and personal characteristics. A comparison of the two sets of interviews showed a considerable lack of agreement, with an average reliability of 0.71 for all items. An explanation for this may be that the respondents were motivated to respond differently to the different interviewers; however, Kahn and Cannell (1957) also found research evidence to suggest that the source of this kind of inaccuracy was not always the respondent. In a study into the causes of destitution, it was noticed that the results reported by one interviewer were very similar for all his interviews, but were very different from the results obtained by another interviewer. The first cited alcohol abuse as the chief cause of destitution, whereas the second interviewer tended to emphasise social and industrial conditions. This suggests that the interviewers' own preconceptions may have influenced their interpretation of what respondents said.

Error and bias can arise for many reasons.

Background characteristics

Background characteristics, such as the age, sex, race or status of both interviewer and respondent may influence the quality of information exchanged in the interview. It was noted in Chapter 4 that the background characteristics of the respondent/speaker can influence what we hear when interviewing others. For example, we may pay more attention to what high-status people say than we do to what low-status people say. There is also a wealth of evidence suggesting that our own background characteristics can affect what respondents are prepared to tell us. Respondents may be reluctant to tell us things that we may find hurtful or things we may disapprove of.

Khan and Cannell (1957) report a study by Robinson and Rohde in which three groups of interviewers questioned New Yorkers on their attitudes towards Jews. The first group of interviewers were people who were non-Semitic in appearance and name, the second group included people who were Semitic in appearance but non-Semitic in name, and the third group comprised people who appeared to be Semitic both in appearance and name. It was found that the more likely the respondents were to identify the interviewers as Jewish, the less likely they were to make anti-Semitic statements.

In terms of the model outlined in Figure 6.1, no matter how hard the interviewer (A) tries to perform a role and project an image that will encourage the respondent (B) to provide full and frank answers, the interviewer's background characteristics may 'give off' signals to B that will have an important influence on the way the interviewee will behave in the interview. Similarly, A may find it equally difficult not to respond to the background characteristics of B.

Psychological factors

Psychological factors, such as motives, attitudes, beliefs and emotionality can also be important sources of error and bias.

MOTIVES

It was noted in Chapter 4 that motivation can affect what we (as information gatherers) attend to. In a similar way, the motivation of respondents can affect the information they will attempt to communicate. In any social encounter, the motivation of both parties to interact with each other may be very different. For example, in an annual performance appraisal interview – where a manager appraises the performance of a subordinate – the manager (interviewer) may be motivated to help the subordinate/appraisee develop and realise his or her full potential. In order to achieve this objective, the appraiser may be motivated to obtain accurate information about the appraisee's strengths and weaknesses. The appraisee, on the other hand, may be motivated to obtain an immediate pay rise or rapid promotion and therefore may be tempted to hide any weaknesses and exaggerate any strengths so that s/he can convince the appraiser that s/he deserves more pay or promotion.

In this example, the conflicting motives of the appraisee and appraiser can have an important effect on the information available to the appraiser. Because the appraisee is motivated to create a good impression, s/he will be alert to cues that provide feedback on how they are regarded by the appraiser. If the appraiser appears to approve of some of the attitudes s/he expressed (or some of the activities s/he has engaged in), the appraisee will tend to emphasise or say more about them. The appraisee will also avoid expressing any feelings or presenting any information about activities the appraiser (interviewer) disapproves of. In this way the appraisee's behaviour can frustrate the appraiser's purpose of collecting accurate information about the appraisee's strengths and weaknesses. If the appraiser is unaware of the appraisee's purpose, s/he may accept the appraisee's statements at face value and fail to appreciate that the appraisee is trying to mislead.

ATTITUDES

Even in interviews where respondents attempt to give full and frank answers to the interviewer's questions, the interviewer's own attitudes, expectations and motives may influence the way s/he interprets what s/he hears. For example, journalists who are committed pacifists may find it hard not to let their own attitudes influence the way they interpret the answers they receive from the chief executive of a company which manufactures battle tanks.

BELIEFS

Similarly, managers who believe that most workers have an inherent dislike of work, will avoid it if they can and must be coerced and closely controlled if they are to perform effectively, may find that these beliefs influence the way they interpret what they are told in an appraisal interview.

EMOTIONALITY

Emotional state can also affect the interviewer's ability to attend to what the respondent has to say. Ostell *et al.* (1999) refer to research which found that appraisers who were in an elated emotional state considered less information than appraisers who were in a more depressed mood.

Interviewer behaviour

The effective interviewer has been described as somebody who is able to behave in ways that will eliminate or reduce as much as possible those forces which cause relevant information to be distorted or withheld during the interview. These behaviours will be discussed under eight headings.

Definition of purpose and preparation

Gratis (1988) argues that clarity of purpose aids preparation and the for-mulation and ordering of questions; enables the interviewer to adopt a more flexible approach to managing problems without losing control of the inter-view; and facilitates a more effective evaluation of the interview once it has been completed.

If, for example, the purpose of a selection interview is defined as 'getting as much relevant information from candidates as might be necessary to allow the interviewer to make an accurate assessment of their suitability for the job as defined by the job specification', this definition would alert interviewers to what they need to do in terms of preparation. This may involve ensuring that they have: (1) an appropriate and sufficiently detailed job specification; (2) given some thought to the kind of information they will require about each candidate in order to be able to assess whether they will be capable of performing the job to the required specification; and (3) considered how they may go about obtaining the necessary information. It is not sufficient to simply have a vague notion about what you hope to achieve from the interview. Interviewers need to be clear about purpose and clear about how they need to behave in order to achieve their purpose.

Dillon (1997) offers a useful review of how the purpose of information gathering in a range of different professional situations can affect the use of questions and the kind of preparation that is required. He argues that there is no template which applies to all situations.

Cognitive scene setting

When the conceptual model of the interview was introduced earlier in this chapter it was argued that early encounters will often be concerned largely with what Wicks (1984) describes as 'cognitive scene setting' and what Hargie *et al.* (1994) refers to as 'set induction'.

When we are seeking information from others, we need to communicate our purpose and establish terms of reference for the interview. This involves inducing a state of readiness appropriate to the task that will follow. If a manager calls some subordinates into the office they may be unsure why they have been summoned and will probably spend the first part of the 'interview' searching for clues that will indicate their boss's purpose. Might it be to enquire into why deliveries have been delayed, might it be to appraise their performance over the preceding twelve months, might it be to assess their suitability for promotion, or what? If the interviewees 'misread' the situation they may respond inappropriately to the manager's questioning. For example, if the manager's opening statement is 'Has there been any improvement in deliveries?' the subordinates may not realise that the manager is enquiring about whether suppliers have made any more progress towards meeting their commitments under the new 'just in time' contractual arrangements. They may go on the defensive and prepare themselves to justify why their department twice failed to get work out on time during the previous month.

Before embarking on the main business of any interview, it is important to ensure that our purpose is understood clearly by the respondents and that we are as aware as possible of the respondents' goals and how these might interfere with the achievement of our purpose. The former is usually easier to accomplish than the latter because respondents, as in the performance appraisal example cited above, may deliberately conceal their own goals and may feel that their purpose would be best served by behaving as though they accepted our goal. None the less, even though it may be difficult, we need to do everything possible to ascertain respondents' purposes and expectations and, where these are inconsistent with our own, take special care when interpreting what respondents tell us.

Inducing an appropriate cognitive set involves preparing others for the main business or purpose of the interview. We can achieve this by providing briefing documents or prior instructions. This kind of information is often provided before a performance appraisal interview when appraisees may be briefed to bring with them to the interview a list of their main objectives and to prepare their own assessment of the extent to which these have been achieved. It can also be achieved by the kind of opening remarks we make and by the non-verbal cues we give off.

The environmental setting in which the interview takes place will also help to key respondents into a particular frame of reference. They may respond differently to an interview on 'expense claims' depending on whether it is held in the local police station or the boss's office. A less dramatic example of how physical setting can induce cognitive set may be seating arrangements. If a manager who usually conducts interviews around a coffee table decides to interview an employee across a desk, this may be interpreted as a signal that the employee is in trouble or that something serious is to be discussed.

Our opening behaviour is important, not only in terms of inducing an appropriate cognitive set, but also in terms of establishing rapport. Gratis (1988) points to the importance of 'meeting and greeting', and Hargie (1994) emphasises the need for what he describes as 'social set induction', a process which involves helping respondents feel more at ease, establishing their confidence and trust in the interviewer and breaking the ice so that the interview can get off to a good start.

Rapport can be established in a number of ways. We may stand up to greet interviewees, shake their hand, use their name and offer welcoming remarks in a tone of voice that puts them at ease. We may demonstrate that we are interested in the interviewees by exhibiting many of the attending behaviours discussed in Chapter 4, and we may break the ice by talking about non-task issues such as the weather or the journey. We may also start the interview by asking the kind of question that respondents will find easy to answer and which will not cause embarrassment or pose a threat of any kind. Empathic listening throughout the interview will also build rapport. Nadler (1977) reports that where more empathic approaches are adopted respondents seem more willing to open up and disclose sensitive information.

Exercise 6.1 is designed to help you identify what it is that we do (intentionally or unintentionally) that affects both the way others view our intent and the quality of rapport that we are able to establish. (*Note*: the early part of Exercise 1.1 also relates to cognitive scene setting.)

Exercise 6.1 Cognitive scene setting

Step 1: Observe others

Identify an opportunity to observe one person seeking information from another. You could view a scene from a film, a clip from an off-air video recording, a role play of an interview or any number of real-life situations such as a manager seeking information from a colleague or a parent seeking information from a child.

Pay careful attention to the information seeker's verbal and non-verbal behaviour and to the setting in which the interaction occurs. Look for and note evidence that indicates how the information seeker's behaviour appears to influence:

- the respondent's early impression of the information seeker's intent;
- the extent to which the respondent is motivated to provide the information seeker with all the information that is sought.

Reflect on your observations. Could the information seeker have done anything to improve the way they communicated their purpose and built rapport?

Step 2: Monitor self

While you are actively seeking information from others open a 'second channel' and observe your own behaviour. Do *not* change your normal approach at this point because the aim of this step is to increase your awareness of your normal cognitive scene-setting behaviour. Follow the same procedure you used for observing others. (An alternative approach is to seek feedback from the respondent or to video the interaction and review the recording.) Make a note of your own behaviour and consider whether it could be modified to be more effective.

Step 3: Experimenting with new behaviours

If you feel that you could improve your cognitive scene-setting behaviour identify what you might do differently, try it out and monitor the consequences.

Rapport and motivation can be closely linked. What happens in the early stage of the interview can have important implications for the interviewee's motivation, which in turn will influence the quantity and quality of information that will be available to us. Where motivation is low the respondent may disrupt the interview, may refuse to answer any questions or may give false answers deliberately, thus defeating our purpose.

Content and coverage

With the purpose of the interview in mind, we need to give some thought to the kind of information we require. Different types of interviewers often have very different purposes; for example:

- Prosecution lawyers may want to ensure that they ask defendants questions that will produce all the information they want the jury to hear.
- Physicians, on the other hand, may want to ensure that they ask patients the questions that will provide them with all the information they need in order to make an accurate diagnosis.

Many selection interviewers still use Rodger's (1952) seven-point plan to reduce the likelihood that they may overlook important information and to ensure that similar kinds of information are collected about all candidates. Roger argues that four points need to be considered when deciding what categories of information to include in an interview plan. (1) They should be relevant to the purpose of the interview; for example, in the selective interview they should pinpoint influences connected commonly and demonstrably with success or failure to perform the job. (2) They should be independent; they should be separable from one another sufficiently to enable the interviewer to avoid making overlapping assessments that could be wasteful. (3) They should be assessable in the circumstances in which the assessment is to be made. (4) They should be few enough to keep the risk of hasty and superficial judgements to a minimum but numerous enough to cover the ground adequately.

Roger's seven-point plan, which has been used extensively in selection and vocational guidance interviews, is as follows:

1   *Physical characteristics*. Physical abilities of occupational importance such as state of health, vision, hearing, speech, appearance and bearing.
2   *Attainments, training and experience*. Educational background and attainment, training, work experience, personal achievements in other areas such as sports, music, etc.
3   *General ability*, especially general intelligence and cognitive skills (words, numbers, relationships). These are best assessed by the use of

110

psychometric tests but the interviewer may be able to make estimates in these areas by seeking information which indicates what the respondents have managed to achieve, especially in those situations where they have been fully stretched.

4   *Special aptitudes,* especially occupationally relevant talents, for example, scientific, mechanical, mathematical, practical, literary, artistic, social skills.

5   *Interests.* Type of interests (intellectual, practical, physical, social, artistic) and how they are pursued can be important because they may indicate the directions in which the respondent's other attributes may be employed most effectively.

6   *Disposition/personality.* Roger argues against the use of abstract nouns such as sociability and leadership, and favours questions that focus the interviewers' attention on facts. For example, how do other people take to the candidates? Do they take notice of what the candidates say or do? Is the candidates' behaviour fairly predictable? Do they work things out for themselves?

7   *Circumstances.* The context of a person's life insofar as it affects their ability to perform the job to the required specification.

A plan of this kind does not represent an ordering of the questions to be asked in an interview; it provides a framework, a set of pigeon-holes into which relevant information may be posted as and when it is obtained. It also provides a check-list to ensure that all the necessary points have been covered before the end of the interview. Exercise 6.2 is designed to help you practise developing interview plans.

Exercise 6.2 Information requirements and interview plans

Imagine that you are planning to drive across part of North Africa for a six-week adventure holiday. You have identified three people in Egypt (from where you plan to start your journey) who have ex-military four-wheeled drive vehicles for sale. You want to identify if any of these vehicles will be suitable for your purpose and to arrange appointments to view any that might satisfy your requirements as soon as you arrive in Egypt.

You intend to speak to the three vendors by telephone but need to plan your conversation carefully in order to obtain all the information you require without incurring unnecessarily large overseas phone charges.

- Make a list of the information you require.

- Compare your list with similar lists drawn up by others.
- Reflect on the relative merits of all these lists and, on reflection, consider whether your original list included all the information you need and excluded unnecessary or low-priority information (bearing in mind the need to keep the telephone conversations relatively short).

Think of an occasion in the near future when you will need to seek information (for example, when choosing a holiday, buying a new computer or deciding the best way to allocate work between members of a project team). Identify your information requirements and draw up a check-list that you might use as an *aide-memoire*.

Organisation of topics

When deciding the order in which topics are to be addressed in an interview, a useful guiding principle is to put ourselves in the shoes of possible respondents and select an order that is most likely to help them understand the questions and motivate them to respond.

Respondents may easily misunderstand complex or subtle questions if they have not been given cues that will key them into an appropriate frame of reference. Topics may be ordered in such a way that the respondent is encouraged to think about a range of issues before answering a question on a more complex topic. For example, before enquiring whether the company's security budget should be cut, the interviewer may first explore the respondent's views on a wide range of security-related issues. These may include data protection, kidnap and hostage policy, whether innovations should be patented or kept secret, pilfering, use of company equipment for personal ends and so on. This approach ensures that the interviewee fully understands the nature of the question on the security budget. However, care must be exercised to ensure that the respondent is not conditioned or led to answer in a particular way by the ordering of topics. An extract from *Yes, Prime Minister* (Lynn and Jay 1986: 106) offers a classic example. Humphrey Appleby shows Bernard, the PM's Principal Private Secretary, how the way opinion pollsters organise the questions they ask can influence the response they receive. Sir Humphrey explains that when an attractive female researcher approaches the man in the street he wants to create a good impression. Above all else he does not want to make a fool of himself. Pollsters are aware of this and may decide to ask a series of questions designed to elicit *consistent* answers so as to produce a desired outcome.

Sir Humphrey proceeded to offer Bernard an example. He asked a series of questions that prompted Bernard to respond in favour of the reintroduction of National Service, and then asked another series of questions that persuaded him to oppose its reintroduction.

Q: Bernard, are you worried about the rise in crime among teenagers?
A: Yes.
Q: Do you think there is a lack of discipline and vigorous training in our Comprehensive Schools?
A: Yes.
Q: Do you think young people would welcome some structure and leadership in their lives?
A: Yes.
Q: Do they respond to a challenge?
A: Yes.
Q: Might you be in favour of reintroducing National Service?
A: Yes.

Bernard volunteered the information that he could hardly say anything but 'Yes' without appearing inconsistent. Sir Humphrey's second series of questions were:

Q: Bernard, are you worried about the danger of war?
A: Yes.
Q: Do you think there's a danger in giving young people guns and teaching them how to kill?
A: Yes.
Q: Do you think it is wrong to force people to take up arms against their will?
A: Yes.
Q: Would you oppose the reintroduction of National Service?
A: Yes.

Thus, while on the one hand the organisation of topics in an interview schedule can provide respondents with a frame of reference that will help them better understand a difficult or complex question, it can also lead them to answer in a particular way. This may be dangerous when our aim is to explore how the respondent really feels about an issue, but it may be helpful when the questioner (for example, a prosecution lawyer) wants to elicit a particular response.

Other considerations may also influence the organisation of topics. It may be that some questions which are seen to be very personal or threatening are best asked in the middle or towards the end of an interview when maximum rapport and motivation have been established.

Formulation of questions

The way in which we formulate questions can have an enormous impact on the quantity and quality of information the respondent will disclose. Three aspects of question formulation will be considered here: choice of words, the extent to which the question signals an expected or preferred response (leading questions), and the degree of freedom given to the respondent to answer (open versus closed questions).

Choice of words is important at one level because, if we use a *vocabulary* that is unfamiliar to the respondents, they may not understand the question we are asking, and in some circumstances may not be prepared to admit their ignorance for fear of losing face. At another level we may phrase questions in such a way that they lack precision, causing different respondents to reply to what they perceived to be different questions. For example, if members of a church congregation are asked about their attitudes towards tithing and if one of the questions is 'Would you be prepared to give a tenth of your income to the church?', the word 'income' may be interpreted differently by different people. Some may take it to mean gross earnings, others may interpret it as earnings after tax, and yet others as disposable income after taxes, mortgage, housekeeping and school fees have been deducted.

Choice of words can facilitate understanding by providing the respondent with a *frame of reference*, the importance of which has already been emphasised. There is a greater likelihood that a supervisor will understand the manager's question and provide relevant information if the supervisor is asked: 'How are things between you and the storeman since you insisted on better record keeping?', rather than if the supervisor is simply asked: 'How are things?' If the respondent is grieving the loss of a partner, this latter question might be interpreted as an enquiry about how s/he is coping with the bereavement.

Acceptability of a wide range of responses. Kahn and Cannell (1957) suggest that if respondents are to be encouraged to answer freely and honestly, questions should be worded in such a way that a wide range of responses are perceived to be acceptable. This can be achieved by incorporating a brief introductory statement into the question. For example, rather than asking a married coal miner: 'Do you ever do the washing and ironing at home?', a more truthful answer might be elicited if the question were worded: 'Recent research has shown that many men share household chores with their wives. Do you ever do the washing or ironing?' Worded in this way, the question informs the respondent that it is not unusual for men to do housework and indicates that the interviewer has no preconceived ideas about what kind of answer would be acceptable.

Leading questions. When phrasing questions we need to take great care to avoid signalling a preferred response. Where the expected or preferred answer is implied in the question this is referred to as a leading question. There are a number of different types of leading question.

Conversational leads are questions that anticipate the answer the respondent would have given anyway, such as: 'Isn't it a lovely day?' They are often used in the early stages of an interview to convey friendliness and interest and to encourage the respondent to participate. Hargie *et al.* (1994) have identified three other kinds of leading question: simple leads, implication or complex leads, and subtle leads.

Simple leads are questions that clearly signal the answer the interviewer expects, for example, 'You are not a member of the Union, are you?' Many writers suggest that leading questions should always be avoided. Gratis (1988) states that the two objectives of questions are to obtain accurate information and to motivate the interviewee to respond freely, and a leading question negates both. There are, however, a number of circumstances where leading questions can contribute to the quantity and quality of information that will be given to the interviewer. It has already been argued that conversational leads can help build rapport, and Hargie suggests that there is evidence that the use of simple leads which are obviously incorrect may induce the respondent to provide information in order to correct the apparent misconceptions inherent in the question. Beezer (1956) who conducted interviews with East German refugees illustrates this point. He found that by using simple leading questions that were obviously incorrect, such as: 'I understand you don't have to pay very much for food in the East Zone because it is rationed?', the refugees gave very full replies in an attempt to correct the interviewer's impressions of life in East Germany.

Implication or complex leads exert much more pressure on the respondent to reply in a particular way. An example of such a question might be: 'At times like this it is important that we all pull together to maintain the stock market's confidence in the company. So don't you feel that all managers should hold on to their bonus shares even though the price is falling?' The kind of introductory statement that prefaces this question, unlike some of those discussed above which are designed to signal that a wide range of responses are equally acceptable, clearly indicates that only one answer is *acceptable* to the interviewer. If respondents offer the 'wrong' answer they have to accept that the interviewer may well label them as disloyal.

Prosecution lawyers are tempted to use leading questions because they can often persuade the defendant to reveal more than s/he intended. Hargie suggests that implication leads put respondents under considerable pressure to justify their position. For example, if asked the question 'Did you know that what you were doing was dishonest?' (Loftus 1982), the respondent must either accept the negative implication of dishonest or respond at length.

Subtle leads are questions that may not be immediately recognised as leading questions. Harris (1973) reports studies which demonstrate that the way a question is worded can influence the response. For example, asking somebody how tall a basketball player is produced greater estimates than when respondents were asked how short the player was. The average guess of those who were asked 'how tall?' was 79 inches, as opposed to 69 inches for those who were asked 'how small?' Hargie describes a study by Loftus (1975) which reported similar findings when forty people were asked about headaches. Those who were asked 'Do you get headaches frequently and, if so, how often?' reported an average of 2.2 headaches per week, whereas those who were asked 'Do you get headaches occasionally and, if so, how often?' reported only 0.7 per week. Some interviewers may deliberately use subtle leads to obtain the answers they desire, but often neither the interviewer nor respondent is aware of the extent to which the wording of the question can influence the response.

Open and closed questions. The degree of freedom given to a respondent to answer a question can have an important influence on the nature of the information available to the interviewer.

Closed questions are those which require the respondent to reply by selecting a response from a series of predetermined categories offered by the interviewer. There are three main types of closed question. The most common is where the respondent is offered the two categories 'yes' and 'no'; for example: 'Are you over 21?' There is usually a correct answer to this kind of question and therefore it can be an effective way of obtaining specific information quickly. In an accident investigation the investigator may need to identify which of the people who were present actually saw the accident occur, and therefore ask the question: 'Did you see the collision?'

A similar kind of closed question, sometimes referred to as the identification question, requires the respondent to identify and offer a correct factual response; for example; 'How old are you?'

The third kind of closed question offers respondents a range of alternative answers from which they are required to select the one which best approximates their own opinion. This form of question is sometimes referred to as a forced choice question; for example: 'Which colour do you want your office painting, grey, red or blue?' The respondent may not be keen on any of these colours and may prefer green, but faced with the choice of grey, red or blue may choose grey on the grounds that it is the least offensive.

The placement of an alternative in forced choice questions can also be important. Dillon (1997) refers to studies which indicate that, no matter what it refers to, the last listed of two or three alternatives is chosen by 10 per cent more respondents than when the same alternative is placed first or second.

Closed questions tend to be easier to answer than open questions and therefore can be useful icebreakers at the start of an interview; for example, 'Can I take your coat?', or 'Would you like some coffee?' They also enable us to exercise control and focus the respondent's attention on relevant issues. A customs officer, for example, may not be interested in whether returning holiday-makers have enjoyed their holiday or whether their flight was delayed. However, the officer may want to know whether they are aware of the duty-free allowances, how many cigarettes or bottles of wine and spirits they have and whether they are importing goods over a specified value. A series of closed questions, for example, 'Are you aware of the duty-free allowance?' (a yes–no question) or 'How many cigarettes do you have?'(an identification question) will enable the officer to elicit this information, and only this information.

Closed questions may also be employed usefully in those situations where it is necessary to collect and compare responses from a large number of respondents. For example, a market researcher may use closed questions when interviewing potential customers because answers to closed questions tend to be brief and therefore easier to record. In addition, since the range of possible responses is likely to be more limited than the range of possible responses to open questions, it is often easier to anticipate, categorise and therefore analyse the responses obtained.

This said, closed questions also have a number of limitations. A question that offers the respondent the choice of answering only 'yes' or 'no' may deny us access to important information. For example, three managers who answered 'yes' to the question 'Should the company introduce the performance appraisal scheme that was discussed at the last executive committee meeting?' may have replied in the affirmative for three very different reasons:

- The first manager may believe that the scheme could help improve productivity by identifying dead wood and making it easier to weed out and get rid of poor performers.
- The second may favour the scheme because it could encourage managers to manage their subordinates more effectively, especially those managers who fail to provide their subordinates with clear objectives and helpful feedback. In other words, the second manager may see appraisal as the key to better staff development.
- The third manager, who may be opposed to the concept of formal appraisal, may support the introduction of the scheme because he or she believes that some form of appraisal will be introduced sooner or later, and that the proposed scheme has fewer disadvantages than most.

The interviewer who receives these three positive answers may assume, mistakenly, that all three managers feel the same way about the scheme. He or she may be unaware that they have very different views; that two are highly committed whereas the third is only lukewarm at best, and that of those who are committed, their commitment is based on different and possibly conflicting assumptions and goals.

Open questions do not restrict the respondent to answering within a framework of a predetermined set of categories. Respondents are left free to reply in their own words and to answer the question in any way they like. Compare the closed question 'Do you like your new job?' with the open question 'What do you think of your new job?' The closed question can elicit only a yes–no reply whereas the open question is likely to not only provide information about the respondents' affective response to their job, but also some explanation of why they feel the way they do.

Open questions can encourage respondents to talk by seeking information about What, Why, When, How, Where and Who. 'Yes' would not be an adequate reply to the question 'What do you think of your new job?'

Open questions also produce answers that the interviewer may never have expected and therefore provide access to information that would not have been revealed by the replies to a series of closed questions. For example, if car owners are asked 'Why did you buy a Rover 400?', they may reply: 'Because the Rover dealership is the nearest dealership to where I live', a reply which indicates that the geographical location of dealerships is a key factor influencing the decision of which make of car to buy. This fact may not be revealed by a series of closed questions that focus on price or design, such as: 'Do you think the Rover 400 is value for money compared with competing models such as the equivalent Ford or the Peugeot?'

It must be remembered, however, that we are not simply faced with the stark choice of using either open or closed questions. The degree of openness, and therefore the degree of control that can be exercised over the way the respondent will reply, can be varied by the interviewer. Compare:

- 'How are things?'
- 'How are things at work?'
- 'How are you getting on with your new assistant?'
- 'How are you managing your new assistant's negative attitude towards working for a woman?'

These are all open questions, but some are more focused than others and impose more restrictions on the way the respondent can answer.

Sequence of questions

The sequence of questions within a topic can take a number of forms. The *funnel* is a sequence that begins with a very open question and then continues with a gradual decreasing level of openness. All the questions in the sequence can be open questions but, as in the 'How are things?' example above, each successive question may become more focused.

Alternatively, the sequence may progress from open to closed questions; for example:

Q: Why did you buy a Rover 4000? [open]
A: Because the Rover dealership is the nearest dealership to where I live.
Q: Why is the proximity of the dealership important? [open]
A: With my last car I was always late for work when I had to take it in to be serviced. The problem was particularly difficult because there wasn't a convenient bus route between the service centre and my workplace.
Q: How many times a year do you expect to have to use the service department? [closed]

The funnel sequence can be useful in problem-solving interviews where the helper wants to find out whether there is a problem and, if so, what the respondent (colleague/subordinate/patient/customer, etc.) believes it to be. This may be achieved by opening the sequence with the question: 'How are you feeling?' or 'What seems to be the problem?' The funnel sequence can also help to motivate respondents by providing them with the opportunity at an early point in the discussion to talk about those things which are important to them. Too many closed questions at the beginning of a sequence may force respondents to suppress their own views and talk about issues which seem unimportant or irrelevant.

None the less there are many occasions when it is useful to reverse the process and start with one or more closed questions. For example:

Q: Do you own your own car? [closed]
A: Yes.
Q: What make and model of car do you own? [closed]
A: A Rover 400.
Q: Why did you buy a Rover 400? [open]

The inverted funnel can be used to help us to gather relevant information (for example, about what happened or how the respondent behaved) before seeking to explore the reasons why.

In some interviews all the questions may exhibit the same degree of openness. For example, if a manager has to interview somebody to assess whether s/he qualifies for a particular benefit or discount the manager may use a predetermined sequence of closed questions that are designed to elicit objective or factual responses as quickly as possible.

Hargie *et al.* (1994) warn against the dangers of inconsistent or erratic sequences of questions, and they point to the research evidence which suggests that a consistent sequence (funnel, inverted funnel, tunnel, etc.) facilitates participation and understanding. However, erratic sequences may be useful in some circumstances. Erratic sequences characterise many of those fact-finding interviews that can be included under the broad heading of cross examination, where the objective is to obtain information the respondent would prefer not to reveal. Not knowing what kind of question to expect next may confuse the respondent. Kestler (1982) suggests that erratic sequences can be effective in the courtroom because the quick change of focus can catch the witness off-balance with thoughts out of context.

Exercise 6.3 involves using the list of information requirements you produced in Exercise 6.2 to develop an interview schedule which incorporates some of the points discussed above.

Exercise 6.3 Planning the schedule of questions

Working on your own, refer to the list of information requirements you produced in the previous exercise and give some thought to how you could go about collecting all the information you need. Map out a schedule of questions you would like to ask, giving attention to the organisation of topics, the formulation of questions and the sequencing of questions (funnel, inverted funnel, etc.).

Working in a small group, compare your interview schedule with the schedules produced by others and, with reference to the content of this chapter, discuss their relative strengths and weaknesses.

In the light of this conversation review your own schedule and make any changes you feel are required.

Probing and seeking clarification

No matter how much care we have exercised in wording and asking a question there will be many occasions when the initial response will be incomplete or inadequate in some way. Probing is the technique we can use to encourage the respondent to provide further information. Kahn and Cannell (1957) suggest three criteria for effective probes:

1   They must enable the interviewer to motivate the respondent to engage in additional communication on the required topic.
2   They must enhance, or at least maintain, the interpersonal relationship between the interviewer and respondent.
3   Most importantly, they must accomplish this purpose without introducing bias or modifying the meaning of the primary question.

Bias and the modification of meaning are aspects of probing that must be managed carefully. Simplifying, shortening or rewording questions can result in the intended meaning of the primary question being changed significantly. Bias can also be introduced if the interviewer fails to give the respondent sufficient time to answer the primary question before posing a supplementary question, or if the supplementary question suggests an expected or preferred response.

One of the easiest ways to press for further information in a way that avoids these problems is to use minimal prompts such as 'uh-huh', 'and . . .', 'tell me more'; attentive silences which suggest to the respondent that the interviewer expects him or her to say more; or accents which offer a one- or two-word restatement of what the respondent has just said. These techniques are discussed in Chapter 4 and are sometimes referred to as non-verbal probes and echo probes.

Another type of non-directive probe is the paraphrase or summary (also discussed in Chapter 4), which indicates the extent of our understanding and provides an opportunity for the respondent to clarify, restate or elaborate what has been said.

These non-directive techniques, while useful, may not provide sufficient focus, and we may wish to use a range of probes that enable us to manage more precisely the kind of information the respondent will feel encouraged to offer. Turney *et al.* (1976) identify seven of these more directive probes.

1   *Clarification probes*, which can be used to elicit a clear, more concisely worded response: 'What exactly do you mean?' Clarification probes can also be posed as closed questions: 'Are you saying that you were not responsible?'
2   *Justification probes*, which seek reasons for what the respondent has said: 'Why did you say that?'
3   *Relevance probes*, which require the respondent to explain the relationship between ideas, people, events, etc.: 'How does that relate to what you said earlier?'
4   *Exemplification probes*, which seek concrete or specific instances of what has been said: 'Does an example spring to mind?'
5   *Extension probes*, which encourage the respondent to elaborate on the initial response: 'What happened next?'
6   *Accuracy probes*, which invite the respondent to reconsider an earlier response and emphasise the importance of accuracy: 'Are you sure it happened before 6 o'clock?'
7   *Consensus probes*, which enable the interviewer, in a group interview situation, to assess the extent to which a view is shared: 'Do you all agree with that?'

Sometimes we may be tempted to ask supplementary questions along with the primary question. The result is a *multiple question* that may leave the respondent confused and provide us with little useful information. For example: 'Why did you change jobs? Were you unhappy with what you had been doing or was it that the new job offered better pay? And are you happy with the new job?' Which question do respondents answer first? Indeed, can they remember all that they have been asked? Their response may be to concentrate on the last question or simply answer 'Yes'.

Hargie *et al.* (1994) suggest that multiple questions may be useful when time is limited and it is important to get some answer from a respondent, for example, in a radio or television interview. However, the information obtained via multiple questions is likely to be inferior to that which may otherwise have been obtained.

Exercise 6.4 is designed to help you review and improve your approach to questioning and probing for information.

Exercise 6.4 Questioning and probing

This exercise involves a three-step approach to the development of questioning skills:

Step 1: Observing others when questioning and probing

This first step involves observing what others do, and thinking about what they could do differently to improve the quality of the information they get from others. It is designed to help you practise observing questioning and probing behaviour and to help you establish a bench-mark of good practice.

1 Types of question used

Record *how often* and in *what context* different types of question are used. Reflect on your findings and consider whether the nature of the questions used helped the questioner achieve their purpose.

Check (✓) number of times used

- Conventional leads (*which anticipate answers respondent would give anyway – 'Isn't it a nice day?'*)

- Simple and complex leads (*which lead responded to an expected or preferred answer*)

- Closed questions: yes–no

- Closed questions: identification
  (*How old are you?*)

- Closed questions: forced choice

- Open questions

- Multiple questions

What might the questioners have done to make better use of questions to achieve their purpose?

2 Probing and seeking clarification

Record *how often* and in *what context* different types of probes are used to seek further information.

Check (✓) number of times used

- Non-directive probes: minimal prompts
- Non-directive probes: summaries
- Directive probes which seek:

  – Clarification (*What do you mean by . . .?*)

  – Justification (*Why do you say that?*)

  – Relevance (*How does that relate to X?*)

  – Exemplification (*Give me an example.*)

  – Accuracy (*Are you sure it was only six?*)

What might the information seekers have done to make better use of probes to achieve their purpose?

Step 2: Assessing your own approach to information getting and identifying possible improvements

This step involves opening a 'second channel' and using your observation skills to observe yourself. Do *not* deliberately try to change your approach to questioning at this point because the aim is to increase your awareness of your normal information-getting behaviour.

Use the same approach to observing yourself as you used in the first step when observing how other people use questions and probes. Record your own behaviour as soon as possible after the event. (If you are able to record yourself conducting an interview you will be able to review the tape and establish a much more accurate record of your questioning and probing skills.)

Note what you might have done differently to improve your approach to questioning and probing.

Step 3: Taking action to improve your information-getting skills

This step involves comparing your behaviour with your standard of good practice and noting what you might have done differently to improve your approach to questioning and probing.

If there are lots of changes you feel you should make, you might think about whether you should try to introduce all the changes at once or draw up a short-list of a few changes to start with. You may, for example, decide to start by focusing attention only on your use of leading questions and attempting to avoid signalling to others your preferred response or by using minimal prompts at some of the points in the interaction where you might normally have asked a question. Once these changes have been successfully introduced you may feel it appropriate to move on and introduce further changes.

Monitor the effects of these changes. Are you able to detect any differences in the way others respond to you? How do you feel about the new approach?

Closure

When we are satisfied that the main purpose of the interview has been ful-filled, we need to check this out and ensure that we have understood fully what the respondent has said. We also need to signal to respondents our view that the interview is drawing to a close so that they can manage their own exit from the interaction. The absence of appropriate closure behav-iour can leave respondents unsure about whether they should wait patiently for another question, continue talking or get up and leave. It can also waste our time because we fail to stop respondents talking, even though we feel that we have obtained all the relevant information the respondents can offer.

One of the most useful closure behaviours is the summary. It helps us to check that we have remembered and recorded the main points discussed. It reassures the respondent that we have listened attentively, and provides them with the opportunity to clarify or elaborate. It also provides the respondent with the opportunity to offer new information on additional issues they feel we need to be aware of.

We may have used summaries at several points during the interview to check our understanding, draw points together and identify themes, and provoke the respondent into offering more information. By prefacing our terminal summary with a remark such as: 'Before we *finish* let me review . . .', we provide a clear signal that the interview is nearing its end.

Other kinds of closure markers may be used to reward the respondent for participating in the interview: 'That's been very useful and has helped me see things from your perspective', or 'Thanks for your time'.

Such remarks help persuade respondents that their participation in the interview has been worthwhile, and can be especially important when we want to engage respondents in a follow-up interview. Closure markers may be non-verbal as well as verbal. Interviewers can gather their papers together, look at the clock, stand up and offer a handshake while thanking the respon-dents for their time and saying goodbye.

Ideally, the information-getting interview will end when we are satisfied that we have elicited sufficient information; however, time sometimes runs out and the interview has to be drawn to a close prematurely. This can happen in the best-managed interviews, possibly because it is only towards the end of the available time that the respondent gives an unanticipated response to an open-ended question (suggesting a new line of enquiry), or develops sufficient confidence in us to reveal important information. However, the effective interviewer will normally ensure through careful time management that it is not a frequent occurrence.

Time management is an important interview skill. We must keep in mind a broad plan of the issues that need to be explored (again emphasising the usefulness of a framework such as the seven-point plan), and a discreet eye on the clock in order to pace the interview appropriately.

Occasionally, it will be possible to extend the interview, and time will not be an important constraint, but often other commitments, on the part of both interviewer and respondent, will render this impossible. In such circumstances we may feel that a follow-up interview would be useful and therefore may attempt to draw the first interview to a close in a way that will encourage the respondent to participate in a further encounter. This end may be achieved by: (1) leaving respondents with the feeling that the interview was worthwhile, that their contribution was useful and that something has been achieved as a result of the interaction: 'Thank you, that has been very helpful'; (2) seeding the idea that a further meeting may be necessary by referring back to the purpose of the interview and indicating that more information will be required: 'I'd like to check out whether these problems persist by talking to you again once the new system has been operational for at least a week', and (3) suggesting a time when the follow-up interview might occur: 'Can we meet again at the end of the month?'

Exercise 6.5 is designed to help you improve the way you manage closure.

Exercise 6.5 Managing closure

Follow the same format as for Exercise 6.4. Begin by observing how others manage closure. When you have honed your observation skills and established a bench-mark of good practice, monitor how you manage closure in a range of different situations. Identify what you could do to improve the way you manage closure and find an opportunity to practise these new behaviours.

You may find it useful to pay attention to:

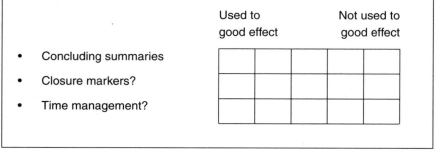

	Used to good effect		Not used to good effect	
• Concluding summaries				
• Closure markers?				
• Time management?				

Improving your overall interviewing style

An important element in all the exercises presented so far in this chapter is the notion of a standard of good practice against which you can compare your normal way of behaving. This provides a bench-mark for skill development. It is important to note, however, that what constitutes good practice will vary, depending on the purpose of the information-getting activity. In a cross-examination, for example, erratic interviewing sequences may be more effective than more consistent sequences such as the tunnel. In a screening interview, on the other hand, tunnel sequences which comprise a series of closed questions may be much more effective than a mixture of open and closed questions presented within a funnel or inverted funnel sequence.

The content of this chapter provides you with a basis for determining which behaviours will be most appropriate for different purposes. While Exercises 6.1 to 6.5 focus attention on the development of specific information-getting skills, Exercise 6.6 focuses attention on your overall interviewing style. It involves comparing your approach to interviewing and the quality of the information you obtain from an interviewee with the approach adopted by other interviewers and the information they obtain from the same interviewee.

Exercise 6.6 Assessing the effectiveness of your interviewing style

This exercise requires you to work in groups of four. Two members of the group (A and C) interview both of the other two members of the group (D and B). The interview topic must be the same for all interviews, for example 'What are the factors that influenced your choice of career/course?'

Step 1

First period of 15 minutes:
A interviews B and notes information obtained.
C interviews D and notes information obtained.

Second period of 15 minutes
A interview D and notes information obtained.
C interviews B and notes information obtained.

At the end of 30 minutes A and C have interviewed both B and D.

Step 2

- A and C compare the information they have obtained from B. They should:
  - Identify similarities and differences in the information they each obtained from B.
  - Invite B to comment on the relevance and accuracy of the information they obtained (was the quality of the information obtained by one of the interviewers perceived to be better than the information obtained by the other?).

- A and C then compare the information they have obtained from D.

- B and D (the interviewees) comment on any differences they observed in the interviewing styles of A and C.

Step 3

All four members of the group share their views on:

- Whether differences in interviewing style may have influenced the quantity and quality of information obtained by the two interviewers.
- Aspects of the interviewing style of A and B that could be improved.

Time permitting, repeat the exercise with B and D taking the role of interviewers and A and C taking the role of interviewees.

Summary

This chapter has presented the interview as a social encounter, and has argued that the nature of this encounter will influence both the way in which the interviewer and respondent interpret the behaviour of the other and the quantity and quality of the information they will exchange.

The effective interviewer has been described as a person who behaves in ways that eliminate or reduce to a minimum those forces which cause relevant information to be distorted or withheld. Critical interviewer behaviours have been discussed under eight headings: definition of purpose and preparation, cognitive scene setting, content and coverage, organisation of topics, formulation of questions, sequence of questions, probing and seeking clarification, and closure. The final section of the chapter discussed ways in which interviewers can begin to modify their behaviour to improve their effectiveness.

References

Beezer, R.H. (1956) Research on methods of interviewing foreign informants, George Washington University, HUM RRO, Technical Report No. 30.

Bingham, N., Moore, J. and Bruce, V. (1941) *How to Interview* (3rd edn), New York: Harper and Row.

Dillon, J. (1997) 'Questioning', in Owen Hargie (ed.) *The Handbook of Communication Skills*, London: Routledge, pp. 103–133.

Farr, R. (1984) 'Interviewing: the social psychology of the interview', in Cary L. Cooper and Peter Makin *Psychology for Managers*, London: British Psychological Society.

Goffman, E. (1959) *The Presentation of Self in Everyday Life*, New York: Doubleday.

Gratis, J. (1988) *Successful Interviewing*, London: Penguin.

Hargie, O., Saunders, S. and Dickson, D. (1994) *Social Skills in Interpersonal Communication*, London: Croom Helm.

Harris, J.R. (1973) 'Answering questions containing marked and unmarked adjectives and adverbs', *Journal of Experimental Psychology* 97: pp. 399–401.

Kahn, R.L. and Cannell, C.F. (1957) *The Dynamics of Interviewing*, New York: Wiley.

Kestler, J. (1982) *Questioning Techniques and Tactics*, Colorado Springs: McGraw-Hill.

Loftus, E. (1982) 'Interrogating eyewitnesses – good questions and bad', in R. Hogarth (ed.) Question Framing and Response Consistency, San Francisco: Jossey-Bass.

Lynn, J. and Jay, A. (1986) *Yes, Prime Minister*, Vol. 1, London: BBC Publications.

Mangham, I.L. (1978) *Interactions and Interventions in Organizations*, Chichester: Wiley.

Nadler, D.A. (1977) *Feedback and Organization Development: Using Data Based Methods*, London: Addison-Wesley.

Ostell, A., Baverstock, S. and Wright, P. (1999) 'Interpersonal skills of managing emotion at work', *The Psychologist* 12 (1): 30–34.

Rodger, A. (1952) *The Seven Point Plan*, London: National Institute of Industrial Psychology.

Turney, C., Owens, L., Hatton, N., Williams, G. and Cairns, L. (1976) *Sydney Micro Skills: Series 2 Handbook*, Sydney: Sydney University Press.

Wicks, R.P. (1984) 'Interviewing: practical aspects', in Cary L. Cooper and Peter Makin, *Psychology for Managers*, London: British Psychological Society.

7

PRESENTING INFORMATION
TO OTHERS

Learning objective

To recognise the ingredients of an effective presentation and understand what the presenter can do to ensure that the presentation achieves desired outcomes such as informing, explaining or persuading.

After reading this chapter you will:

- Be aware of the importance of preparation. This includes clarifying objectives, researching the audience, defining the content, structuring the presentation and reviewing the arrangements such as venue, seating and related factors.
- Understand the steps a presenter can take to gain the attention of the audience at the start of a presentation. These include creating a sense of uncertainty in the minds of listeners so that they are motivated to listen to allay their anxieties, using rhetorical questions, posing intriguing problems and making controversial statements.
- Be aware of how levels of attention can change over the course of a presentation, and understand what the presenter can do to maintain audience interest.
- Recognise five presentation skills that can be used to get the message across (clarity of expression, the use of examples, emphasis, sensitivity to feedback and the ability to answer questions effectively) and be aware of specific modifiable behaviours associated with each of these broad skill categories.
- Be aware of the opportunities and threats associated with question-and-answer sessions and understand what the presenter can do to involve the audience in ways that will contribute to the achievement of the presenter's purpose.
- Recognise the factors that influence the effectiveness of visual aids and demonstrations. These include congruence with the spoken word, visibility, and appropriate levels of complexity and variety.
- Be aware of the importance of drawing the presentation to an appropriate conclusion.

Presenting information to others

Almost everybody who is employed in a managerial or professional role has to present information or offer explanations to others. From time to time the presentation will be before a large audience, in a formal setting. More frequently it will be to a small, sometimes informal, group of colleagues, subordinates, customers or senior managers.

The presentation often represents an important opportunity for the presenter. For example:

- A customer may invite a supplier to come and talk to some of his colleagues about the advantages of a new product. If the manager from the supplying company makes a poor presentation she may fail to win a large order.
- A personnel manager may be invited to address a managers' meeting about the introduction of a new performance appraisal scheme. If he fails to convince them that the scheme is a good one he may lose the chance of winning their support, and his job of introducing the scheme may be made much more difficult.
- A project leader may be required to report on progress to a project review committee. If her presentation is disorganised and she fails to provide committee members with the information they require, she may create the impression that the situation is worse than it actually is.

If, on the other hand, the presentations are successful, the customer may place a new order, the managers may be enthusiastic about the introduction of the new appraisal scheme and the project leader may create the impression that she is very competent, and could possibly manage a bigger project next time around.

A presentation is an occasion when, either literally or metaphorically, the spotlight is on us. We are very exposed and our performance can leave a lasting impression. What would you think of somebody who:

- made a presentation that was difficult to hear and even more difficult to understand;
- if their arguments lacked structure;
- if they failed to mention important information while overwhelming you with irrelevant detail;
- if the session overran its allotted time, making you late for a subsequent meeting?

The answer, almost certainly, is that you would not be impressed. The danger is that members of the audience may not only acquire a poor impression of the presenter's presentation skills, but they may also assume that they

131

lack other work-related skills as well. In other words, because making presentations is a very public activity, it is an aspect of our performance that can have a very important influence on what other people think about us. There are therefore many good reasons why we should consider ways in which we can improve our presentation skills.

This chapter will consider the ingredients of a good presentation and what we need to do to ensure that the presentation is successful. Attention will be focused on:

- preparation, i.e. what we need to do beforehand;
- getting and keeping interest, i.e. what we need to do to involve the audience from the start and to keep them involved until the end;
- getting the message across, i.e. those explaining and presenting skills which enhance clarity of expression and ease the burden of listening;
- aids to understanding, i.e. the use of examples, visual displays and demonstrations;
- closure, i.e. the best way to end the presentation.

Preparation

The importance of preparation cannot be over-emphasised. Pemberton (1982) quotes the old saying that to fail to prepare is to prepare to fail. A sentiment echoed by Jay (1972), who argues that there is a general law applicable to any project that the earlier a mistake is made the more profoundly it will affect the whole project and the harder it will be to recover from. Presentations are no exception. Thorough preparation is the basis of success. We need to define the objective of the presentation, research the audience, identify what information needs to be presented, plan how the presentation is to be structured, and finally, review the environmental arrangements.

Clarifying the objective

The objective of the presentation may be to explain, describe or report what did or will happen. For example, managers may want to brief their team on company results or present a departmental plan for the next operating period. It may also involve more than a descriptive report. It may include an explanation, an account of why something has occurred. Brown and Atkin (1997) define explaining as the attempt to provide understanding of a problem to others. When we offer an explanation, our objective will normally be to help the audience understand a cause-and-effect relationship. For example, a marketing manager may want to explain why profits were affected by fluctuation in exchange rates or an operations manager may want to explain why an increase in the current budget would result in cost savings over the longer term. Explanations are often offered in order to persuade or to sell. In such circumstances it may not be sufficient to ensure that the message is understood. We will need to convince members of the audience that the course of action being advocated is one they should support.

It is a useful discipline to reflect on the purpose of the presentation, to write it down and to refer to it from time to time. For example, if members of a management team are planning a presentation on a new bonus scheme, they may ask themselves whether their objective is to:

- *inform* those who will be affected that a new scheme is to be introduced;
- *explain* to them how the new scheme will work;
- *persuade* them to accept the new scheme in preference to existing arrangements.

If their objective is to persuade them to accept the new scheme their presentation is likely to be very different from one that is merely intended to inform them about its introduction.

Researching the audience

Presentations need to be planned with a specific audience in mind. The background and experience of the audience will influence how much they already know about a subject, their level of understanding of technical vocabulary and the extent to which they will be willing to listen to the presentation with an open mind. The audience's past experience of the presenter may affect the way they interpret what they hear. The status of the audience may also be important because it may be necessary to restrict access to certain kinds of information. A presentation that was originally prepared for the board may need to be modified before it can be given to a group of middle managers or customers.

The size of the audience is also important. How many will be listening: 5, 50 or 500? With large audiences, opportunities for dialogue may be limited, and much of the time we will have to do all the talking and will have to tell the audience what they need to know. With an audience of two or three the presentation may take the form of a structured discussion rather than a formal speech. Audience size will also have implications for the size of the hall and the kind of visual display that will be appropriate. In a large hall visual material may have to be projected on to a large screen rather than displayed on a small flip chart.

Defining the content

Before preparing the script for a presentation, an essential first step is to decide what information the listener will need if the objective of the presentation is to be achieved. This involves identifying the main factors or categories of information and how they relate. For example, if our objective is to persuade a sales team that a new bonus scheme will be to their advantage, we may decide that the presentation should include information that will facilitate a comparative review of how the existing and proposed schemes operate.

Talking to colleagues, brainstorming ideas on to a sheet of paper and consulting reports may suggest a series of headings for our presentation. These may include:

- the target of the scheme (individual or group);
- the aspects of performance that will be measured (total value of sales, number of new customers);
- the methods used to calculate the bonus and so on.

Not all of the headings generated will be of equal importance, and under each heading there may be a range of ideas and subheadings that differ in terms of the contribution they can make to achieving the objective of the presentation. Identifying what information is vital, what is important and what is only desirable can ease the task of pruning and editing material. If we have to make cuts we can focus on eliminating the less important content and retaining all the vital elements. Failure to prioritise material can result in vital content either being omitted or skimmed over, while less important or even irrelevant information is given too much emphasis.

Structuring the presentation

Some presenters organise their material in ways that help the audience understand and assimilate their message. Others manage to confuse both themselves and others. The logical organisation of information can aid understanding. Hargie *et al.* (1994) report that there is a wealth of research into teaching which suggests that the teacher's ability to prepare, structure, organise and sequence facts and ideas with the maximum of logical coherence is related positively to pupil achievement.

Tubbs and Moss (1994) note that research has failed to point to a single pattern of organisation and structure that will always be effective, and they argue that presenters need to identify a structure that is best suited to their particular purpose. Some of the alternatives they have identified are:

- *Topical organisation* – this pattern involves the speaker moving from topic to topic in a way that clearly demonstrates how they are related.
- *Chronological organisation* – a common chronological structure involves starting with a review of the past, moving on to a discussion of the present and, if appropriate, projecting into the future. Another variation starts with an examination of the current situation and moves backwards in time to explore its origins.

- *Spatial organisation* – a structure that uses territory, space or geographical location as the basis for organising the presentation.
- *Problem–solution organisation* – a way of structuring that starts with the statement of a problem and then moves on to consider a way forward or action plan that will lead to a more satisfactory state of affairs.
- *Causal organisation* – a pattern that involves either moving from cause to effect (poverty contributes to low levels of educational achievement) or effect to cause (low levels of educational achievement can be attributed, at least in part, to poverty).

Pemberton (1982) suggests that where the purpose of the presentation is to persuade people to our view, an effective overall structure is to:

1 State the proposition.
2 Anticipate objections and concede possible flaws in the argument. (Even if the presenter decides not to disclose such flaws it is useful to have identified what they may be.)
3 Prove the case. Do this by focusing on the strongest arguments. She argues that quality is better than quantity and cautions against overloading the presentation with too many arguments.
4 Provide practical evidence.
5 End by repeating the proposition.

It has often been argued that, irrespective of the specific focus of the structure adopted, the impact of any presentation can be improved by cueing the audience about what to expect (telling them what we are going to tell them), telling them and, finally, ending by summarising what we have told them.

Reviewing arrangements

On many occasions we have little choice about venue and the arrangement of seating and other environmental factors. Even so, it can be worth the effort to review the arrangements, test the equipment and note the best place to stand so as to ensure that the audience has a clear view of whiteboards, flip charts and screens. Where we are in control of the setting we may consider arranging the seating so as to minimise distractions. If the audience are able to look out of a large window at an interesting scene we may find it difficult to compete for their attention. Similarly, if the only entrance to the hall is by the speaker's table every latecomer will disrupt the presentation. Sometimes it can be fairly easy to change the end of room where the speaker's table is to be located.

Seating arrangements can also be manipulated to either encourage or discourage discussion (Figure 7.1). Seating people in rows makes it more difficult for the audience to assess each other's reaction or to interact

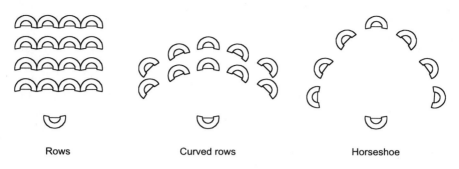

| Rows | Curved rows | Horseshoe |

Figure 7.1 Seating arrangements.

between themselves, whereas curved rows or horseshoe arrangements makes this easier.

The horseshoe, and to a less extent a curved rows arrangement, also encourages interaction between presenter and audience. This is because there are fewer barriers (people) between each member of the audience and the presenter. Eye contact between them is easier and individual members of the audience feel less isolated. They are able to assess whether others have the same reaction to what has been said, and therefore they have more confidence to interact with the speaker.

Keeping the audience's attention

The lecturer who is teaching a recreational class at night school is reasonably safe in assuming that members of the 'audience' are there because they want to be there and because they want to hear what the lecturer has to say. This may not be the case for the manager who is making a presentation about the company's new appraisal scheme. The audience may be enthusiastic, neutral or even hostile to the idea of appraisal. Even those members of the audience who are known to be enthusiastic may be preoccupied and not in the ideal frame of mind to listen.

Motivating the audience to listen

Presenters have to capture the audience's attention. We have to motivate each person to listen. It is difficult to motivate others to listen if they do not understand what we are talking about. Jay (1972) points to the need for the presenter to 'connect up with the audience'. He uses the analogy of a horse and wagon and suggests that speakers need to harness the horse of the argument to the wagon of the audience's interest and understanding. If we gallop straight off we may hurtle along splendidly without realising that the wagon has been left behind. It is important that we start with material and ideas which members of the audience know and understand before taking them off into unknown territory.

Even if members of the audience understand what is being said, they may not see any good reason why they should pay attention. What is in it for them? If they are to be persuaded to attend they must be helped to anticipate that the presentation will be useful, interesting or entertaining. It has been suggested that people will not be interested in salvation until they have experienced the fear of damnation, which is perhaps the reason why some preachers start their sermons by proclaiming the inevitability of Judgment Day and familiarising their congregation with the torments of hell. In the business context the chief executive may begin a presentation on the need for greater effort by forecasting the possibility of cutbacks and redundancies.

Fortunately, inducing a state of fear or unrest is not the only way of capturing attention. The rhetorical question may be used to intrigue or interest the audience; for example: 'What do you think is the major reason why people buy our product? . . . This afternoon I want to share with you the results of our latest market survey and recommend how they should influence our marketing strategy for next year.'

Introductions which use rhetorical questions, pose intriguing problems, include controversial statements or simply offer a concise statement of the purpose of the problem in terms that will appeal to the audience increase the likelihood that the audience will be motivated to attend to our message.

Keeping their interest

Even if we are successful in gaining the audience's attention at the beginning of the presentation there is no guarantee that people will continue to attend. The shorter the presentation the more likely they are to attend throughout. Ley (1983) reports several studies which suggest that both attending and recall are related to the length of the presentation. It was found, for example, that the more information presented, the more patients experienced difficulty understanding and recalling the instructions given to them by doctors.

A number of studies have produced evidence to show that it can be difficult to maintain the attention of an audience for more than a few minutes. Some suggest that after as little as ten minutes (and in some circumstances this may be an optimistic estimate) attention begins to wane, but as the audience begin to sense that the presentation is reaching a conclusion, attention begins to rise again (see Figure 7.2). This has important implications for the presenter. If the message is structured so that key points are presented in the middle, when attention is likely to be at its lowest, the presentation may not have the desired effect. Key points need to be presented when attention is at its highest. This means in the first ten minutes or so, or at the end. If we

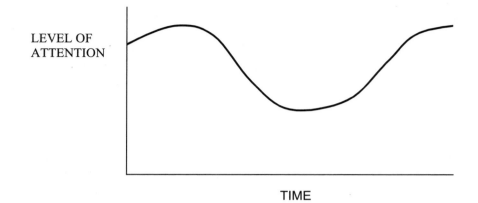

LEVEL OF
ATTENTION

TIME

Figure 7.2 The attention curve.

decide to present key points in the middle of the presentation we need to behave in a way that will increase the audience's attention.

Attention can be heightened if we break up the body of the presentation into logical elements that signal the end of one element and the start of another: 'The third point I want to discuss is. . . .' The effectiveness of this procedure can be increased by offering the audience a framework or structure for the presentation to which they may refer back and use to organise and understand the relevance of the information they receive. The outline of the presentation may be displayed on a flip chart or a handout so that the 'third point' being discussed can be related to the first and second.

Another way of keeping their interest is to anticipate the questions that members of the audience may have in their minds at various points in the presentation: 'You might be wondering where this is leading. Well. . . .' or 'You could be asking yourself whether the market survey was worth the effort. . . .'

Questions can also be useful if we suspect that the audience are losing interest. General questions, targeted at nobody in particular, may fail to evoke a response whereas targeted questions that offer members of the audience an opportunity to contribute can encourage involvement:

> 'Mr. Smith. You have been involved in similar projects in the past. Do you think I have missed any major points in my assessment of how the market is likely to react?'

> 'Mr. Brown. You are the person in the room with the most practical experience. Will the proposal work?'

However, when targeting questions we must take care not to embarrass those whose attention may have drifted so much that they fail to recognise the point of the question if asked, and therefore may find themselves unable to offer a sensible answer.

Visual aids and demonstrations, which are most frequently used to facilitate understanding, may also be used to gain the audience's attention. We can often anticipate those points where attention is likely to flag and introduce a chart, slide or practical demonstration to maintain attention. Examples or amusing stories that illustrate a point can also help to maintain interest, so long as the audience can relate to them. Visual aids, demonstrations and stories that are perceived as irrelevant can distract the audience, as can certain gestures and body movements. The speaker who jingles coins in a pocket can be very annoying, and the actions of the unconscious nose picker can either disgust the audience or divert their attention away from the presentation to a consideration of what the presenter might do next.

Not all movements and gestures are distracting. Chapter 5 cites research evidence suggesting that they can improve understanding by, for example, helping to depict spatial relationships, providing emphasis and communicating enthusiasm.

Delivery and the use of words are also important. When most of us read a script our voice lacks variety in terms of volume, pitch, timbre, rate, rhythm and inflection. We come across as dull and uninteresting. It is often noticeable that when a presentation is followed by a question-and-answer session, the presenter's voice changes. It becomes more alive. Two factors account for this. The answers are fresh and unscripted and the presenter uses spoken not written English.

It can be dangerous to attempt to deliver completely unscripted presentations because we may be tempted to give insufficient attention to the selection and organisation of content, confuse ourselves as well as the audience and get lost and 'dry up' part-way through. Some kind of script can be very useful but too detailed a scripting of the presentation can be dangerous. If we write down everything we want to say we may have a paper fit for publication rather than a script which is to be spoken. Spoken English is very different from written English. There is also the danger that if we rely on a detailed script we may lose our place and miss out a section or have to pause while we locate the next sentence. Another problem is that if we read a script we are likely to keep our head down and have little or no eye contact with the audience.

The important points to remember are that presenters who drone on in a voice that lacks any variety, who evidence little movement, who avoid eye contact, who provide the audience with few signposts regarding the structure of the message and who make little use of visual aids are unlikely to keep the audience involved.

Getting the message across

The previous sections of this chapter addressed the presenter's need to prepare, and the methods that can be employed to attract and maintain the audience's attention. This section considers those presentation skills that help to get the message across. Five main categories of presentation skill will be considered. Turney *et al.* (1972) grouped presentation skills under four headings: clarity, examples, emphasis and feedback. A fifth is the presenter's ability to answer questions.

Clarity

As one might expect, there is a wealth of research evidence which demonstrates that clarity is associated with understanding and recall. For example, Soloman *et al.* (1964) found significant correlations between a global factor 'overall clarity of presentation' and performance on a test of factual material. However, for the purposes of training and the development of presentation skills, it is necessary to operationalise this global factor, namely to identify concrete instances of behaviour that make a contribution to greater clarity. Research results point to the importance of four types of behaviour.

1   *Defining technical terms and jargon.* This has been shown to be correlated with pupil achievement, which is a good indication that the appropriate use of language can contribute both to understanding and recall.
2   *Explicitness.* Reducing the implicit and increasing the explicit information content of a presentation contributes to clarity. An example of implicitness is where our sentence structure requires the listener to infer complete structures. The greater the use of implicit content, the greater the demand on the listener to fill the blanks. For some audiences there will be little need to 'spell things out' but this will not always be the case. It is all too easy for us to assume an unrealistically high level of knowledge and experience and therefore to 'leave blanks' that at least some members of the audience will find it difficult to fill. This point re-emphasises the need for thorough audience research.
3   *Verbal fluency* is another important skill contributing to clarity. Hiller *et al.* (1969) report that verbal fluency (which they measure in terms of sentence length, number of subordinate clauses and hesitations such as 'uh', 'um', etc.) differentiates significantly between those who offer effective and ineffective presentations. Hargie (1994) suggests that speakers often punctuate what they have to say with sounds such as 'eh' or 'mm' when they are trying to put too many ideas or facts across in one sentence. Short, crisp sentences are advocated with pauses in

between, rather than long, rambling sentences full of subordinate clauses.

4   *Avoiding vague expressions.* There will be occasions where it is impossible to avoid the use of a vague term. We may not be able to recall a precise term and may have to substitute a less precise one instead, or may not have concrete and specific data to hand. Problems arise, however, when the use of vague expressions becomes habitual. Turney *et al.* (1975), drawing upon the work of others, has categorised a sample of vague expressions:

- ambiguous designation – 'type of thing', 'all of this', 'stuff';
- negative intensifiers – 'was not too', 'was not hardly', 'was not quite', 'not infrequently';
- approximation – 'about as much', 'almost every', 'kind of', 'nearly';
- 'bluffing' and recovery – 'they say that', 'and so on', 'to cut a long story short', 'somehow';
- indeterminate number – 'a couple of', 'a bunch', 'some';
- groups of items – 'kinds', 'aspects', 'factors', 'things';
- possibility and probability – 'are not necessarily', 'sometimes', 'often', 'it could be that', 'probably'.

An audience will rate a presentation high on clarity when we use appropriate language and define new terms, when we are explicit, fluent and when we avoid vague expressions.

Examples

There is evidence to suggest that the amount of 'concreteness' in an explanation is related to understanding. One way of avoiding excessive abstraction is to use examples. Examples can offer evidence in support of a statement and can be used to relate new and unfamiliar concepts to a situation the audience have already experienced. The selection of examples is important. They need to be ones that the audience can relate to and can use in the way the presenter intended. The use of in-group examples which are not fully explained, for example, 'You will remember what happened last year when we tried to persuade Bill to change his mind', can leave some members of the audience totally confused.

How the examples are used is also important. Turney *et al.* (1975) reports that one pattern which has been recommended strongly by some researchers is the *statement–example–statement* rule.

An alternative, referred to as the inductive pattern, is for us to offer a series of examples and build from these to a statement or generalisation. A marketing manager may try to persuade executive committee members that it would be inappropriate to use price–competition as a way of increasing profits by offering them a series of examples about what has happened in the past, concluding with the statement: 'these examples demonstrate that if we cut prices our competitors will do the same.'

The deductive pattern represents a different approach. It begins with a statement or generalisation and is then followed by a series of examples that confirm and add detail to the original statement.

The research evidence about which of these three rules is most effective is inconclusive, but there is little doubt that the audience benefit from discovering self-evident links between statements and examples and therefore that the use of examples facilitates understanding.

Emphasis

Some presenters confuse their audiences because they fail to differentiate the wood from the trees. At certain points in a presentation it may be necessary for us to call attention to important information while keeping in the background less essential information. If this less essential information is allowed to intrude, listeners may fail to appreciate the significance of an important point or issue. During the course of a presentation a number of different points may need to become the focus of attention. Therefore, as the presentation progresses, the point of emphasis will change. To be effective we need to be able to manage the successive emphasis of crucial points. Turney groups the sub-skills of emphasis into two categories: purposeful variations in aspects of personal behaviour, and providing information that indicates a basic direction or purpose.

Purposeful variations in aspects of personal behaviour

Reference has already been made to how we can vary our behaviour in order to maintain the attention of the audience. Varying behaviour can also focus the audience's attention on specific aspects of the presentation. Examples of how behaviour can be varied to achieve this end include the following:

- *Verbal markers* that highlight main stages in the presentation. They can be used to draw attention to key points so that these points stand out in the listener's mind, ensuring that the 'figure and the ground', to use a Gestalt analogy, do not merge into one. Similarly, phrases such as 'the important point to remember' may serve to draw attention to certain aspects of the presentation.
- *Mnemonics* can also provide a structure for a sub-part of the presentation and an *aide-mémoire* that will assist with recall. For example, a manager talking to some subordinates about objective setting may use a mnemonic modelled on the name of the runner Steve Cram to emphasise the essential ingredient of a good objective:

C Challenging
R Realistic
A Achievable
M Measurable

- *Non-verbal markers*, such as pausing, pointing or changing one's voice, can also be effective.

Providing information that indicates a basic direction or purpose

This involves structuring the presentation so as to emphasise certain aspects of the message. We can use carefully selected repetition at various points in the presentation. This repetition can take a number of forms. Few people will not have heard Martin Luther King's famous speech in which he kept repeating the phrase 'I have a dream' to emphasise his main theme. This technique can leave the audience with a 100 per cent recall of the core message, and is a form of emphasis that is often used by politicians when they are trying to influence large audiences to remember and accept a core message.

Summaries are another form of repetition. Introductory summaries may be used to alert the audience to important points and the main thrust of the presentation, and terminal summaries may be used to re-emphasise selected parts of the presentation.

Feedback

The effective presenter is alert to feedback. The non-verbal behaviour of members of the audience can signal whether they are interested, involved and whether they have understood or been convinced by what they have heard. Useful signs of interest are eye contact, facial expression and posture (are they 'on the edge of their seats' or slumped in a corner and nearly asleep?). Statements, questions and requests for clarification from the audience can also be a useful source of feedback on whether the presentation is being understood and perceived as relevant. The presenter may initiate the questioning to obtain feedback. This often happens naturally at the end of the presentation but may also be helpful during the presentation, especially if we suspect that all may not be well.

Answering questions

There will be occasions when we may want to encourage questions in order to vary the pattern of the presentation, maintain attention, promote a feeling of involvement and avoid the audience feeling steamrollered. Questions also provide feedback on how the presentation is being received, and facilitate clarification and improved understanding.

One way of introducing variety into the presentation is to encourage questions before the end, perhaps after each main point has been presented. A danger with this approach is that we may spend too much time answering questions, and as a consequence may have to severely edit or completely miss out important parts of the message. The audience may also confuse us by asking questions about points that we intend to cover later in the presentation. Responding to all questions as and when they are asked can destroy a carefully thought-out structure and undermine the clarity of the presentation.

We can discourage the asking of mid-point questions by signalling, during the introduction, that questions would be preferred at the end. If, on the other hand, we decide to encourage questions before the end we may, in the event of too many questions, move the presentation on by reminding the audience of the time and offering to continue the discussion later: 'We only have twenty minutes left. If we could move on after this question I will come back to this point, if we need to, at the end.'

If members of the audience ask questions out of sequence and threaten to undermine the structure of the presentation, they might be persuaded to wait for their answer by being told: 'If you bear with me I think you will find that your question will have been answered fully before I finish', or, more simply: 'I will be coming to that later.'

Where questions are reserved until the end there is no guarantee that someone will be ready with a question as soon as the presenter stops talking. It may take a little time for members of the audience to adjust to the possibility of asking a question and it may also take a little time for them to reflect on what they have heard and to formulate a question they want to ask. There is, however, always the possibility that nobody will be comfortable asking the first question and an embarrassing silence may ensue. One way of avoiding this is to have a chairperson or a friendly plant in the audience who is prepared to ask the first question just to get the 'ball rolling'. Another technique is to propose that the audience divide into small groups to discuss the presentation and identify points that deserve to be challenged, or require clarification or elaboration.

A further problem associated with the question-and-answer session is the over-eager person who tries to monopolise our attention. Other members of the audience may become frustrated if their questions remain unanswered. A chairperson can help ensure that the presenter does not ignore parts of the audience by taking questions in turn and only allowing one question (and possibly one point of clarification) from each questioner. Where there is no chairperson, we may be able to disengage from the persistent questioner by noting: 'There seem to be a number of other people with questions. Let me deal with them and, if there's time, we can come back to this.'

People at the back of a large audience may not hear questions asked by those who are sitting near to the front. This problem can be eliminated if we repeat the question so that everybody can relate to the answer.

Sometimes members of the audience may ask questions in an attempt to destroy the presenter's case or make the presenter look foolish or incompetent. If we suspect that we may be confronted by a hostile questioner we may deliberately limit the time available for questions by making the presentation longer than scheduled and then offering to deal with questions privately or over coffee.

If the presenter decides, or is faced with no alternative other than to take the questions, every effort must be made to limit damage and to search out opportunities to gain advantage. One way of limiting damage is to be aware of traps that questioners may try to set. We might ask ourselves 'Why are they asking this kind of question?' Hostile questioners may ask the kind of question they know we will find difficult to answer and then try to destroy our case by demonstrating how inadequate the answer is. This kind of trap can be avoided by not attempting to provide an answer. The safest response, if we do not know the answer, is to say so. The rest of the audience may appreciate this honesty. It may also be possible to move the attention away from the hostile questioner by asking the rest of the audience if anybody else can provide an answer (without re-engaging the questioner in eye contact) and then seeking a 'next question' from somebody else.

Sometimes members of the audience may attempt to put an alternative case or demonstrate their own competence by making lengthy statements rather than asking questions. Acknowledging the statement and then seeking a question from somebody else can be an effective way of moving the session on: 'Yes, I think we need to bear some of these points in mind. May we have the next question please?'

It may not be easy to gain an advantage in the face of a hostile intervention from the audience, but sometimes an opportunity does present itself. Politicians who can make the audience laugh in response to a heckler's interruption often gain such an advantage. Probably the most famous case involved Harold Macmillan at the UN in New York. Krushchev interrupted his speech by shouting and banging his shoe on the table, and Macmillan made Krushchev look very foolish by pausing and then asking the interpreter for a translation. It is not unusual for hostile questioners to ask questions in order to find fault with the presenter's case without having any credible alternative to offer. If we believe this to be the case we may gain the advantage by turning the question around and asking the questioner for an alternative proposal.

Visual aids and demonstrations

Visual aids serve three main purposes. They introduce variety, thereby capturing the audience's attention and interest. They can also aid understanding and assist with recall.

It has often been said that a simple picture is worth a thousand words. A photograph of people dying on the streets of a Third World city can illustrate in seconds a point which may otherwise take minutes to explain. A series of slides showing how an internal combustion engine works can similarly ease the task of explaining, and can help the audience remember key points. However, visual aids do have a number of disadvantages. They cost money and they can take a lot of time to prepare, they can divert attention from the main thrust of the presentation if used inappropriately, and they can go wrong. The bulb may fail in the projector, the computer may malfunction, the plug may fuse, the film may tear, or a slide may be lost or projected upside down or at the wrong time. To get the best out of visual aids we need to plan their use and to have a contingency plan in mind if things do go wrong.

Visual aids can be grouped into a number of broad categories. The first is boards and charts. Flip charts have the advantage that sheets can be torn off and displayed around the room, whereas the white (or black) board has to be cleaned when full. Flip charts can also be prepared in advance and main points or diagrams can be lightly pencilled in so that they can be quickly reproduced 'live' during the session. The main disadvantage with flip charts is size. In a large hall it may be difficult to see what is on the chart.

Slides, either overhead projector, computer-generated or conventional 35mm slides, can be projected onto a screen of appropriate size. The main disadvantage with the overhead projector is that we may misplace slides or display them the wrong way round or upside down. Frequent pauses while we search for a lost slide can be very damaging to concentration. Another problem is that we may fail to check lines of sight, and stand in a position that obscures the view of at least some members of the audience. Similar problems can be associated with conventional 35mm slides. The cassette may be dropped just before the start of the presentation and it may be impossible to reload the slides in time. Even where there has not been this kind of immediate disaster, some slides may have been loaded upside-down and prove difficult to reload without disrupting the session. If another person controls the projector there is also the added complication of synchronising the slides with the script. Computer-based slide presentations can be very effective, and software packages such as PowerPoint can help even the most inexperienced presenter prepare a very professional-looking set of slides and handouts. However, as with 35mm slide presentations, it can be difficult, mid-presentation, to respond to the needs of the audience and change the order of slides or eliminate sections of the presentation.

Films and videos are very effective so long as they are not over-used and they are not allowed to run for too long. If it is planned to use more than one film or video sequence within the same session, video might offer an advantage over film because it can be much easier to change video cassettes (pre-wound on to a required point) than to load and wind on a film.

Demonstrations (for example, using people to show how heavy weights should be lifted or a wind tunnel to illustrate how modifications to the design of a vehicle can affect drag) can be a very effective way of getting a message across. However, the demonstration may not always work or may not be visible to all sections of the audience.

Some general principles associated with the use of visual aids and demonstrations are concerned with the degree of congruence between the spoken and visual message, visibility, complexity and variety.

Congruence with spoken message

Visual aids can be used as a substitute for words or to complement what the presenter is saying. It can be difficult for the audience to concentrate on what we are saying if this does not fit with the message provided by the visual aid or demonstration. When using slides that contain words we may need to pause so that the audience has time to read what is on the screen. If we continue to speak, the words we use should be the same as those which are on the slide. Additional words can be used so long as they provide an elaboration or example which illustrate the point that is being presented and so long as the audience are able to relate the additional words to the message which is on the screen. It can be very distracting for the audience if the presenter uses different words. Do they attend to what we are saying or do they read the slide? Similar distractions may arise if a slide or flip chart is left on display for too long. We may have moved on to a new point while the old display is still visible. If the display is an interesting diagram or photographs the audience may be tempted to continue attending to that rather than listening to the next point.

Visibility

Care needs to be taken with sight lines. Nobody's view should be obscured. Models and displays should also be large enough to be seen by everybody. This point is closely linked to the next point, Complexity.

Complexity

Slides and charts need to be kept simple. Graphs, pie charts and bar charts can be a much more effective way of getting the message across than columns of figures that people may find difficult to read and assimilate. Where slides or flip charts contain lettering the impact can be improved by using as few words as possible. Jay (1972) goes so far as to argue that words are not visuals and should be avoided wherever possible.

> If I could engrave a simple sentence on every presenter's heart, it would be this: WORDS ARE NOT VISUALS. How many times have we sat at presentations and seen slide after slide portraying nothing except abstract nouns: OBJECTIVES, OPERATIONS, PREPARATION, PLANNING, PRODUCTIVITY, PROGRESS, RECONNAISSANCE, RECOGNITION, REPORTING, and so on in an endless and utterly unmemorable series.

Jay possibly adopts a rather extreme position. People differ in terms of the kind of information they prefer to be presented with. Some people are visualisers whereas others are verbalisers (Riding 1991; Riding and Raynor 1998). While too many words can undermine the impact of a slide for some people, the careful use of both words and images can be an effective way of getting a message across. Sometimes, presenters who want to avoid the use of a script use headings on slides to provide themselves with an outline structure of the main points. If you decide to do this take care not to overcomplicate your slides.

Variety

Visual aids and demonstrations can introduce variety, but too much variety can disrupt the smooth flow of a presentation. It can become too bumpy and jumpy if we switch from whiteboard, to slide projector, to flip chart, to video, to overhead projector. We are more likely to forget which aid comes next and to get things in the wrong order if we are continually switching around rather than steadily working through one pile of overhead projector slides which we use at appropriate points in an orderly sequence. Too much variety may result in our failing to take sufficient care over sight lines and talking to the whiteboard or flip chart rather than to the audience. Thus while variety has some advantages it can also lead to problems if it is overdone.

Closure

Presentations have a beginning, a middle and an end. Closure is the management of the end of the presentation. It involves indicating to the audience that we have covered all the appropriate material. This can be achieved through the use of verbal markers such as: 'My final point is . . .' and by non-verbal markers such as collecting papers together and switching off the overhead projector.

It also involves focusing the audience's attention on the essential features of the material covered and encouraging them to relate this material to the purpose of the presentation. The purpose may be for them to better understand how something works, appreciate why a target was not achieved or be convinced of the advantages associated with a particular course of action. This aspect of closure can be achieved by offering a selective summary of the main points. After starting the presentation by telling the audience what they will be told, then telling them, we can conclude by telling them what they have been told.

This process can help motivate the audience to future action. For example, a general manager, after summarising the difficult circumstances facing the company over the next twelve months, may conclude by telling the management team: 'We know the problems, we know what needs to be done. Now it is up to you.'

When we have successfully concluded what we have to say, the transition from the formal presentation to the question-and-answer session is likely to take place without any uncomfortable silences and without people wondering what will happen next. But it is important to remember that the presentation involves more than a formal speech. It may be just as important for us to pay as much attention to concluding the question-and-answer session as concluding the speech. Keep the purpose of the presentation in mind. If, for example, it is to persuade a group to adopt a particular course of action it may be better to end with questions from people who are committed rather than questions from those who appear to be hostile to the proposal.

Developing presentation skills

The final section of this chapter presents Exercise 7.1, designed to facilitate the development of presentation skills. It involves making a presentation to a friendly audience of people who are prepared to give you feedback on both your formal presentation and your management of a follow-up question-and-answer session. You can use this feedback to help you identify what you need to attend to if you are to improve your performance.

Exercise 7.1 Developing presentation skills

This exercise involves making a presentation to others who observe your behaviour and provide feedback on the quality of your presentation. Three presentation assessment forms, each relating to different presentation skills, are presented below. Observers can use these forms to guide their observations and record points for discussion.

Suggested format

1 Presentation (up to 15 minutes).
2 Question and Answer session (up to 10 minutes).
3 Members of the audience provide feedback (up to 15 minutes).
   If the presentation has been video recorded the presenter can also view their own presentation in private and compare their own observations with the feedback provided by members of the audience. (It may be more effective if the presenter observes the recording more than once so that different aspects of their behaviour can be focused on selectively on each viewing.)
4 The presenter reflects on the feedback and identifies a list of learning points that deserve attention if they are to improve their presentation skills.
   If the presentation has not been videotaped, this is best done immediately after the plenary feedback session.
5 The presenter prepares and delivers a second presentation, taking account of the learning points identified above. Members of the audience give feedback on this second presentation.

Specifying the length of the presentation in advance can be helpful because many presenters find it difficult to get the timing right. When people rehearse their presentation they may only read it silently to themselves and this may take more or less time than when they are speaking aloud and supporting their presentation with visual aids. Even if the presentation is rehearsed aloud, the rate of speech used in private may be different from that used in public. It can be useful to be aware of this kind of discrepancy.

Divide the audience into three groups and instruct members of each group to focus attention on the aspects of the presentation covered by one of the three Presentation Assessment Forms. This procedure is recommended because there is so much to observe that any one person may find it difficult to give proper attention to all aspects of the presenter's behaviour. When different groups focus on selected aspects of the presentation the presenter is more likely to receive detailed feedback on a wide range of behaviours.

The three Presentation Assessment Forms are presented on separate pages so that they can be easily copied. Users of this book are permitted to copy these three forms for their personal use.

ASSESSMENT OF PRESENTATION FORM (1)

Name of presenter: ....

	YES	NO

1 Introduction

- Was a brief, clear introduction provided?
- Were the aims clearly defined?
- Did the introduction persuade the audience to listen?

2 Content and structure

- Was all the relevant information provided?
- Was unnecessary detail avoided?
- Was the structure of the presentation clear and logical?
- Was it broken down into appropriate elements?
- Was the relationship between elements adequately explained?
- Was the presentation easy to follow?

3 Closure

- Was there a concluding summary?
- Was it related to the purpose of the presentation?
- Did it contribute to the achievement of the purpose of the presentation?

ASSESSMENT OF PRESENTATION FORM (2)

Name of presenter: . . . .

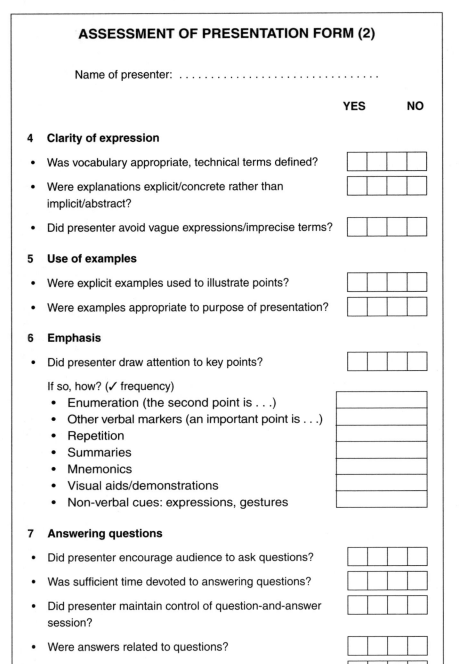

	YES	NO

4 Clarity of expression

- Was vocabulary appropriate, technical terms defined?
- Were explanations explicit/concrete rather than implicit/abstract?
- Did presenter avoid vague expressions/imprecise terms?

5 Use of examples

- Were explicit examples used to illustrate points?
- Were examples appropriate to purpose of presentation?

6 Emphasis

- Did presenter draw attention to key points?

  If so, how? (✓ frequency)
    - Enumeration (the second point is . . .)
    - Other verbal markers (an important point is . . .)
    - Repetition
    - Summaries
    - Mnemonics
    - Visual aids/demonstrations
    - Non-verbal cues: expressions, gestures

7 Answering questions

- Did presenter encourage audience to ask questions?
- Was sufficient time devoted to answering questions?
- Did presenter maintain control of question-and-answer session?
- Were answers related to questions?
- Were answers clear and straightforward?

ASSESSMENT OF PRESENTATION FORM (3)

Name of presenter: ....

8 Getting and maintaining attention

- **What methods were used to motivate the audience to listen at the start of the presentation?**

  - Rhetorical questions

  - The posing of an intriguing problem

  - Controversial statements

  - Concise statements of purpose in terms which appealed to audience

  - Other (specify)

- **What methods were used to *maintain* interest?**

  Visual aids used to capture attention

  Interesting examples and analogies

  Rhetorical questions

  Variety in delivery (voice, gestures, pace, etc.)

  Other (specify)

- **Sensitivity to feedback**

  Did presenter pay attention to non-verbal cues from audience?

  Did presenter ask questions to check understanding and relevance?

153

	YES	NO

9 Use of visual aids

- Were aids well prepared (legible etc)?
- Was level of complexity/detail appropriate?
- Could they be seen by everybody?
- Was the audience given sufficient opportunity to view them?
- Were they effective in:
  Introducing variety and maintaining interest?
  Promoting better understanding?
  Providing an *aid-mémoire*?

10 Manner of delivery and management of session

- Was presenter sure of facts and confident in presenting them?
- Was presenter enthusiastic and committed to message?
- Did presenter speak clearly?
- Was volume about right?
- Was there sufficient eye contact?
- Was the session well paced?
- Did presenter keep to time?
- Was presenter fully in control throughout?

Summary

Most people are required to make presentations or to offer explanations to others. People with poor presentation skills can create a bad impression, miss opportunities and foster misunderstandings. This chapter has examined ways in which we can develop more effective presentation skills. Preparation has been identified as the essential first step. It has been argued that presenters need to clarify their objectives, research their audience thoroughly, define and structure the content of their presentation carefully, and review the venue and other environmental factors.

Consideration has also been given to the ways in which we can attract and maintain the audience's attention. A variety of techniques for capturing people's attention have been considered including creating a sense of uncertainty in the minds of listeners, thus motivating them to listen to allay their anxiety, the use of rhetorical questions, the posing of intriguing problems, and the use of controversial statements. It has been noted that attention often begins to flag in the middle of a presentation, and the presenter therefore needs to behave in ways that will maintain audience interest. The use of interesting examples, visual aids and demonstrations are a few of the techniques considered.

Five presentation skills that help to get the message across have been identified. These are clarity of expression, the use of examples, emphasis, sensitivity to feedback and the ability to answer questions effectively. Attention has been focused on specific modifiable behaviours associated with each of these broad skill categories.

It has been noted that visual aids and demonstrations can be used to introduce variety and interest into the presentation, to facilitate explanation, promote a better understanding and provide an *aide-mémoire*. The advantages and disadvantages of some of the most commonly used visual aids have been considered and a number of principles associated with their use have been discussed.

The importance of drawing the presentation to an appropriate conclusion has also been discussed. It has been suggested that the conclusion should review the key points of the presentation in a way that contributes to the achievement of the purpose of the presentation, be it to inform, explain or persuade.

References

Brown, G. and Atkin, M. (1997) 'Explaining', in O.Hargie (ed.) *The Handbook of Communication Skills* (2nd edn), London: Routledge, pp. 183–212.

Hargie, O., Saunders, C. and Dickson, D. (1994) *Social Skills in Interpersonal Communication*, London: Croom Helm.

Hiller, J., Fisher, G. and Kaess, W. (1969) 'A computer investigation of verbal characteristics of effective classroom lecturing', *American Educational Research Journal* 6: 661–675.

Jay, A. (1972) *Effective Presentation*, London: British Institute of Management.

Ley, P. (1983) 'Patients' understanding and recall in clinical communication failure', in D. Pendleton and J. Hasler (eds) *Doctor–Patient Communication*, London: Academic Press.

Pemberton, M. (1982) *A Guide to Effective Speaking*, London: The Industrial Society.

Riding, R. (1991) *Cognitive Style Analysis*, Birmingham: Learning and Training Technology.

Riding, R. and Raynor, S. (1998) *Cognitive Styles and Learning Strategies*, London: David Fulton.

Soloman, D., Rosenberg, L. and Bezdek, W. (1964) 'Dimensions of teacher behaviour', *Journal of Experimental Education* 33: 23–40.

Tubbs, S.T. and Moss, S. (1994) *Human Communication* (7th edn), New York: McGraw-Hill.

Turney, C., Owens, L.C., Hatton, N., Williams, G. and Cairns, L.G. (1975) *Sydney Micro Skills*, Series 2 Handbook, Sydney: Sydney University Press.

8

HELPING AND FACILITATING

Learning objective

To understand the nature of helping and to develop a critical appreciation of the factors that can contribute to the effectiveness of the helping relationship. After reading this chapter you will:

- Be able to compare and contrast five different approaches to helping.
- Be aware of your own helping style.
- Recognise the factors that will influence the efficacy of different approaches to helping in different circumstances.
- Be able to discuss the nature of the helping relationship within the context of a three-stage model of helping.
- Be aware of the wide range of interpersonal skills that can facilitate the helping process.
- Recognise how the helper can use empathy, probing, feedback and challenging to help others improve their competence to manage problems and exploit opportunities.
- Understand how core values such as respect and genuineness can affect the helping relationship.

Helping and facilitating

The Shorter Oxford English Dictionary defines facilitation as rendering easier, promoting, helping forward, and assisting. To a greater or lesser extent, we are all facilitators. Some of us work in roles that are concerned almost exclusively with helping others, for example, consultants, social workers and AIDS counsellors. Others, such as personnel managers, systems analysts, priests and undertakers are engaged in roles that, while not exclusively concerned with helping, involve helping and facilitation as a major part of the job. However, almost everyone spends some of their time at work (and elsewhere) helping and promoting the effectiveness of others. This may involve working with colleagues who require help to improve

157

their relationship with a major customer, talking with a subordinate who is experiencing difficulties coping with the pressure of work, or supporting a friend who has recently been bereaved.

Sometimes people think of helping as something that is concerned exclusively with assisting others to manage their problems. However, helping is not only concerned with problems. People sometimes require help to identify and take advantage of opportunities offered by changed circumstances or potential career moves, or to recognise their own strengths and to exploit them to the full.

Help and facilitation may be offered informally as part of the normal day-to-day interactions we have with others. A manager may counsel a colleague who is having a difficult time with a new boss, or talk through with somebody how they will cope with working nights when their spouse is admitted to hospital, leaving dependent children at home. Informal help may also take the form of mentoring. Experienced workers may help their less experienced colleagues work out the best way of managing unfamiliar assignments. Sometimes, however, help and facilitation are offered as part of a more formal interaction. In the appraisal interview, appraisers may counsel appraisees about what they could do to improve their performance, or help them clarify career goals, and identify training needs and development opportunities.

Often the person in need of help (the client) will seek out somebody else to talk to, but self-referral is not the only starting point for a helping relationship. A manager may request or even require that a subordinate seeks help from a member of the personnel department, the company's medical officer or even an external consultant, depending on the nature of the problem. There may also be occasions when the manager is both the source of referral and the source of help. A manager may have observed that some subordinates are experiencing difficulties which are threatening the success of an important project and may intervene and require them to accept the manager's help to facilitate their ability to make an effective contribution.

Unfortunately, while many people spend a great deal of time trying to help others, those others often find that what they are offered provides little help. In other words, not all help is 'helpful'. This chapter examines different approaches to helping and facilitating. It also presents the main stages of one approach to helping and facilitation that has been found to be effective in a wide range of different circumstances and identifies some of the most important helping skills.

Helping styles

The Helping Style Profile has been designed to help you think about your typical approach to helping and facilitating. It will enable you to audit your typical approach and provide a point of reference when thinking about how you can improve the effectiveness of your helping interventions. Complete the Helping Style Profile now (Exercise 8.1).

Exercise 8.1 Helping Style Profile

Listed below are five cases (problem situations) and, for each case, five examples of how a helper might respond. For *each* of the five responses to each case, circle the number on the scale that most closely reflects the probability that you would use that response. For example:

A1 NEVER USE → | 1 | ② | 3 | 4 | 5 | ← DEFINITELY USE

There are no right or wrong answers.

Case A

A newly appointed supervisor complained to her manager that her subordinates were hostile, moody, only heard what they chose to hear and often failed to obey instructions. She likened their behaviour to rebellious schoolchildren who were determined to 'break' the new teacher. Her account placed all the blame for the rapidly deteriorating situation onto her subordinates. Her manager had not expected this kind of conversation with the new supervisor because she had joined the company with glowing references and a ten-year record of successful people management. In addition, her work group had never created problems before. All of them had been with the company for at least ten months and most were very well qualified. Two of them had recently been through the company's assessment centre and had been identified as having potential for promotion, and another was an undergraduate on a sandwich course, working for a year in industry.

If you were the manager, how likely is it that you would use each of the following responses? (Circle one number on each of the five scales)

1   Introduce the supervisor to a theory that might help her better understand the situation. For example, the manager might explain the basics of transactional analysis, a theory of personal interaction that can be used to analyse interpersonal problems in terms of the intended and implied messages people send to each other. The

---

supervisor may be asked to apply the theory to her problem and con-sider whether her subordinates see her as a controlling parent dealing with a group of inexperienced children rather than an adult interacting with other competent adults, and speculate how she might apply the theory to improve the situation by changing the way she relates to her subordinates.

A1 NEVER USE → | 1 | 2 | 3 | 4 | 5 | ← DEFINITELY USE

2   Tell her that she has failed to recognise the quality of her subordi-nates, that she is undervaluing the contribution they can make, and that she needs to delegate more and give them greater responsibil-ity.

A2 NEVER USE → | 1 | 2 | 3 | 4 | 5 | ← DEFINITELY USE

3   Listen carefully and attempt to see the problem through her eyes in the hope that by being supportive you can encourage her to open up and tell her story, which in turn may help her to develop a better understanding of the problem and what needs to be done about it.

A3 NEVER USE → | 1 | 2 | 3 | 4 | 5 | ← DEFINITELY USE

4   Suggest to her that it may not be only her subordinates who hear what they choose to hear and ask her if she has really paid attention to all the messages she has been sent by the members of her work group.

A4 NEVER USE → | 1 | 2 | 3 | 4 | 5 | ← DEFINITELY USE

5   Help her to get to the bottom of the problem by assisting her to gather more information which she can use to develop a better understanding of what is going on and what can be done to improve matters.

A5 NEVER USE → | 1 | 2 | 3 | 4 | 5 | ← DEFINITELY USE

Case B

One of your close friends was made redundant ten weeks ago. The news came as a big surprise and he was much disoriented at first. He used to 'eat, sleep and live' work and had few outside interests. However, after the initial shock, he developed a positive attitude and expressed confidence that he would soon be re-employed in the same occupation. Recently, however, you have become concerned because he seems to be giving up hope, is depressed and irritable, hardly ever leaves the house and appears to be doing little to help himself.

How likely is it that you would use each of the following responses?

1   Help him to develop a list of his strengths and weaknesses and encourage him to use this to identify some different kinds of jobs he could apply for.

B1 NEVER USE → | 1 | 2 | 3 | 4 | 5 | ← DEFINITELY USE

2   Give him a newspaper article you came across which explains how people react to unemployment and why some are more successful at finding jobs than others, and suggest that it may give him a few ideas that would help him understand his lack of success and provide a few clues about what he might do to secure a few interviews.

B2 NEVER USE → | 1 | 2 | 3 | 4 | 5 | ← DEFINITELY USE

3   Give him all the emotional support you can and reassure him that he is still an important and valued person.

B3 NEVER USE → | 1 | 2 | 3 | 4 | 5 | ← DEFINITELY USE

4   Tell him to apply for a recently advertised job that you feel he could do.

B4 NEVER USE → | 1 | 2 | 3 | 4 | 5 | ← DEFINITELY USE

5   Confront him with the confusing messages he has been giving to his friends. He is depressed and angry because he is has been deprived of the opportunity to work, and yet he refusing to get off his backside

and take the initiative to find a job simply because there does not appear to be any opportunities in his old line of work.

B5 NEVER USE → | 1 | 2 | 3 | 4 | 5 | ← DEFINITELY USE

Case C

You are the personnel manager of a large utility company. An employee (a 40-year-old widower) was recently promoted and moved from a busy office in the city, where he had spent most of his working life, to manage a small but strategically important office in a relatively isolated rural area. He has come to see you because he is unhappy with the new job. He misses his friends, does not enjoy being the boss in a situation where he has no colleagues to whom he can relate, and he reports that people who live locally are cliquish, aloof and unfriendly.

How likely is it that you would use each of the following responses?

1   Tell him that there is a vacancy at his old grade in the department he used to work in and indicate that you think the best solution would be for him to move back.

C1 NEVER USE → | 1 | 2 | 3 | 4 | 5 | ← DEFINITELY USE

2   Avoid jumping to any conclusions, make sure that you really under-stand why he is unhappy and do everything you can to help him clarify his own feelings about what the problem may be. Listen care-fully to what he has to say and then reflect back to him the essence of what you think you heard. For example, 'What you seem to be saying is. . . . Have I got it right?'

C2 NEVER USE → | 1 | 2 | 3 | 4 | 5 | ← DEFINITELY USE

3   Help him adopt a balanced problem-solving approach and encour-age him to thoroughly explore every aspect of the problem and, where necessary, gather information that might help him identify and evaluate possible solutions (for example, by helping him identify opportunities to meet new people).

C3 NEVER USE → | 1 | 2 | 3 | 4 | 5 | ← DEFINITELY USE

4   Give him the kind of feedback that might push him into taking a new initiative, for example, by telling him that you have listened to what he has said and not once heard him mention anything he has actually done to try to make new friends. All he seems to do is moan about others and complain that they do nothing to make him feel welcome. Try to encourage him into action by asking him if he has thought about what he could do that would make others want to get to know him better.

C4 NEVER USE → | 1 | 2 | 3 | 4 | 5 | ← DEFINITELY USE

5   Lend him a copy of Dale Carnigie's book *How to Win Friends and Influence People* and suggest that if he could master some of the techniques and skills it contains, making friends might be something he could do more easily.

C5 NEVER USE → | 1 | 2 | 3 | 4 | 5 | ← DEFINITELY USE

Case D

You are the general manager of a large manufacturing plant and are in the middle of an appraisal interview with one of your departmental managers. You used to regard her as one of your 'rising stars' but you have been disappointed with her performance of late. You put her in charge of a task force established to conduct a wide-ranging review of the company's manufacturing strategy and you suspect she will not deliver the report on time. You are also concerned that she is involved in too many staff association and other activities that, in your opinion, do little to contribute to the 'bottom line'.

At an early point in the interview she tells you that she has been looking forward to this meeting because she feels overworked and was hoping that you might be able to help. She explains that she believes her subordinates would be unhappy if she tried to delegate more work to them. She also doubts their ability to take on any more of her work.

How likely is it that you would use each of the following responses?

1   Tell her that you are aware of the problem and that you think the first thing she must do is to sort out her priorities and drop all the non-important tasks that are eating into her time.

D1 NEVER USE → | 1 | 2 | 3 | 4 | 5 | ← DEFINITELY USE

2 Suggest that the company's seminars on time management and delegation may help her identify constructive methods of shifting some of her work to others in ways that they will welcome and see as contributing to their own personal development.

D2 NEVER USE → | 1 | 2 | 3 | 4 | 5 | ← DEFINITELY USE

3 Explore how she feels about the situation without passing judgement or telling her what she should do. Encourage her to talk about it and gently persuade her to examine any aspects of the problem she seems to have skirted over so that she is able to develop a more balanced view.

D3 NEVER USE → | 1 | 2 | 3 | 4 | 5 | ← DEFINITELY USE

4 Suggest that it might be useful to find out how the members of her department feel about their work and the way the department is operating, and offer her a copy of an attitude survey form that she may be able to adapt and use.

D4 NEVER USE → | 1 | 2 | 3 | 4 | 5 | ← DEFINITELY USE

5 Make her face up to reality and recognise that she is not the only competent person around. Ask her if she really thinks she is indispensable and suggest that some of her subordinates might be able to do some things better than her if she would only let go of the reins and give them a chance.

D5 NEVER USE → | 1 | 2 | 3 | 4 | 5 | ← DEFINITELY USE

Case E

A colleague has come to you for help. He does not want to be an autocratic boss and believes that people work best when they are given the freedom to get on with their job. However, his department is beginning to get itself a reputation for not getting it right. He has explained that while he always tries to pursue an open-door policy there are some people who never cross his threshold. Consequently he is poorly informed and avoidable mistakes have been made. He is obviously upset and you suspect that his boss has just torn a strip off him.

How likely is it that you would use each of the following responses?

1   Share with him a similar problem you once had and tell him what you did about it. Suggest that there can come a time when democracy has to go out of the window and you have to read the riot act, and that is what he should do now.

E1 NEVER USE → | 1 | 2 | 3 | 4 | 5 | ← DEFINITELY USE

2   Tell him about a theory you are familiar with which argues that the best style of leadership may vary from one situation to another, and suggest that one way forward might be for him to consider whether his current style appears to be a 'best fit' or whether the theory would suggest an alternative leadership style.

E2 NEVER USE → | 1 | 2 | 3 | 4 | 5 | ← DEFINITELY USE

3   On the basis of what you have observed (and been told by others), challenge his view that he always operates an open-door policy. Tell him that you have heard that he is never around when he is needed; also that while he may believe he is approachable others see him as aloof and distant.

E3 NEVER USE → | 1 | 2 | 3 | 4 | 5 | ← DEFINITELY USE

4   You can see that he is upset so decide that the best thing you can do is to sit him down with a cup of coffee and let him get it off his chest.

E4 NEVER USE → | 1 | 2 | 3 | 4 | 5 | ← DEFINITELY USE

5   Help him identify some specific circumstances where things have gone wrong and then question him about a number of these problems to sort out precisely what happened and whether there are any patterns he could do something about.

E5 NEVER USE → | 1 | 2 | 3 | 4 | 5 | ← DEFINITELY USE

Scoring

In the grid below all the available responses to each case have been arranged into columns that reflect five different styles of helping.

- Taking each case in turn, enter the *number* you circled for each response alongside the appropriate response code in the grid. For example, for case A, you may have circled ② for response A1, ⑤ for response A2, ① for response A3, and so on.
  (*Note*: for cases B to E the response codes are presented in different sequences and are *not* arranged in order from 1 to 5.)
- Calculate the total score for each column and enter this in the box provided.

The total score for each column indicates your relative preference for the different helping styles.

Response grid

	THEORISING		ADVISING		SUPPORTING		CHALLENGING		INFORMATION GATHERING	
Case A	A1		A2		A3		A4		A5	
Case B	B2		B4		B3		B5		B1	
Case C	C5		C1		C2		C4		C3	
Case D	D2		D1		D3		D5		D4	
Case E	E2		E1		E4		E3		E5	
TOTAL										

You should now have a score for all five types of helping style. Note whether your scores are spread equally across all five helping styles or whether your response pattern indicates that you prefer to use one or two approaches to helping much more than the other approaches.

(*Note*: The helping style profile presented here is based on an ipsative version of this questionnaire, first published in Hayes 1996.)

Different approaches to helping

The five approaches to helping presented in the Helping Style Profile represent some of the ways in which we might attempt to help others. This section will consider each of these approaches in turn.

Blake and Mouton (1986) describe the essence of helping as cycle-breaking endeavour. They argue that behaviour tends to be cyclical in character; that is, sequences of behaviour are repeated within specific time periods or within particular contexts or settings. Some of these patterns of behaviour are advantageous to the client or client group but some do little to promote their interests and may even be harmful. They go on to argue that individuals, groups or larger client systems (such as entire organisations) may engage in behaviour cycles by force of habit. They may not be conscious of the possibility of harmful or self-defeating consequences. They may be aware that things are not going well, but they may not understand why or what they can do to improve matters. Blake and Mouton define the helper's function as helping the client identify and break out of these damaging kinds of cycle.

This cycle-breaking endeavour can take many forms.

Theorising

The theorising approach involves us in identifying theories and conceptual models that are pertinent to the clients' problem situation, presenting these to clients and helping them to learn to use them to facilitate a better understanding of their situation in an analytical cause-and-effect fashion. We can then build on this understanding and use it to help them identify what they can do to move towards a more desirable state of affairs.

Managers may adopt a theorising approach when they feel that some kind of theoretical framework could help colleagues organise their thoughts and provide the basis for a fresh appraisal of their predicament; for example, a doctor may provide a patient with a simplified theory, which explains why people slip discs in their backs, in order to help the patient adopt a safer approach to lifting. This book offers theories and conceptual frameworks that we can use to help us relate to others more effectively.

We can use theories and conceptual models to facilitate discussion and open the way to an exploration of potentially delicate or sensitive issues. For example, the discussion of the relevance of a theory of group interaction may provide a relatively safe and non-threatening way of exploring how members of a management team work together. The theory-based approach can also provide a way of exploring and testing implicit assumptions and values in a way that avoids direct confrontation, and it can provide a basis for increasing the client's capacity for independent action.

167

Advising

The advising approach involves us in telling clients what they should do to rectify problems in a given situation. The helper diagnoses the problem for the client and prescribes the solution. The advice we offer is often based upon our own direct or indirect experience. It can involve either recommending action that we believe will work or a warning to avoid behaving in ways that we believe will fail to deliver desired outcomes. People tend to adopt this approach to helping when they assume that they have a greater level of relevant expertise than the client. One danger with this approach is that clients become dependent on others. They learn to look to the helper for a solution and they are not helped to learn how to solve problems for themselves.

Supporting

The supporting style of helping involves us in working with clients to help them express any feelings and emotions that impede clear and objective thinking about a problem. The helper listens empathetically, withholding any judgement, and helps clients develop for themselves a more objective view of the situation. It is assumed that this new level of awareness will often be sufficient to help clients go on and solve their problem for themselves. This approach is based upon the Rogerian client-centred counselling model (Rogers 1958) in which counsellors listen, reflect and sometimes interpret what the clients have said about themselves and their relationship with others, but do not intervene or develop any active strategies for dealing with the clients' problem. A feature which distinguishes the supportive approach from the advising approach is that the immediate focus of the supportive approach is the client, whereas the immediate focus of the advising approach is the problem.

An example will help to clarify how this approach can be effective. Blake and Mouton (1986) describe a case in which a consultant, who was working in the Hawthorn Plant of Western Electric, used a supporting approach to help a shop-floor worker. The consultant overheard the worker complaining, in very emotional tones, about his supervisor and decided to intervene. He asked what had been going on and was told, in the same emotional tones, that the bosses were useless because when you had a rise coming to you they would not give it. The worker went on to tell the consultant that he thought the place stank and that he wanted to get out. The consultant's response was to avoid siding with either the worker or the supervisor, but to invite the worker into his office to 'talk it over'. As the interaction progressed, the worker unloaded his feelings about his supervisor. As he talked, he began to ramble from one complaint to another. He had been refused a rise, and because he was at the top of his grade he could not advance any higher. He then complained about the machine setters who did everything they could to protect their own position and stop others learning anything that would help them to improve their work. All the way through this interaction the consultant maintained his neutral stance and refrained from making any evaluation of the worker's complaints. He assumed the role of active listener and did little more than reflect his sympathetic understanding by repeating what he had been told. For example, in response to the complaint about the machine setters he said, 'I see, they seem to be pretty selfish about their knowledge of screw machines.'

In this case the consultant's strategy was to allow the worker to vent his anger because he believed that until he had done so he would be too wound up to think straight. It appeared to work. Slowly, as the tension eased, the conversation moved away from gripes towards problem solving. The consultant confined his interventions to supportive listening and clarifying, but eventually the worker (client) began to work through his problems by himself.

Challenging

This is an approach which involves us in confronting the foundations of the client's thinking in an attempt to identify beliefs and values that may be distorting the way situations are viewed. An assumption underlying this approach is that effective action can be undermined by the clients' inability or unwillingness to face up to reality. They may rationalise or justify their behaviour and in so doing create or perpetuate an unsatisfactory situation. Challenging/confronting interventions are designed to call attention to contradictions in action and attitude or to challenge precedents or practices that seem inappropriate. The aim of this approach is to identify alternative values and assumptions that may lead to the development of more effective solutions to problems. Hayes (1996) illustrates this approach. He refers to a head teacher of a small school who had worked tremendously hard to improve the school's external reputation and had invested a great deal of effort in building a good team spirit among his staff. When one of his staff applied for a job elsewhere the head teacher interpreted this as a sign of disloyalty. He communicated his reaction to the individual concerned and made his disapproval public by excluding him from management team meetings. The deputy head intervened. He confronted the head with his own early career progress and pointed out how this was little different from the progress that the teacher who had applied for the job elsewhere was seeking. The deputy pointed out that the head had rarely stayed in one job for more than three years, whereas this teacher had already been in post and had performed very satisfactorily for almost four years. He also asked the head how he thought others would interpret his action and what effect it was likely to have on the team spirit he prized so highly. Eventually the head accepted that the teacher's application was a timely and appropriate step to take. He also accepted that he had not only overlooked the career development needs of this teacher but had given insufficient attention to the career development of the rest of his staff. He also accepted that his response had been inconsistent with the management culture he was trying to create.

Information gathering

This approach to helping involves us assisting the client in collecting data that can be used to evaluate and reinterpret the problem situation. Hayes (1996) illustrates this with the example of a trainer in the sales department of a machine tool company faced with a very demotivated young representative who had recently lost three important accounts. The trainer suggested that he get in touch with the buyers he used to deal with and ask them why they had changed suppliers. The trainer suspected that it was because the representative had not been attentive enough, but he felt that it would be more effective if the representative discovered this for himself and decided what he needed to do about it.

The assumption underlying this approach is that deficiencies of information are an important cause of malfunctioning. The helpers' objectives are to assist clients in arriving at a better level of awareness of the underlying causes of a problem and to help them identify what action is required to resolve it. Helpers adopting this approach assume that any information they may present will be less acceptable and less likely to be understood than information that individuals (or groups) generate for themselves. Another assumption often made by helpers adopting this approach is that clients will be less resistant to proposals and action plans they generate for themselves.

Is there one best approach?

Some writers adopt a universalistic position and advocate that there is one best style of helping. Others adopt a contingent approach and argue that the best style depends on the client and the problem or opportunities the client needs to manage more effectively. Both of these views will be examined in this chapter. It will be argued that, overall, prescriptive approaches that advise or tell the client what to do are less effective than more collaborative approaches that involve clients and develop their competence to diagnose and manage problems and opportunities for themselves. However, it will also be argued that there is no one best style. Consideration will be given to contingent variables, such as the nature of the client, the situation and the problem that may have some bearing on which helping style is likely to be most effective in a particular set of circumstances (there may even be circumstances where a prescriptive style may be effective). Finally, a different perspective on 'which is the best approach' will be presented. It will be argued that the most effective way of interacting with a client, and therefore the most effective helping style, will vary at different stages in the helping relationship.

Prescriptive vs. collaborative approaches

Many of us adopt a prescriptive approach to helping. We give advice, we tell the client what to do or perhaps even get up and do ourselves whatever we believe must be done to solve the client's problem. We behave as though we are sufficiently expert to discern the real needs of the client, and we assume that clients lack the necessary competence to either make a sound diagnosis or plan corrective action for themselves. The goal of the prescriptive helper seems to be confined to finding a solution to the immediate problem being experienced by the client. One danger with this approach, already acknowledged, is that clients become dependent on the helper. They are not helped to learn how to solve the problem for themselves. Consequently the next time they experience a difficulty they again have to seek help.

Another problem can arise if clients feel that when we are giving advice we are not as expert as we think we are, or if clients feel that we are insensitive to their needs. In these circumstances clients may react by not cooperating with us and withholding information about the problem. They may also reject any advice or solution we may offer.

However, in some circumstances clients do respond well to advice offered by prescriptive helpers, especially when they are under great pressure to find a solution and/or when they are at their wits' end. Steele (1969: p. 193) argues that the needs of both the client and the helper may propel the helper towards exclusive occupancy of the role of expert in their relationship and that in those circumstances where the client accepts the helper as expert there may be some benefits. However, he also identifies some costs. One is the increased dependency, mentioned above, and the other has to do with the helper's neglect of the client's knowledge about his or her own problem. Even where the client does not attempt to withhold this knowledge the helper may choose to ignore it:

> The client often has great wisdom (intuitive if not systematic) about many aspects of his own situation, and an overweighing of the consultant's knowledge value may indeed cause poorer choices to be made than if there were a more balanced view of that which each can contribute to the situation.

Collaborative approaches to helping, such as information gathering, are client-centred, and aim to empower the client to manage his or her own problems or to identify and exploit opportunities more effectively.

People often feel helpless and unable to manage the problems they face. Seligman (1975) defined helplessness as the psychological state that frequently results when events are perceived to be uncontrollable. Much of the original research was undertaken with dogs, but many researchers have also observed learned helplessness in humans. Hiroto (1974), for example, exposed groups of college students to either loud controllable noise which they could terminate by pressing a button four times or uncontrollable noise which was terminated independently of what they did. Another group included in the experiment was not exposed to any noise. All subjects were then tested in a situation in which it was possible for them to exercise control over noise termination. Hiroto found that the groups which had either been subjected to controllable noise or no noise learned to terminate the noise in the later test situation, whereas subjects who had previously been subjected to uncontrollable noise failed to terminate noise during later tests.

Learned helplessness theory, mentioned in Chapter 3, states that when individuals are subjected to events which are uncontrollable (that is when the probability of an outcome is the same irrespective of how they respond), they will develop *expectations* of non-contingency between response and outcome. Furthermore, it is argued that these expectations will produce motivational, emotional and cognitive deficits. The theory suggests that the incentive for clients to initiate activity directed towards resolving a problem depends upon their expectation that responding will produce some improvement to the problematic situation. If clients have no confidence in their own ability to achieve any improvement, they will not try. Abramson *et al.* (1978) distinguish between universal helplessness (where the client believes that the problem is unsolvable by anyone) and personal helplessness (where the client believes that the problem is solvable – for example, by the helper – but not by self). The danger with prescriptive/advising approaches to helping is that they can promote a sense of *personal helplessness* in the client and the client may become dependent on the help of others.

Egan (1998) discusses the notion of *empowerment* in the helping relationship. He notes that some clients learn, sometimes from a very early age, that there is nothing they can do about certain life situations. They engage in disabling self-talk (see Ellis 1977) and tell themselves that they cannot manage certain situations and that they cannot cope. Egan's position is that whether clients are victims of their own doing or the doings of others they can and must take an active part in managing their own problems, including the search for solutions and efforts towards achieving those solutions. He also argues that helpers can do a great deal to help people develop a sense of agency or self-efficacy. We can do this in a number of ways. We can help clients challenge self-defeating beliefs and attitudes about themselves, we can help clients develop the knowledge, skills and resources they need to succeed, and we can challenge them to take reasonable risks and support them when they do so.

The function of the helper, according to Egan, is to encourage clients to apply a problem-solving approach to their current problem situation and to learn from this experience so that, over the longer term, they will also apply a problem-solving approach to future problem situations. In other words, his approach is one that is directed towards eliminating feelings of personal helplessness.

Egan is not alone in advocating empowerment as the aim of helping.

Reddy (1987) defines counselling as a set of techniques, skills and attitudes to *help people manage their own problems using their own resources.* Hopson (1984) offers a similar definition. He defines counselling as a process that involves helping people explore problems so that they can decide what to do about them.

Choice of style and the characteristics of problem and client

It has been argued that the most effective way of helping others is to help them to help themselves. There may, however, be occasions when a more advising/prescriptive style is appropriate. The client may be faced with a critical problem that, if not resolved quickly, could have disastrous consequences. If we have the expertise to help clients avoid this disastrous outcome, it may be appropriate to adopt a prescriptive mode of intervention to provide the required help quickly. However, this is a short-term fix.

Over the longer term, it may be much more effective if we help clients develop the competencies required to manage for themselves any similar situations they might encounter in the future. However, there may be problems where the required level of expertise is beyond the client (or where the opportunity cost of acquiring it is judged to be too high). In these circumstances, the client may have to rely on the advice of an expert helper.

Theory-based interventions assist others to acquire a theoretical basis for managing their problems. Blake and Mouton (1986) argue that theories can help clients free themselves from blind reliance on intuition, hunch, common sense and conventional wisdom, and enable them to see situations more objectively. Theory-based interventions can be applied to all classes of problems in a wide range of situations so long as the theory is valid and the clients are willing and able to internalise the theory and make it a personally useful source of guidance. This kind of intervention may be less effective than other approaches if we introduce the client to a theory they perceive to be invalid, irrelevant or too complicated. It will also be less effective if the client is unreceptive to the possibility of using theory as a basis for managing problems more effectively. Even valid, user-friendly theories may be rejected, for example, when clients are emotionally charged.

Pent-up emotions may undermine an individual's ability to take an objective view. In those circumstances where emotions impede effective problem management, a supportive approach may enable clients to vent their feelings and, eventually, work through the emotional blocks that undermine their ability to view the problem objectively.

Where values affect the individual's ability to manage a problem, a challenging style of helping may be most effective. We can help the client confront potentially invalid or unjustified value positions or draw attention to discrepancies between espoused values and the values that appear to underpin their own behaviour. However, great care needs to be exercised when adopting a challenging style. Egan argues that confrontation can be strong medicine and, in the hands of the inept, can be destructive. Effective challenges are those which are received by clients as helpful invitations to explore aspects of a problem from a new perspective. Helpers who adopt this approach ask questions or provide feedback that draws the client's attention to inappropriate attitudes, values, discrepancies and distortions, but they avoid telling the client how they should think or act. Challenges that clients perceive as punitive accusations or the shameful unmasking of inadequacies are likely to be met with some form of strong defensive reaction and are rarely effective, especially over the longer term. Consequently, even in circumstances where a challenging style of helping promises to be effective, this promise may not be realised if we are inept at challenging and confronting.

Information-gathering interventions can be very effective in those situations where, because of communication problems, perceptions of reality are hampered by a lack of or incorrect information. Exercise 8.2 is designed to help you reflect on the discussion so far and help you identify and bench-mark effective helping behaviour.

Exercise 8.2 Bench-marking effective helping behaviour

The aim of this exercise is to use your own experience to identify a bench-mark standard of effective helping behaviour. Working alone, think of a number of occasions when others have tried to help you.

1   Identify at least two people whose behaviour towards you was very helpful.
    •   What did they do that you found helpful?
    •   How did you respond to this behaviour? (Why was it helpful?)

Record you observations below. Indicate, with an asterisk (*), any behaviours that were used by two or more of the 'helpful helpers'.

List the helpful behaviours	Explain why the behaviours were helpful

---

2   Identify at least two people who, while trying to help, behaved towards you in ways that you found *un*helpful.
   • What did they do that you found unhelpful?
   • How did you respond to this behaviour? (Why was it unhelpful?)

Record you observations below. Indicate, with an asterisk (*), any behaviours that were used by two or more of the 'unhelpful helpers'.

List the *un*helpful behaviours	Explain why the behaviours were *un*helpful

3   Reflect on your findings and consider how they relate to the helping skills referred to so far in this chapter. Does you experience highlight any skills not discussed so far but which appear to have an important bearing on the outcome of the helping relationship?

4   Working in small groups, share your conclusions with others and identify those behaviours you all found to be either helpful or unhelpful. Prepare two lists.
   • Rank order the list of helpful behaviours, assigning the rank of 1 to the most helpful behaviour, 2 to the next most helpful, and so on.
   • Do the same for the unhelpful behaviours, with the most unhelpful behaviour ranked as 1.

In a plenary session, each group presents a summary of its findings. Conclude the exercise with a discussion of how your experience relates to the theories and concepts presented in this chapter.

Choice of style and the stage of the helping relationship

Many of us lack an adequate overview of the helping process and tend to concentrate our efforts on one aspect of facilitation. The supportive mode of helping and facilitation, for example, focuses on the provision of empathy and passive acceptance in order to help clients develop a new level of understanding. This kind of approach may be especially effective at the beginning of the helping process. As well as helping clients clarify their thinking about a problem, it can also contribute to the development of a supportive relationship between helper and client. However, as the process proceeds, it may be necessary for us to modify our initial approach and begin to adopt a more challenging, information-gathering or theorising style of facilitation. We may need to confront clients about discrepancies between what they say and what they do, provide them with feedback or help them gather for themselves new information that will help them view their problem from a different perspective. It may also be beneficial to introduce clients to theories and conceptual frameworks that will facilitate their diagnosis and action planning. In other words, any one approach, used in isolation, may not always lead to an adequate level of understanding about a problem. It may be necessary for us to draw upon a number of different approaches as the client's needs change.

Stages in the helping process

Egan cautions against adopting one dominant approach to helping. He argues that helpers should be competent in all aspects of the helping process because they are all interdependent. For example, helpers who specialise in challenging may be poor confronters if their challenges are not based on an empathic understanding of the client.

Egan (1998) presents a three-stage model of helping that we can use as a cognitive map. He argues that it will help us understand the nature of our relationship with the client and provide us with a sense of direction. While it is a stage model, it does not assume that helping will necessarily involve a sequential progression through each of the three stages. We might move backwards as well as forwards throughout the model because, for example, while planning for action, the client may raise new concerns that have to be clarified and understood before the problem can be resolved.

The three-stage helping model presented here is based upon Egan's integrative approach to problem management. Stage 1 is concerned with identifying and clarifying problem situations and unused opportunities, Stage 2 with goal setting, and Stage 3 with action.

Stage 1: Identifying and clarifying problem situations and unused opportunities

Stage 1 is important because problem situations cannot be managed or unused opportunities developed until clients are able to identify and understand them. Egan originally presented this process of identification and clarification as one that involved two steps. He referred to them as the inward journey and the outward journey (see his first edition of *The Skilled Helper*, published in 1975).

The inward journey is concerned with helping clients tell their stories and develop a subjective understanding of their problems. It focuses on how the client sees things. No attempt is made, at this stage, to persuade clients to consider alternative ways of thinking about their problems. Helpers assist clients to clarify their problem situations *from within their own frames of reference*. We can do this by attending and responding in ways that help clients explore their own feelings, attitudes and behaviours. We can help them consider what it is they do (or fail to do) that has a bearing on their problems. It is important that helpers empathise with clients, that we show we understand what the clients are saying and how they are feeling from within their own frames of reference. We may also have to nudge clients into dealing with concrete and specific issues and feelings if they are to clarify and better understand their problem situations. Vague generalities provide a poor foundation for the generation of strategies to develop unused opportunities or manage problem situations.

Some people find it easy to share their thoughts with a helper, whereas others feel reluctant to talk about their problems. In order to facilitate this sharing we need to be skilled listeners (see Chapters 4 and 5) and good at drawing people out (see Chapter 6).

Relationship building also plays a central role in this phase of the helping process. Strong (1968) defines helping in terms of a social influence process. He goes on to suggest that helpers need to establish a power base and then to use it to influence clients. This is clearly what happens in prescriptive helping relationships where clients define helpers as experts and bow to their expertise. However, in the more collaborative helping relationships advocated here we must be careful to avoid using our ability to influence in ways which will increase clients' feelings of powerlessness. None the less, where clients trust us and believe that the we are 'on their side' and are working 'for' them, they will be more likely to share sensitive information about themselves. It will also help to ensure (in the next phase of Stage 1 – the outward journey) that clients will be receptive to suggestions from us that point to alternative ways of looking at their problems. However, where we are seen to be untrustworthy, incompetent and not 'for' them, clients will be much more likely to reject any feedback we offer. They may also react defensively to any attempt by us to influence their thinking and introducing alternative frames of reference.

177

The outward journey is concerned with helping clients identify blind spots and develop new perspectives. While the inward journey focused on helping clients clarify problems from within their own frames of reference, the outward journey focuses on the development of a more objective assessment. Old and comfortable frames of reference may keep clients locked into self-defeating patterns of thinking and behaving, and we may need to help them identify blind spots and develop alternative frames of reference.

There are a number of ways in which we can persuade clients to consider their problem situations from alternative perspectives. As clients tell their stories we may draw attention to themes:

> 'You have mentioned several times, in several different ways, that you feel uncomfortable when you have to manage people who have more paper qualifications than you. Is this the way you see it?'

We may also draw attention to what appears to be the bigger picture:

> 'The problem doesn't just seem to be that your new boss is a woman, your resentment also seems to be directed at a number of your male colleagues.'

During the 'outward journey', we need to show what Egan refers to as 'advanced empathy'. We need to communicate to clients an understanding not only of what they say but also of what they imply, what they hint at and what they convey non-verbally. In this phase we may also begin to constructively challenge clients in those situations where their old frames of reference appear to be preventing them from identifying better ways of managing their problems.

Stage 2: Goal setting: developing a more desirable scenario

Insight is seldom sufficient, however interesting it may be. The helping relationship aims to promote problem-managing *action*. Egan (1998) suggests that assessment for the sake of assessment, exploration for the sake of exploration or insight for the sake of insight is close to useless. Stage 1 of the helping process – identifying and clarifying problem situations and unused opportunities – can only be judged to be effective to the extent that it helps clients construct more desirable scenarios in terms of realistic and achievable goals. This may involve identifying those aspects of the problem that are to be tackled first. Some problems are too large or too complex to be tackled in one go. If clients set unrealistic goals for themselves they are unlikely to succeed, and failure may reinforce their feelings of helplessness. The identification of realistic and achievable goals is more likely to lead to success and to the promotion of a feeling of self-efficacy. For example, if a problem were identified in terms of 'The quality of my working life is deteriorating', it may be more difficult to identify achievable goals than if it were broken down into sub-problems such as:

- 'I am overworked';
- 'My subordinates don't get along with each other and I am surrounded by conflicts';
- 'I spend too much time away from the office and home';
- 'In my absence problems multiply and nobody seems to care';
- 'My boss and I have different priorities so I am reluctant to ask him to keep a watching brief in my absence';
- 'I seem to have been doing the same old thing for far too long'.

This process not only helps clients identify what a more desirable scenario would look like, but also points to the possibility of selecting alternative scenarios. For example, should clients work at being away less or at building a better relationship with their boss so that fewer problems will arise during their absence? All too often people tend to latch on to the first scenario they generate, and in so doing block out the possibility of considering alternatives.

Clients may need help to think through and anticipate the consequences of opting for different scenarios. Why might they prefer one rather than another?

Goals have important motivational implications. Locke and Latham (1984) argue that they:

- provide a vision and a focus for attention and action;
- mobilise energy and effort (people are motivated to achieve goals to which they are committed);
- increase persistence (people try harder and are less willing to give up when goals are both clear and realistic);
- provide the motivation to search for strategies that will help achieve the objective.

Stage 3: Helping clients act

While Stage 2 is concerned with goals (*ends*), Stage 3 is less concerned with ends and more with the *means* for achieving these ends. It involves identifying different strategies for action, and selecting and implementing the strategy that offers the greatest promise of success. Egan illustrates the importance of Stage 3 with the example of Kate who, on New Year's Eve, decides to lose 20 lb., only to find, some time later, that she had actually gained 5 lb. Her lack of success may be attributed to several factors. First, her goal was not expressed in terms of specific behaviours, such as exercising more or eating less. Second, she failed to think through what losing weight would require in terms of personal commitment and what factors would affect her level of commitment;

finally, she failed to think through how she was going to accomplish her goal. She failed to identify an action programme.

One aspect of the helper's role is to guide clients away from convergent thinking (there is only *one* cause for the present difficult situation, only *one* solution if matters are to be improved or only *one* strategy for achieving that solution) to divergent thinking. In Stage 3 of the helping process we need to encourage the client to identify and evaluate alternative strategies. We can use techniques such as brainstorming to identify different ways of achieving goals, and the chosen route may well end up comprising a combination of ideas derived from different strategies.

The force-field approach to helping clients act

Force-field analysis offers one approach to systematically searching out viable courses of action. It is a method, based on the work of Kurt Lewin, for identifying the psychological and social forces that affect a person's behaviour. If clients can be helped to define realistic problem management goals in terms of the behaviours that would be most desirable, and the behaviours that would be least desirable they will have identified the two extreme points in a force-field. Their current behaviour is likely to be somewhere in between these two points and will usually not vary very much towards one or other extreme.

Returning to the example of Kate, she may have defined her goal in terms of eating less than 1200 calories a day compared to her current consumption of 1800. Over the past few months her calorie consumption may have

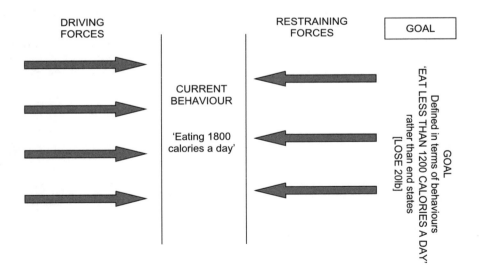

Figure 8.1 A force field

changed very little, perhaps increasing marginally but not approaching anything like the worst scenario of 2200 or the best of 1200. This equilibrium level of consumption of about 1800 is maintained by a set of driving forces (pushing for the lower level of 1200 calories) and a set of restraining forces which work against the achievement of this goal (see Figure 8.1).

These forces can be within the client; for example, Kate may eat constantly between meals because she always feels hungry. Alternatively, some forces may be part of her social environment. Her house-bound mother may express her affection for her daughter by investing a lot of her time in the preparation of elaborate meals, and Kate may feel compelled to eat them in order to avoid hurting her mother's feelings.

Both of these are examples of restraining forces that hinder the achievement of her goals. A driving force may be the desire to wear her sister's dress at a forthcoming dinner-dance but it may be too tight for her at the moment.

The force-field approach fits well with Egan's integrative approach to problem management. When clients have identified and clarified their problem in concrete terms and determined what would be a more desirable state of affairs, they can specify, again in concrete terms, one or more realistic goals. This provides the framework within which they can undertake a force-field analysis. We can encourage clients to list all the restraining forces that are keeping them from their goal and all the driving forces that are helping them reach their goal. At this stage we may encourage them to list as many forces as possible and to make no attempt to list them in order of importance.

The next step is for clients to review these two lists and identify those forces that seem to be the most important and that they might be able to do something about. When these key forces have been identified the clients can review each one in more detail. For each key restraining force, they may think about all the possible action steps they could take to reduce the effect of the force. Similarly, for each key driving force, they may think about all the possible action steps that could increase the effect of the force. At this stage it can be useful to list as many action steps as possible without worrying too much about how practical or effective they would be. The aim is to be as creative as possible. Brainstorming can sometimes help.

Having generated a wide range of ideas, the client then needs to go over them again to identify those which seem most promising, bearing in mind such practical considerations as the availability of people, time and other resources. It is very important, at this stage, that we do not impose our own values. Client commitment to the action plan is crucial, and therefore clients must select action steps that are in keeping with their own values.

The final phase of the force-field approach involves reviewing the chosen action steps from the point of view of how they may be brought together to fit into a comprehensive and workable action plan. It may be necessary to modify or eliminate items that do not fit in with the overall plans. It may also be necessary to add new steps that will round out the plan.

Sharing the helping model with clients

Egan (1998) values the theorising approach to helping. Not only does he present his model as a cognitive map to give direction to helpers when they are interacting with clients. He also believes that clients should be told as much about the model as they can assimilate on the grounds that they, like the helper, will also have a cognitive map that will give them a sense of direction. If they know where they are going they will get there faster.

Blake and Mouton (1986) offer support for this view. The theorising approach facilitates the identification, by clients, of their own self-defeating patterns of behaviour and the identification of possibilities for replacing them with more effective theory-indicated ways of behaving. Blake and Mouton argue that theory can help clients change their behaviour in a number of ways. It offers them a *sense of perspective* that can motivate them to think through the longer-term implications of what they do. This often causes them to reassess the efficacy of their normal, possibly impulsive ways of responding. Theory can also affect *motivation*. It offers a model of excellence that clients may aspire to reach. It can also have an effect on *creativity* in that clients may become more curious about what they observe and more imaginative in their search for solutions. Finally, it has implications for *autonomy* insofar as theory increases the clients' capacity for self-direction.

Helping skills

The focus of attention, so far, has been on helping style and the stages of the helping relationship.

Helping skills are not a special set of skills reserved exclusively for the helping relationship. Helping involves the appropriate use of a wide range of 'everyday and commonly used' interpersonal skills. Hayes (1996) identifies some of the most important as:

- self-awareness (see Chapter 3);
- establishing rapport and building relationships (see Chapter 6);
- empathy (see Chapter 4);
- listening to facts and feelings (see Chapters 4 and 5);
- probing for information (see Chapter 6);
- identifying themes and seeing the bigger picture (see Chapter 4);
- giving feedback;
- challenging assumptions.

Many of these skills have already been considered in earlier chapters. In the final section of this chapter special attention will be given to four skills: empathy, probing, giving feedback and challenging. Attention will also be given to the core values that can have a critical impact on the quality of the helping relationship.

Empathy

Empathy is an essential skill that builds upon the basic skills discussed elsewhere in this book. It involves us in letting clients know that they have been understood from within their own frame of reference and that we can see the world as they see it while remaining separate from it. As noted in Chapters 4 and 5, this involves us in attending, observing and listening to both verbal and non-verbal messages. The client's non-verbal behaviour can be a rich source of data, especially about feelings. However, while these listening skills facilitate understanding, empathy is achieved only when we communicate this understanding to the client. This can be achieved if we:

- respond to what has been said;
- reflect back to the client what it is that we believe the client is thinking and feeling;
- attend carefully to the cues given off by the client which either confirm or deny the accuracy of these responses.

Empathy is a core relationship-building skill. Egan suggests that clients who feel that they have been understood feel encouraged to move on and to explore their problems in greater depth.

Exercise 8.3 is useful in observing the extent to which people show empathy when dealing with others. It is all too easy to deny other people's feelings, to belittle their problem.

Exercise 8.3 Empathic listening

- *Observe others.* Note how often others take the time to engage in empathic listening and try to assess what this does to the quality of the relationship.
- *Monitor your own behaviour.* Without changing the way you normally behave, note how often you communicate empathic understanding.
- *Experiment with new behaviour.* Consciously change your behaviour. Work at increasing the number of times you show empathy and observe the effect it has on others.

People tend to open up when they feel understood; they become less defensive. They not only reveal more of themselves to others but, in the process, often find out more about themselves. The very process of talking openly helps them to reappraise their position.

Blake and Mouton (1986) suggest that a person's ability to deal with a problem can be adversely affected if they exclude intense emotional reactions from conscious awareness. Talking to an empathic listener can help clients get in touch with and work through these repressed reactions, thus enabling them to take a more objective view of their problem.

Probing

Probing has been discussed in Chapter 6. We can use probes to help clients explore their problem. Non-directive probes and minimal prompts such as attentive silences, 'and...' or 'tell me more' can be used to encourage clients to talk and tell their story. Directive probes such as 'How did you feel?' or 'What did you do?' can also help clients clarify their thoughts and think about the problem in more specific terms.

Unless clients think about their problems in concrete, operational terms it can be difficult to develop an effective problem-management strategy. People are being concrete in their self-exploration when they identify and talk about specific experiences, behaviours and feelings that are relevant to their problem. An example of a vague or non-concrete statement may be: 'I'm not too happy about things at the moment.' A more concrete statement from the same client may be:

> 'I took up the company's offer of having my own computer and using it to work from home. Sometimes, when I'm working alone (*experience*) I begin to feel quite lonely (*feeling*). I know the feeling will pass but it makes me restless.'

An even more concrete statement may be:

> 'Sometimes, when I'm working at home alone (*experience*), I begin to feel quite lonely (*feeling*). I even begin to think I don't have any friends – although I know this isn't the case. I begin to feel sorry for myself (*additional feelings*). Finally it gets to me so much that I get up and go to the pub (*behaviour*), not to drink my sorrows away but just to be with people.'

The last statement not only includes more information about feelings, it also describes what behaviour occurred as a consequence. We can assist clients to be more concrete by encouraging them to talk, thus increasing the chance that more concrete data will be revealed, and by probing to seek clarification.

Egan (1998) offers six suggestions for the use of probes:

1 Keep in mind the purpose of probing, which is to help clients tell their stories, to help them focus on relevant and important issues and to help them identify experiences, behaviours and feelings that give a fuller picture of the problem.
2 Use a mix of directive and non-directive probes.
3 Avoid question-and-answer sessions (see Chapter 4).
4 If a probe helps a client reveal relevant information, follow it up with an empathetic response rather than another probe.
5 Use whatever mixture of empathy and probing is needed to help clients clarify problems, identify blind spots, develop new scenarios, search for action strategies, formulate plans and review outcomes of action.
6 Remember that probing is a communication skill that is only effective to the degree that it helps the client.

Giving feedback

Clients' ability to manage their own problems can be fettered by limited or incorrect perceptions, especially about themselves and their relations with others. Feedback that offers clients new information about themselves can help them develop alternative perspectives on problems.

The Johari Window is a model developed by two American psychologists, Joseph Luft and Harry Ingham (see Luft 1970), which can be used to illustrate the process of giving feedback. An adaptation of this model is shown in Figure 8.2. The client's view of self is represented by the vertical columns and the helper's view of the client by the horizontal rows.

The client's view of self

People never know everything about themselves. The left-hand column represents what they know.

- The upper pane, referred to as the *open area*, depicts that knowledge about the self that the client is either willing to or cannot avoid sharing with others, including the helper.
- The lower pane, referred to as the *façade* or hidden area, depicts that knowledge about self that the client would prefer not to share and therefore attempts to keep hidden from the helper.

As respect and trust develop between helpers and clients the clients may be willing to reveal more of what they initially attempted to keep hidden. Façades may be dropped and real concerns discussed more openly. In terms

185

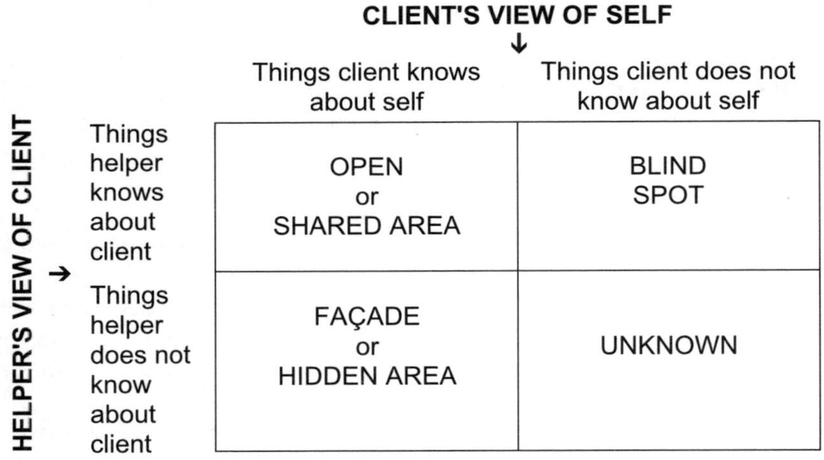

CLIENT'S VIEW OF SELF
↓

		Things client knows about self	Things client does not know about self
HELPER'S VIEW OF CLIENT →	Things helper knows about client	OPEN or SHARED AREA	BLIND SPOT
	Things helper does not know about client	FAÇADE or HIDDEN AREA	UNKNOWN

Figure 8.2 The helping relationship.

of the Johari Window, clients begin to behave in ways that increase the open area and reduce the hidden area.

The right-hand column represents what the client does not know about self. This column contains two panes – the blind spot and the unknown – which will be discussed in more detail above.

The helper's view of the client

What we do or do not know about the client is represented by the rows in Figure 8.2. The bottom row depicts what the helper does not know about the client.

- The bottom left-hand pane (the façade or hidden area) can only be reduced when the client decides to share more information with the helper. However, we can facilitate this process by behaving towards clients in ways that help them tell their story. All the relationship building, exploring, and clarifying skills that are directly or indirectly referred to in this chapter can help achieve this end.
- The bottom right-hand pane, the *unknown*, depicts that knowledge which has not yet been discovered by either client or helper. It was noted earlier that a supportive relationship in which we show empathy towards clients can sometimes enable them to access information, such as previously repressed emotional reactions, that can help them better understand the issues they are trying to deal with.

The top row of the Johari Window represents what the helper knows about the client.

- The top left-hand pane, already referred to, depicts that knowledge which is shared by helper and client.
- The top right-hand pane, the *blind spot*, depicts information which we know about the clients but which the clients do not know about themselves. We may have obtained this information in a number of ways: by observing clients' behaviour, by paying careful attention to all they say, and by searching for and identifying underlying themes, and sometimes by reference to external sources of data such as reports from customers, colleagues, etc.

By offering clients feedback we are disclosing to clients information about themselves to which they may otherwise not have access. In other words, we are revealing to clients information about their blind spots.

Not all feedback is helpful

Given inappropriately, feedback can damage the helping relationship and undermine clients' confidence in their own ability to manage problems effectively. What follows is a set of guidelines for the provision of helpful feedback.

1 *Helpful feedback is descriptive, not judgemental.* To be told that 'You are an arrogant bully' is less helpful than to be informed that: 'Whenever you and I discuss this kind of issue I am left with the feeling that you don't listen to my views and that you attempt to get your way by threatening me.'

   The first example is evaluative: the helper is making a judgement about the client's behaviour. The second example is more descriptive. It describes the effect the client's behaviour had on the helper, which may have been precisely the effect the client wanted. The client may have decided that the best way to influence the other was to issue threats. However, this may not have been the intention, and the feedback may alert the client to important unanticipated consequences of the behaviour.

2 *Helpful feedback is specific, not general.* To be told: 'You never seem to be able to communicate effectively in groups' offers clients few clues about what they might do differently to improve matters. On the other hand, to be told that: 'When you were presenting your case to the group last Thursday you spoke so quickly that I couldn't grasp all the points you were trying to make' provides clients with information that is sufficiently specific for them to determine how they may change their

behaviour if they want to obtain a different outcome at the next meeting.

3   *Helpful feedback is relevant to the needs of the client.* We need to be aware of whose needs we are trying to satisfy when we offer feedback. Sometimes feedback does more for the helper than the client. For example, an angry outburst may help relieve our frustrations but do little for the client. Similarly, the provision of sensitive feedback in public may do more to confirm our superiority than to boost the confidence of the client.

4   *Helpful feedback is solicited rather than imposed.* People seek feedback in many circumstances. However, while they may 'want to know' they may be fearful of finding out. We need to be sensitive to those cues that indicate whether the other person is seeking feedback and to those cues which signal when they have received as much as they can cope with for the time being. Pushing too hard, and continuing to give feedback to people who have already been given as much as they can cope with, can trigger a defensive reaction. It can lead to the client dismissing or ignoring further feedback. People tend to be much less receptive to feedback which they feel is imposed than to that which they have sought out for themselves.

5   *Helpful feedback is timely and in context.* Feedback is best given in the context in which the behaviour to which the feedback refers took place, and as soon after the behaviour as possible. The introduction of formalised appraisal systems sometimes encourages helpers to store up feedback for the appraisal interview when it would have been much more effective if it had been offered at the time the problem was observed by the helper. However, accurate behavioural records such as audio- or videotape-recordings can extend considerably the period over which the feedback is timely; these methods also preserve much of the context and therefore are particularly valuable in training situations.

6   *Helpful feedback is usable and concerned with behaviour over which the client is able to exercise control.* Feedback can improve clients' knowledge of how they typically behave and the effects their behaviour has on others. However, feedback can only help clients secure desired outcomes if it focuses on behaviour they can do something about. To tell clients who have a severe stutter that they are making you impatient, and that they should be quick and say what they have to say or shut up, is unlikely to afford much help.

7   *Feedback can only be helpful when it has been heard and understood.* If in doubt, we need to check with the client to ensure that the feedback has been received and understood.

Exercise 8.4 uses these guidelines to provide a three-step process for developing feedback skills.

Exercise 8.4 Giving feedback

This exercise involves a three-step approach to the development of feedback skills:

1   *Observing others.* The first step involves observing what others do when giving feedback, and thinking about what they could do differently to provide feedback more effectively. One important aim of this step is to practise observing the extent to which the providers of feedback behave in accordance with the guidelines for effective feedback presented in this chapter. Another is to establish a bench-mark of good practice.

2   *Monitoring self.* The second step involves using these observation skills to monitor and assess how you give feedback and to identify what you could do differently to improve the effectiveness of the feedback you give to others.

3   *Experimenting with new behaviours.* The third step involves identifying and taking action to improve the way you behave when giving feedback to others.

Step 1: Observing other people giving feedback

Accurate observation is more difficult when you are actively involved in giving or receiving feedback, so start by observing others. The feedback observation record presented below can provide a useful framework for recording your observations.

FEEDBACK OBSERVATION RECORD

Assess the feedback on each of the following seven dimensions:

Descriptive		Judgemental
Specific		General
Relevant to client's needs		Irrelevant to client's needs
Focused on behaviour client can control		Focused on behaviour client cannot control

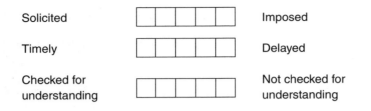

Solicited		Imposed
Timely		Delayed
Checked for understanding		Not checked for understanding

Step 2: assessing your own approach to giving feedback and identifying possible improvements

This step involves opening a 'second channel' and using your observation skills to observe yourself. Do *not* deliberately try to change your approach to giving feedback at this point. The aim of this step of the exercise is to increase your awareness of how you normally go about giving feedback to others.

Use the same approach to observing and assessing your own behaviour as you used in the first step of this exercise when you were observing others. Record your observations of your own behaviour when giving feedback on a second copy of the feedback observation record.

When you have collected sufficient information to identify your typical approach to giving feedback, compare how you behave with the recommendations presented in this chapter (and reflected by the content of the left-hand column of the feedback observation record).

- How satisfied are you with your approach to giving feedback?
- Does your feedback normally produce the outcome you intended it to produce?
- Could you improve the way you go about giving feedback in order to make it more helpful for those receiving it?

Step 3: Taking action to improve the feedback you give to others

This stage involves attending to those aspects of your own behaviour where you feel there is scope for improvement. Identify what you want to do differently and find opportunities to practise the new way of behaving.

Monitor the effects of these changes. Are you able to detect any differences in the way the other party responds to you? How do you feel about the new approach?

Make a note of the outcome of your efforts to improve your approach to providing feedback.

Challenging

The goal of challenging or confronting in the helping relationship is to help clients explore those areas of experience, feeling and behaviour that they have so far failed to explore. Blake and Mouton (1986) suggest that confrontational interventions can be among the most effective in reducing the efficacy of defence mechanisms. By challenging clients, we can persuade them to face up to contradictions between what they say and do or between how they see themselves and the way others see them.

We may also challenge clients because we suspect that they distort reality and use these distortions to avoid facing up to things. For example, a client may view a subordinate's application for a better job as disloyalty rather than as a timely and appropriate career move, or a client may disguise (even from self) the fear of change. The fear of change may be rationalised as a commitment to a well-tried and effective way of doing things.

Egan (1998) suggests that, in its simplest form, a confrontation is an invitation. An invitation to examine some form of behaviour that seems to be self-defeating, harmful or both, and an invitation to change that behaviour if it is found to be so. Effective challenges are never punitive accusations. They are invitations to explore contradictions and distortions, or invitations to identify and employ unused strengths and resources. The term 'invitation' cannot be emphasised too strongly. The client who experiences the challenge as a shameful unmasking or some other form of attack will not be receptive to the alternative perspective that the challenge may offer. A likely outcome is that clients who feel under attack will direct their energy towards a defensive action and possibly a counter-attack aimed at discrediting the 'helper'.

Consider how you might react to the following challenges:

- 'Why don't you start being honest. You feel so sorry for yourself most of the time that you never even give a thought to the possibility that you might be the cause of most of your own problems. You mope around and never face up to things. Grow up!'
- 'Let me check something out with you. You say that you have been feeling very low because everything seems to be going wrong. You also indicate that there is nothing you can do to change things. Now I'm not sure about this. From what I've observed you appear to behave as if you believe that you can't change things and therefore you don't even try, even in circumstances where you could. For example, you didn't even try to make a case for an increase to your budget at the last managers' meeting. You seem to blame others for your problems but do nothing to change things. Does this make sense to you?'

The second challenge was based on what the client had said and on what the helper had observed. It started by acknowledging the client's point of view, thus signalling that the client was understood and that the helper was 'with' rather than against the client. It was specific and offered examples. It was also presented tentatively. The phrases 'Now I'm not sure about this' and 'Does this make sense to you?' offered the client the options of accepting, modifying or even rejecting the confrontation without feeling accused by the helper.

Helpful challenges are those which encourage the client to seek greater self-understanding. As well as being based on accurate empathy and presented tentatively, they must also be made when the client is in a fit state to respond. To paraphrase Egan, a confused and disorganised client may be further disoriented by a challenge that adds to the confusion. Exercise 8.5 is designed to help you develop your challenging skills.

Exercise 8.5 Constructive confronting

Follow the same format as used for Exercise 8.4.

1   ***Observe others when they are confronting and challenging.*** The first step involves observing what others do when challenging others.
    - Use the confronting observation record form presented below to record your observations.
    - Think about what they could do differently to confront and challenge others more effectively.

One important aim of this step of the exercise is to practise observing the extent to which confronters behave in accordance with the guidelines for effective challenges presented in this chapter. Another is to establish a bench-mark of good practice.

CONFRONTING OBSERVATION RECORD

Based on accurate empathy   YES ☐☐☐☐ NO

Specific (illustrated with specific examples)   YES ☐☐☐☐ NO

Offered tentatively (providing the   YES ☐☐☐☐ NO
opportunity for discussion, even rejection)

Supportive (made in circumstances where   YES ☐☐☐☐ NO
the person confronted is unlikely to feel
humiliated or defensive)

---

2   ***Monitor self***. The second step involves using these observation skills to monitor and assess how you confront others and to identify what you could do differently to improve the effectiveness of your confrontations.

Do *not* deliberately try to change your approach to confronting at this point. The aim of this step of the exercise is to increase your awareness of how you normally go about confronting others.

Use the confronting observation record form to record your observations.

3   ***Experiment with new behaviours***. The third step involves identifying and taking action to improve the way you behave when confronting others. Identify what you want to do differently and find opportunities to practise the new way of behaving.

Core values

The behaviour of effective helpers appears to be influenced by certain core values. Rogers (1958) identified these as unconditional positive regard for the client (i.e. respect) and genuineness.

Respect

Egan (1998) and Reddy (1987) elaborate the core value of unconditional positive regard or respect to include:

- *Being 'for' the client.* This involves helpers behaving in a manner that indicates that they are 'with' or 'for' the client in a non-sentimental, caring way. If clients feel that we might be against them they are unlikely to put their trust in us or reveal anxieties, weaknesses or specific information that they fear could be used against them.
- *Signalling that the other's viewpoint is worth listening to.* This reflects the helpers' willingness to commit themselves to working with the clients. It also suggests a minimum level of openness to the other's point of view. Without this openness, empathic listening is impossible. Too often, even when we go through the motions of asking the other for their viewpoint, we are not really committed to listening. For example, parents, before visiting their wrath upon a child who has been seen to behave inappropriately, may ask for an explanation of the child's

behaviour. However, although they asked, they may not really expect to receive a satisfactory explanation, and therefore may not prepare themselves to listen. The effective helper needs to respect the client's point of view and to clearly signal this respect if the client is to be encouraged to work with the helper.

- *Suspending critical judgement.* We need to keep an open mind and avoid reaching premature conclusions. This does not mean that helpers should signal approval of everything they hear or observe. An effective response is to communicate that we understand the client's point of view. Reddy (1987) suggests that communicating understanding in this way can help clients change. Rather than making judgements and pushing clients into a position they may resist, the act of suspending judgement (and trying to understand the other's viewpoint) can encourage them to explore their position and give them the freedom to change their viewpoint. According to Reddy, suspending judgement and keeping an open mind does not come naturally. He argues that we have been conditioned to persuade others to our point of view. At school, there is nearly always a debating society but rarely a listening club. It may be that we often fail to keep an open mind because if we listen we may end up agreeing, and if we agree we may appear to have lost. However, the aim of the helping relationship is not to win. Suspending judgement encourages clients to believe that we are 'for' them and have their interests at heart.
- *Working with the client as a unique individual.* This involves being willing to support each client in his or her uniqueness and not relating to them as just another 'case'. It requires the helper to personalise the helping process and tailor it to the needs, capabilities and resources of each client.
- *Respecting clients' right to determine their own fate.* The role of the helper in the collaborative helping relationship is to help clients develop a sense of agency or self-efficacy rather than to promote a state of dependency and a feeling of helplessness. This implies an attitude, on your part, that clients have the necessary resources to manage their own problems more effectively. The helper's role is to facilitate the development of these resources. It is not our role to take over clients' problems and prescribe solutions. If clients opt for courses of action that, in our opinion, will not offer the best way forward, we may encourage them to re-examine their chosen solution. Ultimately, however, we must respect their right to determine their own fate.
- *Assuming the client is committed to the goal of managing problems more effectively.* It has already been noted that some clients may not have referred themselves for help. They may therefore engage in the helping relationship with some reluctance. However, their initial reluctance to work with the helper does not necessarily imply that they are

not committed to finding ways of managing their problems more effectively. Egan (1998) suggests that respectful helpers will assume the client's goodwill and will continue to work with the client until this assumption has been clearly demonstrated to be false. Clients who recognise that we respect them and are oriented to their needs are more likely to engage positively in the helping relationship than clients who observe little evidence of any respect.

Genuineness

Genuineness is important in the helping relationship. If respect for the client is faked, and if such attitudes as openness and interest in the client are not genuine, there is a high probability that this will be detected by the client and that it will seriously damage or even destroy the helping relationship. Being genuine involves being honest, sincere and without façade. It involves a refusal to take on a stylised helper role. Egan (1998) defines it as a value that can be expressed as a set of behaviours that include being oneself, being open, spontaneous, assertive and consistent.

Exercise 8.6 Monitoring core values

Next time you are involved in a helping relationship, observe yourself. Open up a second channel and monitor what you are *thinking* when you are relating to the client. Consider what this tells you about your values.

- Are you able to suspend critical judgement?
- Do you believe that the client's point of view is worth listening to?
- Is what you are saying and thinking consistent with the value that clients have the right to determine their own fate?

Developing helping skills

In this chapter, reference has been made to almost all of the skills discussed in previous chapters. Exercise 8.1, presented at the beginning of this chapter, is designed to help you identify and critically appraise your typical approach to helping. Exercise 8.2 is designed to help you reflect on your own experience in order to identify good practice. Exercises 8.3, 8.4, 8.5 and 8.6 are designed to help you develop specific aspects of your helping style, and Exercise 8.7 is designed to provide an opportunity to practise and receive feedback on your helping skills.

Exercise 8.7 Exercise consultation

Aims

- To provide an opportunity for you to assume the role of helper and apply the three-stage problem management model to a real problem situation.
- To provide you with feedback (from both a client and an observer) on your helping style. You can compare this feedback with your own assessment of your style (as reflected in your scores for Exercise 8.1).
- To provide you with an opportunity to identify behaviours that contributed to or undermined the effectiveness of the helping process by observing other people engaged in a helping relationship.
- Provide an opportunity for you to receive help with a 'hot' problem.

Overview

This exercise involves working in groups of three. In each group there is a client, a consultant and an observer. The consultant's role is to help the client manage his or her problem more effectively. The process is watched by an observer who, at the end of the consulting session, provides feedback to the consultant and client. This cycle is repeated three times so that everybody has the opportunity to take the role of consultant, client and observer.

Preparation

In order to prepare to play the role of client, identify a problem that you feel you need to manage more effectively. You will be asked to present this problem to others. They will work with you to help you identify what you might do to improve the current state of affairs. For the purpose of this exercise, think about a problem that directly involves you and that you have a responsibility for doing something about. It should be a 'hot' problem; that is, it should be a problem that is important and, as yet, unresolved. Do not think about a problem that has already been satisfactorily resolved or one that you are not in a position to do anything about.

Observation check-list

Did the consultant appear to be guided by the three-stage model of helping?

1   Identifying and clarifying the problem

Was it possible to distinguish between the 'inward' and 'outward' journeys? Did the consultant attempt to view the problem from within the client's own frame of reference (empathise) before attempting to persuade the client to consider alternative ways of framing the problem?

Did the consultant behave in ways that helped the client:

- *Own the problem?* (Indicated by a recognition that the client will have to take action to resolve it.)
- *State the problem concretely?* (The more concretely the problem is presented the easier it will be to identify concrete, achievable goals.)
- *Break the problem down into manageable units?* (Especially if the problem is too large or too complex to be tackled in one go.)

2   Goal setting

Did the consultant behave in ways that helped the client:

- *Identify priorities?* (There are often some aspects of the problem that are more pressing than others.)
- *Generate more than one possible outcome?* (There is a natural tendency to lock on to the first acceptable goal rather than to invest a little more time in exploring other possibilities.)
- *Carefully consider the criteria to use when selecting which goals to pursue?*

3   Action planning

Did the consultant help the client:

- Gather information about factors that might obstruct or facilitate change?
- Identify possible action steps?
- Review the most promising action steps and formulate an action plan?

How did your observation of the consultant's helping style compare with the consultant's score on the helping style profile?

(*Note*: helpers often find that they are inclined to be more prescriptive and give clients more advice than suggested by their score on the helping style profile.)

Suggested timing

Round 1: 35 minutes

The first 30 minutes is for the consultation exercise

The final 5 minutes is for feedback and discussion. The observer will be the first to provide feedback, but the client may also have some useful observations to make on the consultant's helping style.

Round 2: 35 minutes

Allocated as for Round 1.

Round 3: 35 minutes

Allocated as for Round 1.

Round 3: 35 minutes

Allocated as for Round 1.

Review within groups: 10 minutes

Each group should appoint a spokesperson to summarise the key learning points in a plenary review session. (*Note*: it is not necessary for the presenters to refer to the content of the problems discussed. The focus of attention should be what you have learned about your approach to helping.)

Plenary review: 15+ minutes

Time required for the plenary review will be determined by the number of groups reporting back.

Summary

Different approaches to helping have been reviewed and some of the factors that can affect the efficacy of different helping styles have been considered. A three-stage model of helping has been discussed. The first stage of the model is concerned with identifying and clarifying problems and unused opportunities, the second with goal setting and the third with action planning.

This chapter draws heavily on some of the basic interpersonal skills discussed in earlier chapters, and highlights four skills that are particularly relevant in the context of helping relationships. These are empathy, probing, feedback and challenging. The importance of two core values, respect and genuineness, have also been discussed in the context of their impact on the helping relationship.

References

Abramson, L.Y., Seligman, M.E.P. and Teesdale, J. D. (1978) 'Learned helplessness in humans: critique and performulations', *Journal of Abnormal Psychology* 87 (1): 49–74.

Blake, R.R. and Mouton, J.S. (1986) *Consultation: A Handbook for Individual and Organization Development*, Reading, MA: Addison-Wesley.

Egan, G. (1998) *The Skilled Helper: A Systematic Approach to Effective Helping*, Belmont, CA: Wadsworth.

Ellis, A. (1977) 'The basic clinical theory of rational-emotive therapy', in A. Ellis and G. Grieger (eds) *Handbook of Rational-Emotive Therapy*, Monterey, CA: Brooke/Cole.

Hayes, J. (1996) *Developing the Manager as a Helper*, London: Routledge/Thomson Business.

Hiroto, D.S. (1974) 'Locus of control and learned helplessness', *Journal of Experimental Psychology*, 102: 187–193.

Hopson, B. (1984) 'Counselling and helping', in C. Cooper and P. Makin (eds) *Psychology for Managers*, Leicester: British Psychological Society.

Lewin, K. (1951) *Field Theory in Social Science*, New York: Harper & Row.

Locke, E.A. and Latham, G.P. (1984) *Goal Setting: A Motivational Technique that Works*, Englewood Cliffs, NJ: Prentice Hall.

Luft, J. (1970) *Group Processes: An Introduction to Group Dynamics*, Palo Alto, CA: National Press Books.

Reddy, M. (1987) *The Manager's Guide to Counselling at Work*, London: British Psychological Society/Methuen.

Rogers, C.R. (1958). 'The characteristics of a helping relationship', *Personnel and Guidance Journal* 37: 6–16.

Seligman, M.E.P. (1975) *Helplessness*, San Francisco, CA: W.H. Freeman.

Steele, F.I. (1969) 'Consultants and detectives', *Journal of Applied Behavioural Science* 5 (2): 193–194.

Strong, S.R. (1968), 'Counselling: an interpersonal influence process', *Journal of Counselling Psychology* 15: 215–224.

9

ASSERTING AND INFLUENCING

Learning objectives

To understand the nature of assertive behaviour, identify those situations where asserting can help an individual achieve desired outcomes, and to be able to conceptualise influencing as a political process.

After reading this chapter you will:

- Be able to distinguish between assertive, non-assertive and aggressive behaviour.
- Understand why some people do not assert themselves.
- Recognise the characteristics of effective assertion messages in terms of content.
- Recognise the characteristics of effective assertion messages in terms of non-verbal behaviours.
- Recognise the characteristics of effective assertion messages in terms of social interaction skills such as escalation, persistence and the management of defensive reactions.
- Be aware of the risks associated with asserting.
- Understand what you can do to improve your ability to assert yourself and influence others.
- Know how to assess your power and ability to influence others in different situations.
- Identify the steps you can take to minimise your dependence on others and limit their ability to influence you.
- Identify the steps you can take to increase others' dependence on you and increase your power to influence their behaviour.

Influencing others

Many people working in organisations experience problems when attempting to influence others. Sometimes the source of difficulty is perceived to be rooted in a particular relationship and sometimes it is experienced as a more general inability to exercise influence.

People react to these perceived problems in different ways. Some give up trying. They accept the impossibility of introducing any significant change and become apathetic and passive. Some respond by trying harder. They devote more energy to influencing others and achieving results, but when things do not go their way their frustrations surface in the form of abrasive and coercive behaviour. They continue to push their ideas, but they become aggressive and behave like the proverbial bull in the china shop, upsetting others and creating unnecessary resistance to their proposals. The most effective people, however, seem to be those who expect to experience resistance to their attempts to influence others and get things done. Nevertheless they keep on taking carefully selected initiatives in ways that eventually tend to produce the results they desire.

This chapter (and Chapter 10 on negotiating) attempts to identify what we can do in order to exercise more control over the outcomes available to us. Two approaches to influencing are examined.

- The first focuses on assertiveness, and examines those behaviours that help individuals stand up for their rights and communicate important messages to others.
- The second adopts a more macro perspective, and considers influencing as a political process.

Assertive and aggressive behaviour

Some people, even many of those who occupy senior positions in organisations, seem to find it difficult to influence others. They do not find it easy to ask others to do things and they seem unable to refuse requests, even unreasonable requests, others make of them. They feel powerless when it comes to bringing about a state of affairs which they desire. It is possible to identify a number of different styles of interacting with others which range along a continuum from non-assertive/submissive to aggressive (see Figure 9.1).

People who are non-assertive find it difficult to express their needs and influence others. For example, even though they may be allergic to cigarette smoke they are the kind of people who would be reluctant to tell colleagues working in the same office that their smoking makes life uncomfortable for them, and they would find it even more difficult to ask them to stop. If they ever do express their honest feelings they tend to do so in an apologetic way.

NON-ASSERTIVE   ASSERTIVE   AGGRESSIVE
SUBMISSIVE

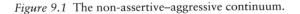

Figure 9.1 The non-assertive–aggressive continuum.

Phrases like 'but it really doesn't matter' and non-verbal behaviours such as low eye contact, soft voice and submissive postures signal to others that what has just been said is not really important. Guirdham (1995) suggests that over-submissive behaviour can lead to a person being 'trampled on', which in turn can lead to a loss of self-respect.

Assertive people express their needs and stand up for their own rights, but do so in ways that respect the rights of others. They are unlike the many non-assertive people who are so preoccupied with the need to avoid conflict that they fail to let others know where they stand on issues or what they hope to achieve. An assertive interpersonal style involves communicating clearly with others, stating one's own position in a confident manner, avoiding phrases that devalue the message and using appropriate non-verbal behaviours which signal to others that they should pay attention to the speaker's point of view.

People who adopt an aggressive style of interacting with others tend to be those who are determined to win, regardless of what happens to the other people involved. They often express their feelings and pursue their needs at the expense of others, and they fail to pay attention to what others value. In behavioural terms aggressive people tend to talk loudly, look angry and use phrases that abuse, blame or undervalue others. In the short term aggressors often win, but because they do so at the expense of others, in the longer term their aggressive style tends to foster opposition and resistance.

Guirdham (1995) argues that it is worth trying to hold a middle course and work at behaving assertively because the two extremes of behaving either submissively or aggressively typically yield undesirable outcomes over the longer term.

	Situation	Non-assertive	Assertive	Aggressive
1	If you were allergic to cigarette smoke and shared an office with a smoker, would you:	Say nothing and suffer in silence.	Tell your colleague about your allergy, explain the consequences of his smoking for you and politely ask if he would refrain from smoking in the office.	Get angry, tell him that he is inconsiderate and uncaring and demand that he stops smoking immediately.
2	If your boss asked you for help, when you were busy trying to meet an important deadline, would you:	Seethe inside but shrug your shoulders and agree to help.	Tell him about the important deadline, apologise and refuse immediate assistance but offer to help as soon as you are free.	Complain that he is always interfering and demand to be left to get on with your own work.

Figure 9.2 Ways of responding to a situation.

Think about your own interpersonal style. Consider the hypothetical situations presented in Figure 9.2 and identify the response that most closely reflects the way you would deal with each situation. Exercise 9.1 is designed to help you diagnose your interpersonal style.

Exercise 9.1 Diagnosing your interpersonal style

Think about four or five recent occasions when you wanted to change somebody else's behaviour or refuse a request. For each incident place a check-mark at the points on the non-assertive–aggressive continuum which best describes your response.

NON-ASSERTIVE	ASSERTIVE	AGGRESSIVE

Ask yourself whether the way you behaved produced the outcome you wanted and consider whether you are satisfied with your interpersonal style.

If you are able to work with others on this exercise, take turns to summarise the main features of each incident and describe how you responded (the ideal group size is three). After each incident and response has been described, the other members of the group should agree how the response should be classified. If the presenter disagrees with this classification, s/he should explain why. The process is repeated until each member of the group has had the opportunity to share four or five incidents.

The nature of assertiveness

Over the past thirty years many books and hundreds of research studies have been published on the topic of assertiveness and assertiveness training. The evidence clearly supports the view that assertion skills are related to interpersonal effectiveness in conflict situations. Schroeder *et al.* (1983) identified seven different classes of assertive response which they grouped under two headings: positive and negative expressiveness. The focus of attention here will be the conflict (or negative) assertion skills which include:

- *Expressing unpopular or different opinions*: 'I disagree with Jim's pro-posal that we should settle the pay claim at 8 per cent. I think we should hold out for a better deal.'
- *Requesting behaviour changes*: 'I feel that I am being kept in the dark when you don't keep me informed about customer complaints. From now on I would like you to provide me with a daily report.'
- *Refusing requests*: 'No, I will not change the date of your appraisal interview.'

People who are able to express their rights by using these kinds of assertive responses are more likely to influence others and achieve desired outcomes than those who are unable to assert their rights in such ways.

One reason why some people do not assert themselves, and therefore find it difficult to influence others is because they have a strong need for approval and acceptance, and fear that if they stand up for their rights others may reject them. Consequently they are reluctant to refuse requests, express unpopular opinions or request behaviour changes. Assertive behaviour is not without risks. It may be necessary to chance dissension and accept some level of conflict if established relationships are to be changed and the assertor is to become more influential. However, these risks can be minimised if the people who want to stand up for their rights and influence others have a well-developed set of asserting skills.

Assertion skills

The skills of asserting can be grouped under three headings:

1 Content skills – what the assertor says.
2 Non-verbal skills – how the assertor looks and sounds.
3 Social interaction skills – the way the assertor behaves in the process of the interaction including escalating, persistence and the management of defensive reactions.

Content skills

Effective assertion messages tend to be *brief and direct* statements. Rambling, non-specific or ambiguous responses are much less effective because they are open to misinterpretation. It has been found that the more assertion messages are elaborated, the greater the danger that side issues will intrude and undermine the impact of the message.

Effective assertion messages are also *respectful*. They express our con-cerns without blaming or attacking others. Respectful messages are more effective because the non-judgemental statements they contain are less likely to elicit a defensive reaction. Other people are more likely to receive our assertion as a new input that offers a different perspective on the reasonableness of their requests or on the consequences of their behaviour rather than as an attack. These new inputs may encourage the recipients to re-evaluate their behaviour and may motivate them to take steps to modify their relationship with us.

If we assert our rights without paying attention to the rights of others, we are more likely to encourage resistance and we increase the risk of damaging our relationships with others. According to Rakos (1997), the assertive expression of rights is more effective when it is presented as part of a process which involves a chain of behaviours, some preceding and some following the actual assertion. He argues that prior to emitting an assertion we should engage in whatever behaviours may be necessary to determine the rights of the other people involved, and we should develop a verbal and non-verbal response repertoire which will enable us to influence others' offending behaviour without evaluating their 'worth' . We should also consider all the potential negative consequences others might experience as a result of our assertive response. He suggests that after emitting the assertive response we should elaborate our assertion in a way that makes it more acceptable to others.

A review of the literature led Rakos (1997) to suggest a number of ways in which standard assertive messages can be elaborated and made more acceptable without undermining their potency. They include:

- *Offering a non-defensive, honest explanation of the need to assert oneself*: 'I cannot change the date of your appraisal interview because I have to visit the factory in Germany next week.'
- *Offering an empathic statement which recognises the effects on other parties*: 'I cannot change the date of your appraisal interview. I know you will be disappointed because you have been invited to attend the project review meeting.'
- *Offering a short apology for the consequences*: 'I cannot change the date of your appraisal interview. I'm sorry because I know it will mean that you will have to miss the project review meeting.'
- *Attempting to identify a mutually acceptable compromise*: 'I cannot change the date or time of your appraisal interview, but would you like me to ask Graham if he could start the project review meeting in the morning?'
- *Praising or offering another positive comment directed towards the other person*: 'Graham told me that he had invited you to the project review meeting because of the contribution you made towards getting the project back on schedule. I'm sorry I cannot change the date of your appraisal interview.'

Developing a verbal response repertoire

Many people are unable to assert themselves because they find it difficult to formulate appropriate assertive responses. In conflict situations they feel under pressure and cannot think what to say. As a result they either say little or nothing and engage in flight behaviour, or they let their frustrations and anger get the better of them, become aggressive and engage in fight behaviour.

Anticipating the need to assert and preparing appropriate assertion messages can help us overcome these problems. Bolton (1986) offers a simple formula for constructing assertion messages that can be very effective in those circumstances where the assertor desires to change the behaviour of another. He suggests that assertive responses should include a non-blaming description of the behaviour that is being confronted, a disclosure of the assertor's feelings and a clarification of the tangible effect the other's behaviour has on the assertor. It is similar to the first approach suggested by Rakos, which involves the provision of a non-defensive explanation. This formula takes the following form:

- *When you* (a non-evaluative description of the other's behaviour)
- *I feel* (disclosure of assertor's feelings)
- *Because* (clarification of effect).

Although this three-part assertion message formula may seem rather mechanistic and its structure may not be appropriate for all situations, it has been found that using it for planning, writing down and assessing the likely impact of alternative assertion messages can help people develop their assertive response repertoire. This kind of practice makes it more likely that when assertors eventually confront another, even though they may be under pressure, they will speak with precision and convey precisely the meaning they want to convey.

Describing the other's behaviour

Some of the issues that we might need to pay attention to when formulating non-evaluative descriptions of behaviour have already been mentioned. Writing them down can help us differentiate between direct respectful responses such as: 'When you are late for project review meetings . . .', and fuzzy, imprecise and judgemental responses such as: 'When you are selfish and waste others' time . . .'

Disclosure of feelings

Writing down how we feel about others' behaviour can help us formulate statements that accurately communicate our feelings. Bolton argues that the

Behaviour description	Disclosure of feelings	Tangible effects
When you are late for project review meetings	I feel frustrated	Because my time, and that of others, is wasted while we wait for you
When you make last-minute changes to production targets	I feel *very* annoyed	Because I have to work late and do not see my children before they go to bed

Figure 9.3 Three-part assertion messages.

genuine disclosure of feelings can increase the potency of assertions by making the recipients aware of how we feel about their requests or behaviours. However, he cautions against over- or understating feelings. If we feign stronger emotions in the hope that they will be more convincing, our pretence may be detected, thus undermining our efforts to influence others. On the other hand, understating the intensity of our feelings will deprive others of important data that could motivate them to change their behaviour.

Clarifying effect

Bolton also argues that if we can convince others that their attitudes or behaviour have concrete and tangible effects (e.g. as unnecessarily costing us money, harming our possessions, consuming our time, causing us extra work, endangering our jobs and/or interfering with our effectiveness), the probability of change will be even greater. Figure 9.3 offers some examples of the kind of three-part assertion message advocated by Bolton.

Non-verbal skills

The potency of an assertive response can be influenced by paralinguistic characteristics such as volume, firmness of delivery and inflection, and non-verbal behaviours such as facial expression, eye contact, gestures and posture.

Rakos (1997) summarises some of the main results of research on the paralinguistic components of assertive communication. Findings indicate that:

- Assertive people speak louder than non-assertive people but not as loud as aggressive people. Rakos refers to a study by Rose and Tryon which suggests that non-assertive people speak at a level of 68dB, assertive at 76dB and aggressive at 84dB.

- Laypeople, when asked to judge whether others are assertive, point to the importance of inflection as well as volume. While the research evidence presents a fairly complex picture on this, there does seem to be agreement that intermediate levels of inflection are associated with greater impact. Inflection can be used to direct the listener's attention to important parts of the assertive communication.
- Firmness of delivery is another paralinguistic characteristic associated with assertiveness. Although the research evidence suggests that both assertive and non-assertive individuals can exhibit voice firmness, it appears that the absence of firmness can detract from the impact of an assertion.

Rakos also reports that even though many assume that speed of response, duration of response and response fluency are important characteristics of assertive communication, the research evidence regarding the effect of these variables is inconclusive. For example, one view is that non-assertive individuals have a greater tendency to offer long explanations, excuses and apologies. However, empathic assertions (which can be very effective) typically include elaborate verbalisations.

Research on facial expression (see e.g. McFall *et al.* 1982; Kolotkin *et al.* 1984) points to the importance of mouth, eyebrow and forehead cues. It has been found that an uncontrolled fidgety mouth, wrinkled forehead and constantly moving eyebrows undermines the potency of an assertive response. Eye contact is also important. While assertive people tend to engage in more eye contact than non-assertive people, this contact, especially when the assertor is talking, tends to be intermittent. As noted in Chapter 5, the fixed stare tends to be associated with aggressive behaviour.

Rakos (1997) reports that gestures and body posture have been found to enhance the impact of assertive responses. With reference to gestures, he cites McFall *et al.* (1982), who note that extraneous or restrained movements tend to undermine impact, whereas smooth and steady arm movements while speaking, and inconspicuous, non-fidgety gestures while listening, increase the impact of assertion messages. With reference to posture, he notes that while experts tend to discount its importance, laypeople consider it significant. Effective assertors tend to adopt upright torso positions and face others squarely. It appears that stooped or hunched posture and shrugging and squirming movements seriously undermine the impact of any attempt to be assertive.

Social interaction skills

Under this heading special attention is given to three aspects of asserting: escalation, persistence and the management of defensive reactions.

Escalation

Rimms and Masters (1987) suggest that the initial assertion should be what they refer to as 'the minimal effective response' (MER). Common sense supports this view. The aim of the assertive response is to encourage others to reassess the reasonableness of their behaviour and to consider modifying it so as not to infringe the rights of the assertor. The more intense our initial assertive response, the less likely recipients are to perceive it as an invitation to reassess their position and the more likely they will be to interpret it as an attack which threatens their own rights. The most effective sequence appears to be to start with an assertion which we perceive to be the minimal effective response. If this proves to be ineffective, the way forward is to gradually escalate the intensity of the assertion messages issued.

Intensity can be increased by changing both the verbal and non-verbal content of the assertion. Rakos (1997) illustrates the principle of escalation with an example of a salesman selling a product that the assertor does not want. The interaction could take the following steps.

Minimal effective response 'No thanks, I'm not interested.'
Escalation 1 'No, I told you I'm not interested. Good day.'
Escalation 2 'I am not interested.' (Louder volume and firmer delivery.)
Escalation 3 'I told you I am not interested. If you do not leave immediately I will contact your supervisor and register a complaint against you.'

The impact of the escalation may be lost if we allow ourselves to get side-tracked on to other issues. For example, an encyclopedia salesman may attempt to sell his product by suggesting that encyclopedias will help children with their school work, and he might try to divert assertors by asking whether they are concerned about their children's education. To maximise the impact of an assertion, we need to avoid being side-tracked and to persist with our core message: 'I'm not interested in purchasing encyclopedias.'

Another form of escalation involves us in becoming increasingly explicit about the nature of the change we are seeking to achieve. There is a body of opinion which suggests that the initial assertion message should not specify the desired change. For example, Bolton's *When you . . . I feel . . . Because . . .* formula does not present others with a solution but leaves them free to offer one which satisfies both their and our needs.

Assertion messages that do not back others into a corner or attempt to impose a solution may be more effective because they are less likely to provoke a defensive response and counter-attack. However, there may well be occasions when the recipient either offers no solution or one which we judge to be unsatisfactory. We may therefore need to escalate by becoming increasingly explicit about what we want. For example, an initial assertive message might be: 'My steak is cold.' If this does not elicit a satisfactory response it may be necessary to escalate by being more explicit about the consequences this has for us: 'My steak is cold and I cannot eat it.' If this still does not work, the only way forward may be for us tell others what we want done about it. '*My steak is cold and I cannot eat it. Please bring me another.*'

Persistence

It is sometimes necessary to reassert several times before recipients will respond as desired. One reason for this is that the recipients' defensiveness may get in the way of their hearing and understanding what we have said. Assertors too often fail to get what they want because they give up too soon. They fail to persist.

Managing defensive reactions

We can minimise the effect of defensive reactions by reflectively listening to other people's responses. Reflecting skills have been considered in detail elsewhere (Chapter 4). They are effective because, when other people's defensive responses are reflected back with respect, it gives them confidence that their views have been recognised and understood. Reflecting skills are especially important when we are attempting to change an ongoing relationship. Simply repeating the core assertion message, even though effective when judged in terms of securing specific behaviour changes, may hurt others and damage the relationship. Reflective responses can help minimise feelings of hurt, anger or disappointment.

An example may illustrate this point. A young product engineer may feel that, if she is to progress, she needs to break free of her mentor and demonstrate to herself and others that she is ready to assume more responsibility. However, she may value her relationship with the person who has given unstintingly of his time and taught her much of what she needed to know to make a success of her early career. Her initial assertion, therefore, may contain both elements of praise and explanation to make her expression of rights more acceptable.

- *Assertion*: 'Jim, you've given me a first-class apprenticeship but I think the time has come for me to begin to stand on my own two feet. I think it's time to end our regular daily meeting.' However, what Jim hears may be that Chris is rejecting him. He may not be conscious of her need for independence or her feeling that it is time to prove herself to others. He may therefore reply:

- *Response*: 'So you don't think an old hand like me has anything useful to offer any more. You think I'm past it.' If Chris recognises Jim's concerns about rejection she can respond to them by offering a reflective response before going on to reassert her need for independence.
- *Reflective response and reassertion*: 'You feel I don't value your advice because I think you are out of touch with new developments. That is not the case. I want to break off the daily meetings because I feel it's time I took more responsibility for my own work.'

Bolton's (1986: 173) view is that effective asserting hinges on a rhythm of asserting and reflecting. He argues that:

> Shifting between these two different roles is the most demanding interpersonal skill we teach. After asserting most people forget to listen. When the other person makes her defensive response, they clobber her with another confrontative statement and a battle ensues. . . . Other people get stuck in the listening role and neglect to assert.

Assertion and cultural values

Assertive behaviour involves an element of risk. Even when we take care to assert in a way that respects the rights of others, the recipients may not recognise the empathic nature of the assertion and may respond negatively. It is also possible that even if the recipients of the assertion deliver the requested outcome, they may still harbour some resentment. Consequently, it can be helpful to assess the long- as well as the short-term costs and benefits before engaging in any assertive behaviour.

Rakos (1997) argues that the values which legitimise assertion are grounded in American democracy which promotes the concepts of individual activism, pragmatism, rationality and ethical relativism. He goes on to argue that the behaviours and attitudes that foster assertion are not consistent with the cultural assumptions of all societies and ethnic groups. This is an important point. Assertion needs to be regarded as a situation-specific skill.

Before moving on to consider influencing as a political process, you may find it useful to reflect on the above and consider how the content of the first part of this chapter relates to your interpersonal style (Figure 9.2).

Exercise 9.2 Diagnosing the need for assertive behaviour

The aim of this exercise is to help you develop a greater sense of aware-ness of how you respond to situations where you feel a need to:

- express an unpopular or different opinion;
- request somebody else to change their behaviour; or
- refuse their request/demand that you act in a particular way.

You can adapt this exercise and do it by yourself, but the format pre-sented here assumes that you will be working on this exercise with others.

Step 1

Working alone, reflect on your answers to Exercise 9.1 when you were asked to think about four or five occasions when you wanted to change somebody else's behaviour or refuse a request. What was the pattern of your responses? Was your style assertive, non-assertive or aggres-sive?

If your responses indicate that you were *assertive* in all (or most) of the cases you identified, consider:

- Whether you are always as assertive as you would like to be. Are there some *situations* or *specific relationships* where you are not as assertive as you would like to be? Why is this? What could you do about it?
- Consider *how others respond* to your assertions. Do others resist or comply? If they resist, why do they react in this way? If they comply, do they do so with good grace and without cost to the quality of the long-term relationship? If not, why? What could you do about this?

If your responses indicate that you fail to be assertive (when asserting might be a more effective way of helping you achieve a desired outcome), consider why you are not as assertive as you would like to be.

- Is it because you do not want *to offend* others? If you suspect this is the reason, consider what you could do to be more assertive without adversely affecting the quality of your relationship.
- Is it because you find it *difficult to formulate appropriate assertive responses* as and when the need arises? If you suspect this is the reason, practise writing down a number of different 'three-part assertion messages' (When you . . . I feel . . . because . . .) and identify which of them would be most effective in a particular situation.

If your responses indicate that you tend to be aggressive (when asserting might be a more effective way of helping you achieve a desired outcome), consider why you tend to be aggressive rather than assertive.

- Is it because you tend to be too focused on immediate outcomes and neglect the long-term implications of your behaviour? If so, would it help if you set aside a little time to anticipate how an imminent interaction might unfold and assess the long-term costs and benefits of assertive versus aggressive behaviour on your part?
- Is it because you have not given much thought to alternative ways of behaving and lack skills in asserting? If so, think of particular instances and consider how you might have used content, non-verbal and social interaction skills to achieve a more beneficial outcome.

Step 2

Share your analysis and conclusions with a partner or the other members of a small group. After each member has shared their analysis and conclusions others should reflect on what they have heard and draw attention to any aspects of the presenter's diagnosis or their conclusions that they feel might merit further exploration. It may be necessary to set a time limit for the discussion of each case.

Step 3

Each group should appoint a member to present a summary of the discussion and any useful learning points to a plenary session.

Influencing as a political process

The final part of this chapter switches attention to a different set of factors which can affect the probability that an attempt to influence will be successful. Influencing is examined as a political process.

Most of us do not work alone. We are members of complex organisations. Many people working in organisations are less influential than they could be because they do not fully understand the nature of organisational life. One widely held assumption is that organisations are well-integrated entities within which everybody works harmoniously together in order to achieve a set of shared goals. People who support this view assume that decisions are made logically and rationally, and that organisational members select the alternatives that maximise the achievement of these shared goals. Little attention seems to be given to self-interest and to the competing personal goals of organisational members.

An alternative view of organisations is that they are political organisms within which individuals and groups attempt to influence each other in the pursuit of self-interest. Decisions and actions result from bargaining and negotiation between people who have different goals. They often represent a compromise; they are the result of explicit or implicit working agreements that interested parties are prepared to live with, at least temporarily. When preferences conflict, it is the power and influence of the individuals and groups involved that determines the outcome of the decision process, not logic and rational argument.

The acquisition and exercise of power and influence can be viewed as a political process. Some people are too political in the sense that they pursue their self-interest without paying any attention to the rights of others or to the survival and growth of the organisation. Their aim is that they should win. Others are too passive and accepting, and fail to contribute as effectively as they might to the organisation's survival and growth. These non-assertive people may react to events, but rarely, if ever, engage in proactive behaviour to bring about the kind of changes that they think are desirable. However, there is a middle ground. There are people who acquire power and exercise influence in order to bring about what they perceive to be a more desirable state of affairs, and they use their power and exercise their influence in ways that do not unnecessarily deny others their rights.

The acquisition and exercise of power and influence

We can increase our ability to influence others by paying attention to ourselves, others and the kinds of relationships we have (see Hayes 1984).

Developing the capacity to satisfy others' needs

First we need to look to ourselves. We need to ensure that we are professionally competent. Others may view people who are incompetent or possess obsolete skills as irrelevant because they have little to offer. Such people are unlikely to be able to exercise much influence. To develop and maintain a power base we need to invest time and effort in maintaining existing and/or developing new areas of professional competence.

In order to be in a position to exercise influence we not only need to be competent, we also need to be seen to be competent by others. Consequently we need to pay attention to the promotion of our own and our department's reputation. Others pay more attention to those who are known to be motivated, competent and capable of making an effective contribution.

Assessing others' dependence

We will also benefit from taking stock of the information and resources we provide to others. We need to know how important these are to the achievement of their goals, and we need to assess how readily they can obtain them from alternative sources. This appraisal will provide some indication of how dependent others are on us. This is vital information. As Emerson (1962) so clearly stated, power is inherent in any relationship in which one person is dependent upon another.

> It would appear that the power to control or influence the other resides in control over the things he values, which may range all the way from oil resources to ego support. In short, power resides implicitly in the other's dependence.

Increasing others' sense of dependence

In order for us to exercise power, other people have to be aware that they are dependent upon us. We can make others aware of their dependence in a number of ways. For example, we may threaten to withhold some vital product or service. However, such heavy-handed measures may frighten the dependent others. It may provoke them into initiating a thorough search for alternative sources which, if successful, could reduce their dependence on us. It may also provoke them into seeking out counter-dependencies which they may use against us as bargaining points. Neither of these responses is unreasonable; indeed, as will be noted below, in certain circumstances they are to be encouraged. However, there is a danger that coercive, bullying-type attempts to raise awareness may promote the kind of win–lose climate which could easily deteriorate into one where everybody loses. The objective of any awareness-raising exercise must be to raise an awareness of dependency but to do so within a climate that supports the ideal of mutual help and cooperation.

When, through our interactions with others, we can convince them that they need the information or other resources we control, we can increase our influence over them. (Whether or not we actually control or are the only available source of that resource is less relevant than the impression we manage to create. However, as will be noted in the chapter on negotiating, some people are less comfortable than others with bluff and concealment. They feel bluff involves unfair manipulation.)

The ability to 'define reality' for others and convince them that they are dependent on us is probably one of the most effective ways of enhancing our power in practice.

Assessing own dependence

In order to acquire and exercise power it is not sufficient for us to ensure that we are competent, have a good reputation and that others are aware of the extent to which they are dependent upon us. We also need to pay attention to our dependence upon others and identify the 'significant others' on whom we are dependent. These 'significant others' are important because they can help or hinder the achievement of our goals.

Minimising own dependence

We can reduce our dependence on others by searching for alternative sources of required resources, thus minimising our reliance on any one individual or unit. We can also challenge established working agreements where we suspect that others are exercising power over us based on dependency relationships which may have prevailed in the past, but which no longer reflect the current situation. As available resources, market conditions or any number of similar factors change, so does the nature of dependency relationships and therefore the distribution of power.

Once the 'others' on whom we are dependent have been identified, we can build direct or indirect links with them. Such links can serve a number of purposes.

- If one of the 'significant others' is responsible for allocating a scarce resource, it may be helpful to improve communications with them in order to persuade them to allocate the scarce resource to us. Projects are often starved of resources simply because people are unable to communicate with important decision makers.
- Another benefit is that closer contact may help us identify information or resources the others require that we can provide, thus establishing a basis for negotiation and trade.

Significant others may also be able to influence third parties which are inaccessible to us, or they may be able to champion our cause to a much wider audience than we could ever reach on our own. Sponsorship of this kind is typically a reciprocal relationship. The sponsor gives support but expects something, perhaps loyalty, in return. By seeking and accepting sponsorship, people unavoidably become dependent on others, and therefore vulnerable to their influence attempts.

Negotiating advantageous agreements

Most working agreements within work organisations and other social systems are based on some degree of reciprocity or interdependence. Effective influencers are likely to be the kind of people who are aware of this and able to assess, realistically, what they can offer to others and what they in turn need from others. They will be able to set this alongside an equally realistic assessment of what others have to offer them and what others need from them. They are also those who can use these assessments to negotiate the best working agreements and bargains for themselves and their department.

Ineffective influencers tend to be the people who constantly enter into explicit or implicit agreements that are to their disadvantage. Not only does this ensure that they are exploited and unable to fulfil their own goals, it means that they are unlikely to be able to adequately fulfil their role in the organisation and contribute to its success.

It is not necessary to erode the power of one organisational member to enhance that of another. Interactions within organisations do not occur within the fixed framework of a zero-sum ('I win, you lose') game. More political awareness and greater participation in the negotiation of a new organisational order and in the establishment of new working agreements up, down and across the hierarchy may best be viewed in the context of an increasing-sum game. Effective participation in the political process can lead to a better definition of organisational problems and to the generation and implementation of more successful solutions.

People who are able to relate to others in ways that enable them to achieve their goals are less likely to feel that the system gets in their way and frustrates their attempts to exercise influence. They are more likely to:

- have a clear idea of what they want to achieve;
- believe in their own ability to manage events and get things done;
- be clear about how best to invest their time and energy;
- possess a well-developed set of assertion and political skills.

They also need to be able to negotiate advantageous agreements for themselves. Negotiation skills are considered in the next chapter.

Improving our ability to influence others

People are often reluctant to assert themselves because they assume that they have a weak power base. Sometimes this may not be the case. They may be unaware of their potential ability to influence because they have never attempted to consciously assess how dependent they are on others and compare this with the extent to which these others are dependent on them. Thinking about relationships in terms of relative dependencies can point to ways in which the balance of power may be changed in your favour, and can radically change expectations about the probable outcome of any attempt to assert your rights and influence others. This is the focus of Exercise 9.3.

Exercise 9.3 Check-list for the acquisition and exercise of power

One way of identifying any deficiencies in your influencing skills is to undertake a personal audit.

- Think about those situations in which you are *satisfied* with your ability to influence others. Using the check-list presented below, build a profile of what you typically do *to acquire and use power* in those situations.
- Next, think about those situations in which you are *dissatisfied* with your ability to influence. Repeat the procedure and build a profile of what you do when you are less successful.
- Compare the two profiles and look for differences in your behaviour. Differences between the two profiles may point to ways of changing your behaviour that could help you achieve desired outcomes in those situations where you typically fail.

A weakness with this approach is that different situations may demand a different approach. In other words, an influencing style that works in some situations may not be effective in all situations. An alternative approach, therefore, is to compare your unsuccessful profile with the profile of somebody who, in the same situation, tends to be consistently more successful. This approach can also be used when you want to identify ways of improving your ability to influence in a range of different situations. Observe others who have this ability and compare their profiles with your own.

Check-list for the acquisition and exercise of power

1   Developing the capacity to satisfy others' needs

Have you invested enough effort in maintaining
relevant skills, keeping well informed and being
professionally competent?   Yes ❑   ❑ No

2   Assessing others' dependence on you

Have you taken stock of what others want from you?   Yes ❑   ❑ No

Have you attempted to identify alternative sources of
supply or substitutes?   Yes ❑   ❑ No

Have you assessed how important to others are
the resources you provide?   Yes ❑   ❑ No

3   Increasing others' dependence on you

Have you raised others' awareness of their
dependence on you?   Yes ❑   ❑ No

Did you do this in a way that minimised the threat
to others?   Yes ❑   ❑ No

Have you attempted to persuade others that what
you offer is necessary and only available from you?   Yes ❑   ❑ No

4   Assessing your dependence on others

Have you taken stock of what you want from
others?   Yes ❑   ❑ No

Have you built links with significant others?   Yes ❑   ❑ No

5   Minimising your dependence on others

Have you sought alternative sources of supply
and/or substitutes?   Yes ❑   ❑ No

Have you sought to develop interdependencies
with significant others?   Yes ❑   ❑ No

Have you challenged or reassessed established
relationships?   Yes ❑   ❑ No

There are people who are aware that they occupy potentially powerful positions yet who experience difficulty influencing others. This is often because they do not assert themselves. Developing assertion skills involves diagnosing the most important areas for skill development, identifying new behaviours and practising them in low-risk situations. This is the focus of Exercise 9.4.

Exercise 9.4 Effective asserting

This exercise involves a three-step approach to the development of asserting skills:

1 *Observing others.* The first step involves observing what others do, and thinking about what they could do differently to assert themselves more effectively. One important aim of this step is to practise observing the skills presented in this chapter. Another is to establish a bench-mark of good practice.
2 *Monitoring self.* The second step involves using these observation skills to monitor and assess how you assert yourself and to identify what you could do differently to improve your asserting skills.
3 *Experimenting with new behaviours.* The third step involves identifying and taking action to improve the way you assert yourself.

Step 1: Observing other people asserting

A useful starting point is to train yourself to observe and recognise what is happening in situations where you suspect that one party wants to change somebody else's behaviour or refuse a request. Are they assertive, non-assertive or aggressive? The asserting skills check-list presented below can provide a useful framework for recording your observations of any assertive behaviours.

ASSERTION SKILLS CHECK-LIST

1   Content skills
   Are assertion messages:

Brief and direct?	❏	❏	Rambling and ambiguous?
Respectful?	❏	❏	Blaming and judgemental?
Empathic?	❏	❏	Blunt?

If assertion messages are empathic, do they?

Offer an explanation of the need to assert?	Yes ❑ ❑	No
Offer a short apology?	Yes ❑ ❑	No
Recognise effect on others?	Yes ❑ ❑	No
Attempt to identify a compromise?	Yes ❑ ❑	No
Offer praise to others?	Yes ❑ ❑	No

2 Non-verbal skills

Is voice	Soft? ❑ ❑	Loud?
Is inflection used to emphasise message?	Yes ❑ ❑	No
Is delivery firm?	Yes ❑ ❑	No
Is facial expression controlled?	Yes ❑ ❑	No
Is eye contact (a)	High? ❑ ❑	Low?
(b)	Intermittent? ❑ ❑	Staring?
Is posture square and upright?	Yes ❑ ❑	No

3 Social interaction skills

• Escalation:
Is initial response a minimum effective response?　Yes ❑　❑ No

If the initial response is *in*effective is the intensity
of successive responses gradually increased?　Yes ❑　❑ No

Do the assertion messages become more explicit
in terms of required outcomes?　Yes ❑　❑ No

• Focus:
Does the assertor avoid being side-tracked and
stick to the core message?　Yes ❑　❑ No

• Persistence:
How many times does s/he assert before giving up?　❑

• Management of defensive reactions:
Does the assertor listen to the other's reply?　Yes ❑　❑ No

Before reasserting, does the assertor reflect back
the other's response?　Yes ❑　❑ No

Step 2: Assessing your own approach to asserting and identifying possibilities for improvement

This step involves opening a 'second channel' and using your observation skills to observe yourself. Do *not* deliberately try to change your approach at this point because the aim is to increase your awareness of your normal asserting/non-asserting style. Use the same approach to observe and assess your own behaviour as you used in the first step when you were observing how other people behave. Record your observations on a copy of the check-list presented above.

After a while you will be able to build up a profile of your normal asserting/non-asserting style. How satisfied are you with the outcome you typically achieve? Do you think you could do better?

Step 3: taking action to improve your asserting skills

This stage involves attending to those aspects of your own asserting behaviour where you feel there is scope for improvement. If there are lots of changes you feel you should make, you might think about whether you should try to introduce all the changes at once or draw up a short-list of a few changes to start with. You may, for example, decide to start by paying more attention to your content skills. Once you have practised a few new ways of behaving you may feel it appropriate to move on and introduce further changes.

Monitor the effects of these changes. Are you able to detect any differences in the way the other people respond to you? How do you feel about the new approach?

Make a note of the outcome of your efforts to improve your asserting skills in the space provided below:

Summary

Consideration has been given to the nature of assertion and the differences between assertive, non-assertive and aggressive behaviours. Three types of assertion skill (content, non-verbal and social interaction) have been examined. This chapter has considered a number of ways in which the impact of assertive responses can be increased, thus raising the probability that the desired outcome will be achieved. Attention has also been given to the cultural factors that might influence the effectiveness of assertive behaviour in particular situations.

Influencing has also been considered from the perspective of the acquisition and exercise of power. Assertive behaviour is more likely to lead to desired outcomes in those situations where assertors are seen by others to be 'powerful'.

References

Bolton, R. (1986) *People Skills*, Sydney: Prentice Hall of Australia.

Emerson, R.M. (1962) 'Power-dependence relations', *American Sociological Review* 27: 31–41.

Guirdham, M. (1995) *Interpersonal Skills at Work* (2nd edn), London: Prentice Hall.

Hayes, J. (1984) 'The politically competent manager', *Journal of General Management* 10 (1): 24–33.

Kolotkin, R., Wielkiewicz, R. and Judd, B. (1984) 'Behaviour components of assertion: comparison of univariate and multivartiate assessment strategies', *Behavioral Assessment* 6: 61–78.

McFall, M., Winett, R. and Bordewick, M. (1982) 'Non verbal components in the communication of assertiveness', *Behaviour Modification* 6: 121–140.

Pitcher, S. and Meikle, S. (1980) 'The topography of assertive behaviour in positive and negative situations', *Behaviour Therapy* 11: 532–547.

Rakos, R. (1997) 'Asserting and confronting', in O. Hargie (ed.) *A Handbook of Communication Skills*, London: Croom Helm, pp. 289–319.

Rimms, D. and Masters, J. (1987) *Behaviour Therapy: Techniques and Empirical Findings* (3rd edn), New York: Academic Press.

Schroeder, H.E., Rakos, R. and Moe, J. (1983) 'The social perception of assertive behaviour as a function of response class and gender', *Behaviour Therapy* 14: 534–544.

10

NEGOTIATING

Learning objectives

To understand how parties with different preferred outcomes seek agreement, and to develop an awareness of how negotiating skills can affect the outcome of the process.

After reading this chapter you will:

- Be aware of the difference between explicit and implicit negotiation.
- Recognise how limits and targets can affect the process of negotiation.
- Understand how motivational orientation can influence a person's preferred negotiating style.
- Be aware of some of the contingent variables that can influence a negotiator's choice of strategy in practice.
- Recognise the circumstances in which different strategies may be effective.
- Be aware of how choice of strategy affects choice of tactics.
- Recognise, and be able to categorise, a range of frequently used tactics.
- Be aware of some of the main negotiating behaviours and how they can be structured and sequenced to provide a range of different negotiating tactics.
- Understand the importance of opening bids and counter-bids and the relationship between bids and outcomes.
- Be aware of the factors that influence how people tend to respond to contending tactics.
- Be aware of the factors that influence how people tend to respond to concessions.
- Understand what you can do to improve your ability to negotiate effectively.

Negotiating

We are all negotiators. Negotiation is a process of joint decision making in which people with different preferred outcomes interact in order to resolve their differences. It can be an explicit process when, for example, we bargain with a supplier over the price of a component, argue for an increased budget with our boss or seek to establish a new rate for a job with a group of workers. However, it can also be an implicit process through which the nature of our relationships with others is determined. We all have many demands on our time, so if a colleague calls for assistance we have to weigh the costs and benefits of helping out. A failure to help colleagues achieve their desired outcomes may provoke them to reappraise their priorities and offer us less assistance in the future when we seek help. Generous support, on the other hand, may cement an alliance that could be mutually beneficial. Much of the give and take of everyday life represents an implicit process of negotiation. Everybody who occupies a managerial or supervisory role is inevitably drawn into a process of explicit or implicit negotiation whenever there is a need to reconcile differences between group members or between manager and subordinate. Some people are better negotiators than others and consequently are more successful in terms of achieving their desired outcomes.

Negotiation is not necessarily a win–lose process; it need not involve one party seeking to improve its lot at the expense of the other. Negotiation can often be a win-win process through which an agreement may be reached which helps both parties achieve their preferred outcomes. This chapter aims to help you develop a better understanding of the process of negotiation and will consider a number of different strategies, including competitive and collaborative. It will also help you to identify the skills you need if you are to become a more successful negotiator.

The questionnaire presented in Exercise 10.1 is designed to help you assess your views about negotiating. Think about your answers as you read this chapter. It may be useful if you complete the questionnaire a second time once you have read the chapter so that you can note any changes in your views.

A simplified model of negotiation: targets and limits

When people begin to negotiate they normally have some idea about the level of benefit they hope to secure. This is their *target* outcome. They also have some idea about the level of benefit below which they will not go. This is their *limit*. A settlement can only be achieved when the limits each party brings to the negotiation coincide or overlap.

This can be illustrated with a simple example in which only one issue (price) is being negotiated.

In the situation represented by Figure 10.1 a settlement is not possible.

- The buyer, seeking to purchase a component from a supplier, refuses to pay more than £1.50 per unit. This is the buyer's limit. It may be set at this level because the buyer cannot afford to pay more or because the buyer is aware of an alternative supply at £1.50.

Exercise 10.1 Negotiating style questionnaire

1 Is your aim to achieve
   - ❏ The best result for all involved?
   - ❏ The best deal for you/your department/your company?

2 Are there any circumstances when you would sacrifice benefit for self in order to ensure benefit for the other party?
   - ❏ Yes
   - ❏ No

3 Are you more or less competitive than the people with whom you typically negotiate?
   - ❏ I am more competitive
   - ❏ I am less competitive

4 When you are selling do you ask:
   - ❏ A price much higher than your target price?
   - ❏ A price close to your target price?

5 If you were buying, how would you feel if you made an offer a long way below the seller's asking price?
   - ❏ Comfortable?
   - ❏ Uncomfortable?

6 During a negotiation, do you tend to:
   - ❏ 'Stay firm' and refuse to make any concessions?
   - ❏ Try to open up the negotiation with an early concession?

7 If you decide to make a concession, do you tend to:
   - ❏ Offer very little and make only the smallest of concessions?
   - ❏ Make a very generous concession to get things moving?

8 Do you believe that making a large concession will:
   - ❏ Weaken your position?
   - ❏ Encourage the other party to reciprocate?

9 Do you believe that most people respond to threats by:
   - ❏ Giving way and conceding?
   - ❏ Making counter-threats?

10 Which do you do most in a negotiation:
   - ❏ Listen?
   - ❏ Talk?

- The supplier refuses to sell at anything less than £2.50. The seller's limit may be set at this level because it is possible to achieve a better price elsewhere or because a lower price would result in the seller making a loss.

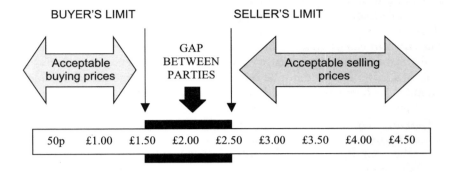

Figure 10.1 Settlement not possible.

Figure 10.2 Overlapping limits offer possibility of settlement.

The black portion of the bar in Figure 10.1 indicates the extent of the gap between the two parties' limits.

In the situation represented by Figure 10.2, a settlement is possible because the buyer is prepared to pay up to £3 a unit and the supplier, if pushed, will sell for as little as £1.50. The overlapping limits (indicated by the black portion of the bar) offer the possibility of a settlement that would be acceptable to both parties.

The motivational orientation of the negotiators and their relative skill will help determine what the settlement price will be. If the negotiators are motivated to adopt a competitive strategy, and the supplier (seller) is the more skilled negotiator, the agreed price is likely to be towards the £3 limit of the buyer. If, however, the seller adopts an accommodating strategy and is concerned to ensure that the buyer secures some benefit, the seller (despite being the more skilled negotiator) may be motivated to settle nearer his own limit of £1.50. (It would not be unusual for parents, negotiating the sale of a family car to one of their children, to adopt an accommodating rather than a competitive strategy.)

Planning can make a vital contribution to the outcome of a negotiation. Skilled negotiators, whatever their motivational orientation, attempt to discover their opponents' limit. To push an opponent beyond this limit will lead to a breakdown in the negotiation. Competitive negotiators seek to secure an agreement as close to their opponent's limit as possible, thereby maximising their own benefit. To achieve this outcome, skilled negotiators need to know how to research their opponent's case before coming to the negotiating table and, during the negotiation, need to be skilled at probing and listening, so that all available information is gathered and can be used to maximum advantage.

Anticipate the need to negotiate: targets and limits

Preparation takes time and the negotiators' case is often weakened because they do not have the time to prepare adequately.

The members of an area management team of a petrol company, which is looking for a new site for a filling station, know that at some point they will have to negotiate with the owners of potential sites. This knowledge may alert them to the need to start planning for this negotiation.

Two possible sites may be identified. At this stage an analysis of traffic flows, the proximity of other filling stations and similar considerations could facilitate the calculation of potential profit. This, in turn, could help determine the maximum rental or purchase price that would be commercially viable for each site (i.e. the petrol company's *limit* for each site).

Researching alternative uses for these sites, and the profits these alternative uses may generate, could also provide an indication of the kinds of bids competitors for these sites may make. This knowledge can provide vital clues about the site owner's bargaining power and *limit* (determined by the maximum alternative bid).

Usually this kind of information cannot be acquired overnight, so it pays to think ahead.

Exercise 10.2 is designed to help you engage in some pre-planning.

Exercise 10.2 Planning for a negotiation

Before you enter into a negotiation give some thought to the following points and make some notes on the negotiation preparation sheet presented below.

- Think about your *target* outcome. Ensure that you have taken account of the main variables this will involve (product specification, price, delivery, payment terms, etc.).
- Think about your *limit* or ultimate fall-back position. What is the limit you must not go beyond?
- Assess the importance of each variable for you and for the other parties involved in the negotiation. It will be to your advantage if you can restrict any concessions you make to your low-priority variables (especially if they are high priority for the other party) and if you can persuade the other party to concede on the variables that are most important to you.
- Seek out clues that will help you identify what your opponent's target and limit are likely to be. Even though you will only be able to make a subjective assessment of the other party's target, limit and key variables, this assessment will provide a useful basis for planning your own strategy and tactics.
- Decide on the most appropriate opening bid.

NEGOTIATION PREPARATION SHEET

MY		THEIR	
Key variables	Priorities	Key variables	Priorities
_____	____	_____	____
_____	____	_____	____
_____	____	_____	____
_____	____	_____	____
_____	____	_____	____
Limit: _____		Limit: _____	

My intention is to: ❏ Open first
                       ❏ Wait until the other party has made an opening bid before responding

If I decide to make an opening bid it is likely to be: _____

_____

Morley (1997) identifies five broad models that examine the psychological aspects of negotiating. They are synthetic models, behavioural models, information-processing models, models of the personal characteristics of effective negotiators, and discursive models that focus on the social construction of cognition and action. The remainder of this chapter focuses on behavioural models. It examines negotiation from the perspective of behaviours, tactics and strategies, and it explores how the process of negotiation can affect outcomes.

The hierarchical nature of negotiating skills: behaviours, tactics and strategies

The primary components of negotiating skills are behaviours such as information sending, information seeking, argumentation, compliance seeking, bidding and yielding. These behaviours can be structured and sequenced into sets that are often referred to as negotiating tactics. The wide range of available tactics can be categorised in a variety of ways. In this chapter they are grouped under four headings: contending, non-contending, flexible and complex. Strategies are the highest level in the hierarchy and reflect the negotiator's overall approach or style.

The next section of this chapter focuses on the factors that affect choice of negotiating strategy. Attention is then focused on the primary elements of negotiating behaviour before consideration is given to a range of commonly employed negotiating tactics. Exercises are presented at the end of each section to help you improve your negotiating skills.

Motivational orientation and choice of negotiating strategy

Carnevale and Pruitt (1992), in their overview of the literature on negotiation, refer to two traditions of thought. The cognitive tradition argues that it is the negotiators' approach to information processing that determines the outcome of a negotiation. The motivation and strategy tradition, which provides the conceptual framework for this chapter, focuses on how the negotiators' motivational orientation influences their preferred strategy, which in turn influences the outcome of the negotiation.

Early theories in the motivation and strategy tradition were based on a single dimension of motivational orientation (cooperation–competition), but Thomas' (1979) two-dimensional model of conflict behaviour provided the basis for a dual-concern model of motivational orientation and strategic choice. The two independent dimensions in Thomas' model are cooperation (which reflects a negotiator's concern for the other party's benefit) and assertiveness (which reflects the negotiator's concern for own benefit).

It is the relationship between these two motivational orientations (cooperativeness and assertiveness) that predicts the negotiators' preferred strategy, and it is the negotiators' preferred strategy that determines the way they behave and the tactics they will adopt. Figure 10.3 illustrates five strategic orientations.

1   The competitive negotiator is motivated to achieve maximum benefit for self at the expense of the other party (win–lose). Carnevale and Pruitt (1992) suggest that negotiators who adopt this strategy will favour contentious tactics that involve behaving in ways that will persuade the other party to concede.
2   The accommodative negotiator is primarily concerned with ensuring that the other party achieves some benefit even if this requires the sacrifice of benefit to self. Negotiators who adopt this strategy engage in tactics that involve yielding or conceding.
3   The collaborative negotiator is motivated to achieve maximum benefit for both parties (win-win). Those who adopt this strategy utilise problem-solving tactics that involve behaviours such as empathic listening, providing information about one's own priorities and joint brainstorming in search of solutions.
4   The inactive negotiator neglects both own and the other's benefit by avoiding any attempt to resolve differences in preferred outcomes.

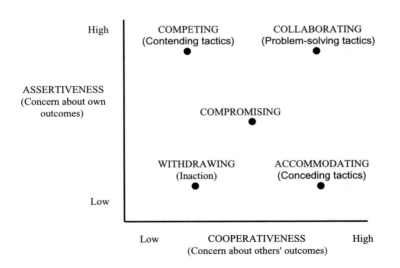

Figure 10.3 The dual concern model of motivational orientation. Adapted from Ruble and Thomas, 1976.

5 The compromising negotiator adopts an intermediate strategy and is motivated to seek a satisfactory (rather than maximum) level of joint benefit by splitting the difference on issues of concern.

Thomas (1979) suggests that it is possible to gain more insight into the consequences, in terms of outcomes, of adopting any of these five strategies by elaborating the model with two additional dimensions. They are the integrative and distributive dimensions that were originally identified in the context of labour–management negotiations. In terms of game theory, an integrative orientation reflects a search for a positive-sum outcome whereas a distributive orientation reflects a search for a zero-sum outcome.

The *integrative* dimension is concerned with the total benefits available to all parties, sometimes referred to as the 'size of the pie' dimension. Collaborating involves seeking outcomes that enable both parties to satisfy their needs as completely as possible (which involves behaving in ways that offer the possibility of 'enlarging the pie' of potential benefits). Inaction, on the other hand, involves doing nothing to satisfy either party's needs, thereby 'reducing the pie' of potential benefits available to both parties (Figure 10.4).

The *distributive* dimension is concerned with the negotiators' motivation

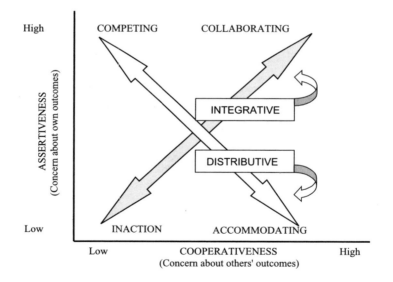

Figure 10.4 The integrative and distributive dimensions. Reproduced with permission of the authors and publisher from Kilmann, R. H. and Thomas, K. W. Interpersonal conflict-handling behaviour as reflections of Jungian personality dimensions. *Psychological Reports*, 1975, 37, 971–980 © Psychological Reports 1975.

to distribute the benefits between the parties (sharing out the pie). At one end of this dimension is competing, which reflects extreme 'taking' behaviour, and at the other is accommodating, which reflects extreme 'giving' behaviour.

Many people regard collaboration as the negotiating strategy that will be most effective in all circumstances. This universalistic perspective is less helpful than a more contingent view which asserts that a variety of factors (contingencies) can determine which strategies will be most effective in a range of different circumstances. Thomas (1977) illustrates this point. He found that chief executives used all five strategies, depending on the needs of the situation (see Table 10.1). Inspection of some of the entries in Thomas' table illustrates how a range of factors can affect choice of strategy in practice. For example, negotiators who might normally be motivated to adopt a collaborative strategy may be fiercely competitive on issues vital to company welfare. Alternatively, a competitive negotiator may adopt a collaborative strategy when it is necessary to gain commitment from others.

Other factors affecting strategic choice

While the negotiators' motivational orientation will exert a strong influence on an individuals' preferred negotiating strategy, a number of more immediate factors can affect the choice of strategy in any given situation.

Continuity of the interaction

Sometimes negotiations are one-off episodes and whatever happens between the parties is unlikely to have any long-term consequences. Often, however, they are embedded in ongoing relationships. A manager (whose preferred negotiating strategy may be competitive) needs to be aware, when negotiating with union officials, that the current negotiation is part of an ongoing relationship. It may be possible to compete and push the other party into making heavy concessions today, but this may motivate them to seek ways of 'evening the score' sometime in the future. Accommodating some of their demands, on the other hand, may create a sense of indebtedness that could have a beneficial affect on their approach to subsequent negotiations.

Definition of the situation

The way parties to a negotiation define the situation will influence their choice of strategy. For example, if they conceptualise the situation in terms of a zero-sum struggle and perceive the other party to be hostile, they may feel that the only option is to adopt a competitive strategy. The way negotiators conceptualise the situation is inevitably subjective, and often egocentric. Consequently real opportunities for cooperation may not be recognised even where they exist.

Table 10.1 Uses of the five conflict modes, as reported by a group of chief executives.

CONFLICT HANDLING MODE	APPROPRIATE SITUATIONS
COMPETING	1 When quick, decisive action is vital – emergencies. 2 On important issues where unpopular actions need implementing – cost cutting, enforcing unpopular rules. 3 On issues vital to company welfare when you know you are right. 4 Against people who take advantage of non-competitive behaviour.
COLLABORATING	1 To find an integrative solution when both sets of concerns are too important to be compromised. 2 When your objective is to learn. 3 To merge insights from people with different perspectives. 4 To gain commitment by incorporating concerns into a consensus. 5 To work through feelings that have interfered with a relationship.
COMPROMISING	1 When goals are important, but not worth the effort or potential disruption of more assertive modes. 2 When opponents with equal power are committed to mutually exclusive goals. 3 To achieve temporary settlements of complex issues. 4 To arrive at expedient solutions under time pressure. 5 As a back-up when collaboration or competition is unsuccessful.
AVOIDING (Inaction)	1 When an issue is trivial, or more important issues are pressing. 2 When you perceive no chance of satisfying your concerns. 3 When potential disruption outweighs the benefits of resolution. 4 To allow people to cool down and regain perspective. 5 When gathering information supersedes immediate decision. 6 When others can resolve the conflict more effectively. 7 When issues seem tangential or symptomatic of other issues.
ACCOMMODATING	1 When you find you are wrong – to allow a better position to be heard, to learn, and to show your reasonableness. 2 When issues are more important to others than yourself – to satisfy others and maintain cooperation. 3 To build social credits for later use. 4 To minimise loss when you are outmatched or losing. 5 When harmony and stability are especially important. 6 To allow subordinates to develop by learning from mistakes.

Local culture

In some organisational settings the local culture places a high value on team-work and cooperation, whereas in other settings there is a high premium on individual achievement and competition. This kind of cultural pressure can influence an individual's choice of strategy.

Stakes

Competing and collaborating take more time and energy than other strate-gies. When one or more of the parties conceptualise the situation as involving issues that are of little consequence, they will be more likely to con-cede (accommodate) or avoid the need to negotiate. The low stakes make them reluctant to invest the necessary time and energy (irrespective of their motivational orientation) because they prefer to focus their attention on more important issues.

Constituents

Carnevale and Pruitt (1992) refer to the people whom negotiators represent as their constituents. It is often the case that negotiators are anxious to please their constituents. When constituents are highly motivated to win, negotiators frequently adopt a competitive strategy, employ contending tac-tics and concede as little as possible. This tendency is most marked when negotiators are insecure about their standing in the group and/or when they are aware that they are being observed by their constituents.

Attribution of others' intent

There is often a strong bias in the way negotiators perceive the intention of the other party. Thomas and Pondy (1977) asked sixty-six managers to recall a recent conflict. They were all asked to state which conflict-handling mode they used and which mode was used by the other party. The results showed that there was a strong tendency for them to see themselves as coop-erative and to see the others as overwhelmingly competitive.

This has important consequences for choice of negotiating strategy. Once the negotiation is under way each party responds to the other on the basis of their interpretation of the other's behaviour (see discussion of this point in Chapter 6). The general tendency to see the other party as competitive increases the likelihood that negotiators will respond in kind in order to pro-tect their interests. Collaborative strategies are unlikely to be adopted unless there is an acceptable level of trust between the parties. This is because col-laboration involves providing information about one's own position and offering concessions in the hope that they will be reciprocated.

Early encounters and choice of strategy

People's behaviour can be interpreted in many different ways. An enquiry from someone whom the negotiators know and trust may be interpreted very differently than one from a stranger or someone they do not trust.

When strangers meet, first impressions can be very important. If one party creates the impression that they are unsure of their ground, believe that they have a weak case, that it is important for them to reach an agreement or that they are anxious to settle quickly, they will encourage the other party to believe that they have the stronger case. The other party may then adopt a competitive strategy and make high demands, stand firm and push the first party into making large concessions.

If, on the other hand, the first party appears confident and launches into an immediate attack, the other party may be pushed into a defensive position or be provoked into making a counter-attack. However, this kind of win–lose struggle is not inevitable. If the negotiators are able to present themselves as people who are genuinely seeking a mutually beneficial agreement, the possibility of a collaborative negotiation exists.

When negotiating, especially with strangers, it is easy to be drawn into a competitive interaction where one party seeks to maximise their benefit at the expense of the other. Careful management of the initial encounter can increase the possibility of discovering a common purpose and establishing the trust that is necessary for a collaborative negotiation. Responding immediately to the other party's competitive thrusts will, almost inevitably, eliminate this possibility and encourage, at least initially, a competitive interaction. Scott (1981) emphasises the importance of not being drawn in this way if the negotiators want to test the possibility of a collaborative relationship. He advocates the introduction of a neutral topic (such as a discussion of procedures) that can provide the space necessary for the parties to assess each other's aims and intentions.

As the negotiation begins to unfold, each negotiator will provide the other with clues which indicate their desired outcome and preferred approach together with information about their negotiating skills and experience. Careful listening and gentle probing in the early stages of the negotiation can help each negotiator judge whether there is any common ground and shared goals. An initial assessment of the other's intention may also be possible, thus providing some basis for deciding what would be the most appropriate negotiating strategy to adopt.

Benefits associated with possible outcomes

When the reward structure encourages the belief that a mutually beneficial exchange and outcome is possible, a collaborative approach to negotiation is likely to be more attractive than a competitive approach. This can be the case when, for example, each party controls resources that would cost little to give up but would have high value for the other. It can also be the case when all parties believe that a problem-solving approach to negotiating their differences may lead to a more beneficial solution than might be achieved through a win–lose competitive approach.

Perceived balance of power

A negotiator may be reluctant to adopt a competitive strategy when the other party is seen to be more powerful and capable of winning.

Modifying strategies as the negotiation proceeds

Negotiators often modify their strategy as the negotiation progresses. One of the parties may begin by adopting a collaborative approach but, in response to the other's fierce competitive stand, may have to modify their strategy to match their opponent's contending tactics. Alternatively, competing parties may recognise that their opponents have equal power. They may come to realise that the only way to reach an acceptable settlement may be via compromise or by working together to find a win-win collaborative solution. Exercise 10.3 is designed to help you identify the strategies that you and others typically adopt.

Exercise 10.3 Negotiating strategy

Observe others role playing or in real-life situations when they are negotiating and invite others to observe you when you are negotiating.

When you are *observing others*, focus your attention on the behaviour of one of the negotiators.

1   What was their typical style/strategy?
- Withdrawing/avoiding   [   ]
- Accommodating   [   ]
- Compromising   [   ]
- Collaborating   [   ]
- Competing   [   ]

---

2 Did they adopt a consistent strategy or did they modify it as the negotiation progressed?

- Consistent   [ ]
- Modified   [ ]

If they modified their strategy, describe *how* it changed and speculate *why* it changed.

3 Was their overall strategy effective in the context of this negotiation?

4 Compare your assessment with the negotiator's own assessment.

- Did the negotiator agree with your assessment of their negotiating strategy?
- If not, did they view their own style/strategy as more or less collaborative than your assessment of their style?

When others are *observing you*, ask them to comment on your overall style.

1 Did they see it as:

- Withdrawing/avoiding   [ ]
- Accommodating   [ ]
- Compromising   [ ]
- Collaborating   [ ]
- Competing   [ ]
- Do you agree with this assessment?

2 Did they report that your strategy changed or remained consistent throughout the negotiation?

- Consistent   [ ]
- Modified   [ ]

If they observed that you modified your strategy, *how* did it change? Did they speculate *why* it changed?

3 Did they view your overall strategy as effective in the context of this negotiation?

4 Compare your assessment of your own style with their assessment of your style.

- Did the observer(s) agree with your assessment of your own style?

- If not, did they view your negotiating style as more or less collaborative than your own assessment of your style?

Negotiating behaviours

Behaviours are the primary components of negotiating skills. Table 10.2 lists some of the main types of negotiating behaviour (such as information sending, information seeking, bidding and yielding) and indicates how the negotiators' intention influences how these behaviours are expressed. For example, where the negotiator's intention is to contend, information-sending behaviour is more likely to involve some element of deception than when the intention is not to contend.

- Contending behaviours are those behaviours that are often woven together to produce tactics that support a competitive negotiating strategy.
- Non-contending behaviours are those which tend to typify the problem-solving tactics that support a collaborative negotiating strategy. However, they can also form part of tactics that are associated with compromising and accommodating strategies, such as splitting the difference or conceding.

Greenhalgh (1987: 243) lists a number of source references that offer a more detailed discussion of many of the behaviours listed in Table 10.2.

Table 10.2 Contending and non-contending negotiating behaviours.

BEHAVIOUR	EXPRESSION WHERE INTENTION IS TO CONTEND	EXPRESSION WHERE INTENTION IS TO COLLABORATE
Information sending	*Demonstrates lack of interest* in other party's well-being and focuses attention on strength of own position. (Egocentric statements)	*Demonstrates an interest* in other party's well-being and a willingness to explore solutions that will benefit both parties. (Empathic statements)
	Deception regarding the situation, and own concerns and preferences. (Bluffing)	*Honesty.* No intention to alter information in order to gain a personal advantage.
	Withholds information in order to create a false impression without actually telling lies.	*Full disclosure* of information to foster a climate of openness and cooperation.
Information seeking	*Focus:* Only seeks information that will *benefit self*.	Adopts an empathic approach to seeking information *about the other party's* concerns and preferences.
	Type of question and probe. Use of questions and probes that restricts the other party's freedom to answer (e.g. closed and semi-closed questions).	Heavy use of open questions.
	Body language that communicates lack of interest in other party's views (little evidence of 'SOLER' non-verbal signals).	Body language that signals negotiator is listening to other: S Facing other party Squarely O Adopting Open posture L Leaning towards speaker E Maintaining Eye contact R Appearing Relaxed.
	Attending behaviour. Interrupts other and/or fails to give others the opportunity to present their case.	Using minimal prompts and attentive silences to *encourage other to communicate* all the information they feel is important (see Chapter 4).
Idea generating	Rejects invitations to engage in joint idea generation or problem-solving discussions. Restricts idea generation to helping self/own side.	Initiates or engages in joint brainstorming or problem-solving discussions.
Argumentation	*Debating posture* to assert own case.	*Open exchange* and receptivity to others' case.
Compliance seeking	*Demands compliance* with little or no justification.	*Explains* own position and requests compliance.
Bidding	Use of bids and counter-bids to *challenge other's target* outcome.	Bids and counter-bids used to *communicate own target* to other.
Yielding	*Size:* Small concessions. *Rate:* Concessions granted slowly.	Large concessions. Concessions granted quickly.
Sanctioning	Threats and conditional concessions (promises)	Unconditional concessions.

Exercise 10.4 is designed to help you identify and develop more effective negotiating behaviours.

Exercise 10.4 Negotiating behaviours

This exercise involves a three-step approach to the development of effective negotiating behaviours.

Step 1: Observing other people negotiating

A useful starting point is to train yourself to observe others and recognise what is happening during a negotiation. The negotiation behaviour observation record presented below provides a framework for recording your observations.

It can be difficult to pay attention to all that is going on at the same time. One way of managing this potential information overload is to restrict your attention to just some of the behaviours included on the negotiation behaviour observation record form.

For example, you might restrict your attention to:

- The relative frequency of information-sending and information-seeking behaviour and/or the focus and openness of this behaviour.
- Argumentation – the extent to which a negotiator is receptive to the other's case or adopts a debating poster to assert own case.
- Compliance seeking – whether this comes across as demanding compliance without justification or as explaining own position and requesting compliance.
- The timing and purpose of bidding. Does the negotiator make the first bid, and if so at what point in the negotiation? What appears to be the purpose of any bids made – to communicate own target or to challenge the other party's target and limit?
- Yielding behaviour – the frequency, size and nature of any concessions that are made.

If there are several observers, each observer might pay attention to different aspects of the negotiation. If you are observing a video recording, the tape can be viewed on more than one occasion, giving you the opportunity to pay attention to different aspects of the negotiation on each viewing.

NEGOTIATION BEHAVIOUR OBSERVATION RECORD FORM

1   Information sending

Record (with a check-mark in the box provided) the frequency of each information-sending statement in terms of:

- *Focus*. Does the negotiator give others:
  - Information about strength of *own* position.
  - Information about potential mutual benefit?

- *Openness*:
  - Overall impression; Allocate 10 points between
    - ❏ *Bluff*, distortion, part disclosure
    - ❏ *Honest* and full disclosure

2   Information seeking

Record (with a check-mark in the box provided) the frequency of each information-seeking behaviour in terms of:

- *Focus*. Does the negotiator seek:
  - Information that will primarily benefit self?
  - Information that has potential mutual benefit?

- *Openness:*
  - Overall impression; Allocate 10 points between
    - ❏ *Restricting* (closed questions, interrupting, blocking out)
    - ❏ *Encouraging* (e.g. open questions, minimal prompts, attentive silences)

3   Argumentation
  - Overall impression; Allocate 10 points between
    - ❏ *Debating posture* to assert own case
    - ❏ *Open exchange* and receptivity to others' case

4   Compliance seeking
  - Overall impression; Allocate 10 points between
    - ❏ *Demanding* compliance without justification
    - ❏ *Explaining* own position and requesting compliance

5 Bidding
- Overall impression;
  Allocate 10 points between

☐ To *challenge* others' target and limit
☐ To *communicate* own target

6 Yielding

Record (with a check-mark in the box provided) the frequency of yielding behaviour in terms of:

- *Size of concessions given:*
  - Small concessions

  - Large concessions

- Does negotiator concede faster
  than other party?

  ☐ Yes
  ☐ No

- *Conditionality of concessions:*
  - Conditional
    (Threats and promises)
  - Non-conditional

It is not unusual for people to modify the way they behave as a negotiation progresses. In order to identify whether – and if so, how – a person's behaviour changes you may decide to use separate forms for the early and later stages of the negotiation (or change the colour of the pen you use to record your observations). You may have to decide on the length of the first period without knowing how long the negotiation will last (this will not be a problem when viewing a video recording of a negotiation).

Step 2: Assessing your own approach to negotiating and identifying possible improvements

This step involves opening a 'second channel' and using your observation skills to observe yourself. Do *not* deliberately try to change your approach to negotiating at this point because the aim is to increase your awareness of your normal negotiating style. Use the same approach to observing and assessing your own behaviour as you used in the first step when you were observing how other people negotiate. Record your observations on a second copy of the negotiation behaviour observation record form presented above.

Step 3: Taking action to improve your negotiating skills

This stage involves attending to those aspects of your own negotiating behaviour where you feel there is scope for improvement. If there are lots of changes you feel you should make, you might think about whether you should try and introduce all the changes at once or draw up a short list of a few changes to start with. You may, for example, decide to start by paying more attention to your opening bid or the size and rate of concessions. Once you have practised a few new ways of behaving, you may feel it appropriate to move on and introduce further changes.

Monitor the effects of these changes. Are you able to detect any differences in the way the other party responds to you? How do you feel about the new approach?

Tactics

Tactics are sets of behaviours that are structured and sequenced in ways that help negotiators achieve their desired ends. Choice of tactic is heavily influenced by choice of strategy. For example, if negotiators adopt a competitive strategy they are likely to adopt contending tactics designed to convince the other party that the only way to reach an agreement is for them to concede.

Tactics can be classified under four headings: contending, non-contending, flexible and complex.

Contending tactics

This first category includes negotiating tactics that are designed to help a negotiator push the other party into accepting the negotiator's demands. As noted above, they tend to emphasise behaviours that persuade the other party to concede. Examples include:

1 *Defining issues.* The aim of this tactic is for one party to impose its own agenda on the other party in order to define the issues that are negotiable. It is usually most evident in the early stages of a negotiation. The dominant behaviour is information giving, and involves asserting the importance of issues to self. Little attention is paid to the other party's concerns. If they are expressed they are typically rejected as non-negotiable.

2 *Demonstrating a commitment to hold firm.* This is a set of competitive tactics that involves negotiators in convincing the other party that they are determined to hold firm and that they will not (or cannot) give ground. If agreement is to be reached it is the other party who will have

244

to concede most. Behaviours associated with this set of tactics involve information giving, demonstrating the strength of one's own position, small and infrequent concessions, and some element of deception. This type of tactic often takes one of the following forms:

- *Indicating that 'the cupboard is bare' and that there is no room for concessions.* The essence of this tactic is to convince the other party that the current offer is at or very near the negotiator's limit, and that there is no room for manoeuvre. Travel agents, for example, may attempt to convince customers that if they insist on using a credit card to pay for their air ticket it will be impossible to offer a discount. The agents may reinforce the point by quoting the high commission rates charged by the banks and the narrow margins they have on ticket sales.
- *Demonstrating a limited mandate to negotiate.* A variation on the above tactic is to convince the other party that one's mandate allows little or no room to negotiate certain variables. For example, negotiators may claim that they are bound by company policy which only allows staff to offer goods for sale at list price. The mandate tactic can also be used to make it appear that it is not the negotiators who are being difficult but some third party, thus helping them to appear firm without creating personal resentment.
- *Making small concessions and conceding slowly.* There is evidence that small concessions, offered slowly, are more likely to reinforce a firm image than large concessions or a series of small concessions offered in rapid succession.
- *Resisting the other party's persuasive arguments or threats.* An example of this tactic is to counter the opponent's attempt to impose time pressure by asking if they can suggest a good hotel, thereby demonstrating that time is maybe less important to you than to them.

3   *Imposing time pressure.* This is a set of contending tactics that can be used to persuade the other party to concede by increasing the perceived cost or risk of continuing to negotiate. It often involves deception, less than full disclosure of information, frequent reliance on non-verbal behaviour, threats and so on. Carnevale and Pruitt (1992) refer to several studies which indicate that time pressure produces lower demands, a faster rate of conceding and faster agreement. This type of tactic often takes one of the following forms:
   - *Imposing deadlines to dramatise the likelihood of breakdown.* There are various ways negotiators can use time pressure to convince others that they must concede. A group of diplomats, for example, may put pressure on others to reach an agreement by declaring that they have

been recalled to London and that they have to catch the four o'clock flight. A buyer may state that the deal must be concluded before the end of the financial year; otherwise the available funds will be lost.

- *Making preparation to leave.* Collecting papers together, packing a briefcase, standing up and looking around for a coat are all powerful non-verbal signals which communicate that unless the other party makes some concessions there is little point in continuing the negotiation.

- *Dragging out the negotiation.* Pruitt (1981) suggests that this tactic is often embodied in the familiar routine of consulting with superiors. He offers the example of a car salesperson keeping a customer waiting for twenty minutes while checking with a more senior manager whether it will be possible to offer a marginally better price. Customers who value their time may capitulate rather than accept other such delays. Dragging out negotiations can also be a very effective technique when the cost of lost time is higher for one party than for the other. Examples might include the need to reach agreement about the delivery of perishable vegetables or the completion of work before an important deadline.

4 *Positional bidding to lower the other's expectation regarding the overall level of benefit that can be achieved from an agreement.* This is a contending tactic that often focuses on the opening bid and counter-bid.

Opening bids tend to be influenced by a number of factors. These include the negotiators' desire to provide room to trade concessions, to protect their limit from detection and to challenge the opponents' expectation regarding the likely outcome of the negotiation. It is this latter point that is the focus of attention here.

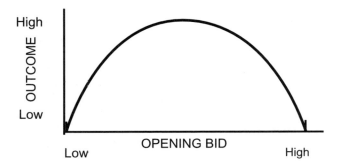

Figure 10.5 The relationship between opening bid and outcome.

The aim of challenging expectations is to persuade the other party that their *target* outcome is unrealistic. For example, the owners of a canal barge may be hoping to sell it for about £40,000 (their *target* price) and may have decided that they will accept nothing less than £35,000 (their *limit*). If the potential buyers make the first bid and this is only £19,000 it may shock the sellers into revising both their *target* and *limit*. If, however, the prospective buyers' opening bid is £37,000 this may convince the sellers that their target selling price of £40,000 is realistic and that they should hold out for it. Consequently, they may counter the buyers' opening bid of £37,000 with an opening offer to sell for £45,000 (£5000 above their actual *target* and £10,000 above their *limit*).

When deciding what the opening bid should be, negotiators may find it useful to know that research evidence suggests that those who ask for little usually reach an agreement, but one which yields little benefit for themselves. Those who demand too much may fail to reach any agreement at all. Those who make realistically high demands are the ones who have the best chance of obtaining the greatest benefit.

The normal relationship between initial demand and outcome is illustrated in Figure 10.5. It is worth noting, however, that if a negotiator's initial demand is too low the other party may believe it is too good to be true and ask themselves 'what's wrong with it?' For example, if the prospective buyers expect to pay £35,000 for the canal barge and the sellers open the bidding by only asking for £700, the buyers may be concerned. They may worry about whether the hull is rotten or whether something else is wrong with it. They may have a similar reaction if, after the sellers have opened with an initial high demand, say £45,000, they then offer large concessions in rapid succession. People, especially where they expect to engage in a competitive negotiation, are more likely to value an outcome if they have had to work hard to achieve it.

5   *Reducing the other's resistance to making concessions.* This is a set of contending tactics designed to increase the other party's willingness to yield, and involves many of the contending behaviours listed in Table 10.2. (However, it can also include non-contending behaviours such as explaining one's own position and requesting rather than demanding compliance.) This type of tactic usually takes one of the following forms:

*   *Making it costly to continue to negotiate.* Examples of this tactic are legion. A company trying to agree a claim for damages or divorced parents fighting over the custody of a child may attempt to increase the cost of continuing to negotiate for the other party by initiating

expensive legal proceedings. This kind of tactic is most effective when one party has more power than the other because they have access to more resources and can more easily afford the extra costs.

- *Undermining the other party's case.* This can be done by challenging the assumptions on which the opponent's case is based. For example, when negotiating the number of established posts in a hospital, a negotiator may challenge the assumption that certain duties can be performed only by professionally qualified staff. A negotiator may also gain some advantage by questioning the facts of an argument and the conclusions drawn from the facts. If the other party can be convinced that their case is weak there is a greater likelihood of them making concessions.

To use this tactic effectively, negotiators need to be skilled at asking questions and listening (see Chapters 4, 5 and 6). The more they can persuade the other party to talk, the more information they are likely to give away. This includes revealing inconsistencies and omissions in their argument and disclosing weaknesses that can undermine their case.

- *Persuasive argument.* The most persuasive arguments are those which convince one party that the other party's proposals offer them valuable benefits. Advocacy of this kind is likely to be most effective when a negotiator is able to empathise with the opponent's point of view, understand their needs, even some of those which may not be directly related to the issue being negotiated, and frame arguments which go as far as possible towards satisfying those needs. For example, an employer wanting to acquire tighter control over the hours worked by employees may persuade the union to consider the introduction of flexi-time. While it could have many advantages for union members, the employer would benefit because, in order to obtain the benefits of flexi-time, employees will have to clock on and clock off.

- *Contingent concessions.* Threats involve the declared intent of imposing some sanctions if the other party refuses to concede. Employees may threaten to strike unless a new wage rate is agreed. Buyers may threaten to go elsewhere for a product or service, hinting that alternatives could be found that are better, cheaper or more reliable. Threats will be most effective when the party issuing the threat is seen to have the power to impose it. However, they must also be seen to have the will to carry it out. The threatened party will search for evidence regarding whether previous threats have been implemented. Threats will also be taken more seriously in those circumstances where all parties are aware that it will cost very little to follow through and implement a threatened sanction.

Promises offer rewards for conceding. A promise is conditional, a reciprocal concession. 'If you do this then I will do that.' Nothing is given away until the other party concedes. Promises are most likely to be believed when the party issuing the promise is seen to have the ability to deliver it. They must also have a track record that will convince the other party that they can be relied on to keep their promises.

Resistance to contending tactics

In some cases contending tactics appear to produce the desired effect whereas in others they provoke retaliation. Pruitt (1981) suggests that the reaction of the other party to the use of competitive tactics is influenced by the 'heaviness' of the negotiator's efforts to influence. Heaviness, in this context, refers to the extent to which negotiators put pressure on the other party to the point of creating a feeling of resentment. Making 'if-then' promises or attempting to influence the other by improving the relationship does not normally produce a feeling of resentment. Making threats and imposing time pressures, on the other hand, are examples of tactics that are more likely to generate such feelings.

People are more likely to resist when they experience the other party's behaviour as heavy-handed. This resistance tends to develop into active retaliation when the pressured party judges their bargaining power to be equal to or greater than the other's. Retaliation is even more likely when the negotiators are aware of being observed by their constituents. There is also evidence that where the resentment is very strongly felt some people will be prepared to retaliate, even when they believe that their chances of winning are small or non-existent. They would prefer to go down fighting rather than let the other party win. In these circumstances the win–lose competitive relationship deteriorates into one which can best be described as lose-lose.

The other party's response to concessions

The normal convention is that the opening bid does not represent the final position. It is anticipated that agreement will be reached, irrespective of whether the climate of negotiation is competitive or collaborative, after a process of trading concessions.

Concessions are more likely to be reciprocated when the negotiator offering the concession has a 'firm' image. A firm image is promoted by resisting the other party's threats and creating the impression that movement will not be achieved easily.

When the negotiator has a 'soft' image, concessions are more likely to be interpreted as a sign of weakness. Instead of reciprocating, the other party may be encouraged to stand firm and press for even more concessions. Thus where one party is seen to be relatively soft (i.e. to have a weaker bargaining position), there is a greater chance that the negotiation will become competitive.

Non-contending tactics

These are tactics that are commonly employed when the negotiator's intention is to search for a mutually beneficial agreement or to ensure that the other party's requirements are accommodated. They involve more openness and a greater willingness to offer concessions than the tactics associated with more competitive strategies. This type of tactic may involve the joint definition of an agenda of negotiable issues as well as a more open exchange of views as the negotiation proceeds.

Non-contending tactics involve higher risk than many competitive tactics. The type of non-contending tactic that negotiators may choose to employ will be determined by the extent to which they feel they can trust the other party. Pruitt (1981) has identified some high- and low-risk collaborative (non-contending) tactics.

1 *High-risk non-contending tactics.* Negotiators may offer a large concession to the other party in the hope that this will be reciprocated. This kind of move is high risk because if it is not reciprocated they will have seriously weakened their position.
2 *Lower risk tactics.* Where negotiators wish to collaborate but are unsure whether they can trust the other party, they might favour the kind of move which is reversible, disavowable and covert. These moves minimise the risk of image loss (appearing 'soft'), position loss (offering concessions which cannot be taken back) and, to a lesser extent, information loss (providing information which competitors might use to their advantage). Some examples are:

   • *Signals and hints.* Signals can be used to suggest a willingness to make a concession or reciprocate if the other concedes. Early signals tend to be more ambiguous so that they can be more easily disavowed, thus enabling the signaller to avoid image loss if the other party does not reciprocate. An amorous young man may smile at a female colleague. If she returns his smile he may seek an opportunity to get closer to her. If she does not move away he might initiate some physical contact, he may touch her hand. If she delays slightly before withdrawing it he may feel reasonably confident in risking a more direct approach and invite her out for the evening. The initial use of ambiguous sign language followed by more noticeable signals enables him to minimise the risk of being rejected. If the initial smile had not been reciprocated or if she had physically distanced herself as soon as he sat close to her, he could have maintained the earlier working relationship and denied any suggestion that he was hoping for anything more. When negotiating a pay deal the parties involved may use gestures or phrases to hint that a concession may be possible if the other party would also be willing to move. This kind of tactic can be particularly useful part-way through a negotiation to test whether there is any possibility of moving from what, so far, may have been a competitive confrontation towards a more collaborative interaction. For one party to directly introduce this possibility could be very risky. The opportunities offered by indirect communication minimise such risks.

- *Messages transmitted through intermediaries* can be used in the same way. A colleague may suggest to a manager that the person she has been negotiating with would be willing to agree the transfer of staff she wanted if he could feel confident that she would not block his application for an increased computing budget. If she felt unable to offer this assurance the negotiation could continue as if no concession had been offered. On the other hand, if she were to inform the intermediary that she would agree not to oppose the other manager's application he may feel confident enough to directly propose the compromise next time they meet.

- *Informal problem-solving sessions.* These can take place over lunch, on the golf-course, in the lift or on the telephone. Because they are discussions which occur outside the framework of formal negotiation they provide the opportunity to informally explore possible moves. Such discussions tend to be very tentative and liberally peppered with 'what if'-type statements. They are often conducted in secret, away from the eyes of constituents and even fellow negotiators. This approach has been used very effectively on many occasions to find a way out of a seemingly deadlocked situation. Because such discussions take place outside the formal negotiations, if they fail to produce an agreement the negotiators are able to return to the bargaining table without prejudice and continue from where they left off. (This tactic is sometimes referred to as 'arena screening'; see below.)

- *Small concessions, followed by larger ones if reciprocated.* If the initial concession is not reciprocated, relatively little will have been lost. If, on the other hand, it produces movement, it may lead to further concessions and eventual agreement.

Flexible tactics

There are also a number of tactics that can be used to support any one of a range of strategies such as competing, collaborating, compromising or accommodating. Two examples are offered below.

1   *Improving the relationship with the other party or improving the other's mood.* There is ample evidence to suggest that we tend to help those people whom we like, identify with or depend on. Knowing this, skilful negotiators may attempt to make others like them in order to increase the likelihood that they will make concessions to help them. These kinds of tactics can be used competitively to manipulate or deceive the other party in order to gain a personal advantage. However, they can also be used as part of a genuine attempt to build mutual trust and encourage a more collaborative approach to the resolution of differences. Tactics that can be used to improve a negotiator's relationship with the other party include:

   - *Being warm and friendly.* The 'warm and friendly' tactic can also include an element of ingratiating, agreeing with the other party and appearing to value their opinion. These are all behaviours that encourage the other party to develop a positive attitude towards the negotiator.
   - *Doing favours for the other party.* The objective of this tactic is to generate a feeling of indebtedness and dependence as well as encourage the other party to like the provider of favours. Being told by a group of negotiators that it took hours to convince their boss that their company should consider a contractor's tender, even though it was submitted one hour after the deadline, makes it more difficult for the contractor to squeeze the negotiators too hard.
   - *Behaving in accordance with the other's values.* The other party is more likely to identify with someone who shares their values than with someone who offends them. For example, when negotiating an agreement in some Islamic countries, a company may find that male negotiators are better received than female negotiators.
   - *Choosing a pleasant setting for the negotiations.* Helpfulness can be induced by being in a good mood. Many factors can affect mood. One is the setting for the negotiation. A negotiator may decide that the relaxed atmosphere of a restaurant is more conducive to a productive negotiation than meeting in the client's office. The office setting may be one where the client will be subject to interruptions, competing demands for attention and the many immediate irritations which may be a feature of the client's working environment.

2   *Soft concessionary behaviour.* Reference has already been made to how large concessions can be used to support a collaborative strategy and encourage the search for a mutually beneficial agreement. However, large concessions can also be offered with manipulative intent. Negotiators may, for example, offer large concessions on an issue that is of low value to them in order to persuade the other party to reciprocate with concessions on a variable that is much more valuable to them. The important issue is intent. Large concessions can be offered either to secure personal advantage or mutual benefit.

Complex tactics

Reference has also been made to how the parties can sometimes modify their strategies as the negotiation proceeds. They may, for example, switch from competing (and the use of contending tactics) to collaborating (and the use of problem-solving tactics). The advantage of an alternative strategy may become apparent as the negotiation proceeds or it may have been planned in advance to gain tactical advantage. Carnevale and Pruitt (1992) provide examples of how contending and non-contending tactics can be linked together. They refer to:

- *Rapid sequencing.* This involves successive switching between conceding and contending.
- *Arena shielding.* This involves employing different tactics in different situations, for example, contending at the negotiating table and problem solving in unofficial meetings or over drinks (see the discussion of informal problem-solving sessions, above).
- *Personnel shielding.* This involves one team member taking a contentious approach while the other engages in a conceding or problem-solving approach. One variation of this 'good guy–bad guy' routine is to substitute, on a temporary basis, a more reasonable negotiator. The contrast between the two can encourage the other party to enjoy a sense of relief during the bad guy's absence. They may feel that it would be productive to progress the negotiation – to a conclusion if possible – before the bad guy returns. They may feel this way because they are less fearful of being exploited by the good guy. They may also believe that it would be to their advantage, in the long run, if the 'other side' could be persuaded that the good guy is the better negotiator. This makes them willing to make concessions in order to progress the negotiation in the absence of the 'bad guy'.
- *Issue shielding.* This involves standing firm on some issues while conceding on others. Feints offer an example of how this tactic can be used in practice. A negotiator may focus attention on an unimportant issue. This is done to make the other party believe that it is critical. The

negotiator then concedes on this issue in order to divert attention away from what is really a much more important issue. The important issue is one on which the negotiator is determined to hold firm.

Creating opportunities to take time out and think

It is difficult to anticipate every move in a negotiation. Sometimes an unexpected opportunity presents itself or an opponent makes a move that puts the negotiator under pressure. At times like this it can be useful to create the space to think through what to do next. This space can be created in a number of ways.

- The most obvious is to ask for a recess in order to 'take stock' or to consult with constituents. However, the negotiator may wish to take time out without making this obvious to the other party.
- A more covert approach is to ask an irrelevant question. While the other party is providing an answer the negotiator can do some thinking. A similar technique is to offer a summary, but to deliberately misstate the other party's position. They will demand the opportunity to clarify where they stand, again creating a breathing space.

Exercise 10.5 is designed to help you recognise (and assess the effectiveness of) the negotiating tactics that others use.

Exercise 10.5 Negotiating tactics

At the level of tactics, note [✓] whether the negotiators you are observing engage in any of the following tactics.

(If these tactics are not used, describe the tactics that are used in the space provided below).

_____

Contending tactics

Defining issues for all parties . . . .   [ ]
Demonstrating commitment to hold firm.

- Indicating the cupboard is bare – no room for concessions   [ ]
- Demonstrating limited mandate to negotiate . . . .   [ ]
- Tough conceding (small concessions granted slowly)   . . .   [ ]
- Resisting others' persuasive arguments and threats   . . . .   [ ]

Imposing time pressure.

- • Imposing deadlines to dramatise possibility of breakdown . [ ]
- • Making preparations to leave . . . . [ ]
- • Dragging out the negotiation . . . . [ ]

Positional bidding to gain competitive advantage . . . . [ ]

Reducing others' resistance to making concessions.

- • Making it costly to continue to negotiate . . . . [ ]
- • Undermining other party's case . . . . [ ]
- • Persuasive argument . . . . [ ]
- • Contingent concessions . . . . [ ]

Non-contending tactics

Generous non-contingent concessions . . . . [ ]

Reciprocating concessions offered by other party . . . . [ ]

Exploring possibilities for collaboration

- • Signals and hints re readiness to concede . . . . [ ]
- • Messages transmitted through intermediaries . . . . [ ]
- • Problem-solving discussions . . . . [ ]

Flexible tactics

Improving relationship with other party/improving others' mood.

- • Being warm and friendly . . . . [ ]
- • Doing favours for other party . . . . [ ]
- • Behaving in accordance with others' values . . . . [ ]
- • Choosing pleasant setting for negotiation . . . . [ ]

Soft conceding (large concessions given quickly) . . . . [ ]

Complex tactics

Rapid sequencing (switching between conceding and contending)   [ ]
Arena shielding (using different tactics in different arenas)   . . . . .   [ ]
Personnel shielding (good guy/bad guy)   . . . .   [ ]
Issue shielding (feints)   . . . .   [ ]

Other tactics

Specify:

Did they create opportunities to take time out to think?

Request recess   . . . .   [ ]
Ask irrelevant questions   . . . .   [ ]
Deliberately misstate others' position   . . . .   [ ]

How did other party respond to contending tactics?

By conceding   . . . .   [ ]
By retaliating   . . . .   [ ]

How did other party respond to concessions?

By reciprocating   . . . .   [ ]
By holding firm   . . . .   [ ]

Improving your ability to negotiate effectively

An essential first step is to train yourself to observe and recognise what is happening during a negotiation. Many of the exercises presented in this chapter have been designed to help you observe others, and also to monitor your own behaviour and identify areas for improvement. Working on these exercises can help you build up a profile of the way you typically behave when negotiating. For example:

- How do you respond to others? Are you easily put off? If your opponent fails to answer a probing question do you typically repeat the question and then stay silent until it is answered? Or do you typically respond by asking an 'easier' (and from your point of view less satisfactory) question, suggest an answer for the other party, or simply move on?

- Consider whether you tend to favour certain tactics and ignore others?
- Are you inclined towards being more competitive or more collaborative?
- Do you vary your style depending on the circumstances?

How satisfied are you with the outcomes you achieve? Do you think you could do better? If so, where do you need to focus attention – on specific behaviours, tactics or your overall negotiating strategy?

Preparation is also important. In addition to some of the points highlighted earlier in this chapter, and specified in Exercise 10.2, it can be helpful to know as much as possible about your opponents. What kinds of assumptions do they make about negotiating? Do they see it exclusively in terms of a win–lose competition or are they prepared to consider the possibility of a win-win collaborative activity? At a different level, are they likely to ask probing questions? Can they be easily put off? How persistent are they? Researching your opponent in this way can be extremely useful when deciding which negotiating tactics and strategies to employ.

Summary

The aim of this chapter is to help you develop a better understanding of the process of negotiation and to help you identify the skills you need if you are to become a more successful negotiator.

The factors that influence the strategies that negotiators adopt have been examined, and a range of different negotiating tactics have been reviewed. Attention has also been focused on some of the specific negotiating behaviours that underpin these tactics and strategies. The chapter concludes with a discussion of how you can improve your ability to negotiate more successfully.

References

Carnevale, P.J. and Pruitt, D.G. (1992) 'Negotiation and mediation', *Annual Review of Psychology* 43: 531–582.

Greenhalgh, L. (1987) 'Interpersonal conflicts in organizations', in C.L. Coopper and I.T. Robertson (eds) *International Review of Industrial and Organizational Psychology*, New York: John Wiley, pp. 229–271.

Morley, I.E. (1997) 'Negotiating and bargaining', in O.D.W. Hargie (ed.) *The Handbook of Communication Skills* (2nd edn), London: Routledge.

Pruitt, D.G. (1981) *Negotiation Behaviour*, New York: Academic Press.

Ruble, T. and Thomas, K. (1976) 'Support for a two-dimensional model of conflict behavior', *Organizational Behavior and Human Performance* 16: 145.

Scott, W.P. (1981) *The Skills of Negotiating*, Aldershot: Gower.

Thomas, K.W. (1977) 'Uses of the five conflict modes, as reported by a group of chief executives', *Academy of Management Review* 2: 487.

Thomas, K.W. (1979) 'Organizational conflict', in S. Kerr (ed.) *Organizational Behaviour,* Columbus, OH: Grid Publications, pp. 151–181.

Thomas, K.W. and Pondy, L.R. (1977) 'Toward an "Intent" model of conflict management among principal parties', *Human Relations* 30: 1089–1102.

11

WORKING WITH GROUPS

Learning objectives

To understand how the behaviour of group members can affect group performance and to recognise how and when to act in order to achieve desired outcomes.

After reading this chapter you will:

- Be able to define group effectiveness in terms of three different kinds of output.
- Understand the importance of being able to identify powerful and manageable factors that can affect group performance.
- Recognise the factors that influence the amount of effort group members expend on carrying out the task.
- Recognise the factors that determine the quantity and quality of task-relevant information available to the group.
- Recognise the factors that will help ensure that the group utilises the most appropriate performance strategy.
- Be able to describe and use a number of diagnostic tools that can determine what is going on in a group and what kind of action needs to be taken to improve group performance.
- Be aware of how you typically behave when interacting with other group members.
- Recognise what you could do to improve your contribution to group performance.

Working with groups

Groups provide an important context for work activity. Boards of directors, management committees, planning groups, project teams, task forces, quality circles, safety committees and autonomous work groups are but a few of the many different kinds of group within which organisational members have to work. Handy (1985) estimates that, on average, managers may

259

spend 50 per cent and senior managers 80 per cent of their working day in one sort of group or another.

The ability to work effectively with a group of other people, either as leader or member, is an important interpersonal skill. Hayes (1997) makes a distinction between groups and teams. Work groups can be any set of people whose work keeps them in regular contact. Teams, on the other hand, are groups of people that work together to achieve a specific task. In this chapter the terms are used interchangeably.

Katzenbach and Smith (1993) believe that effective team work is the key to organisational success. Sometimes groups are very productive. They are valued because they create ideas, make decisions, take action and generate commitment in ways that might otherwise be difficult to achieve.

On the other hand, some groups can be anything but productive. They can waste time, make poor decisions, be ridden with conflict and frustrate their members.

The first part of this chapter identifies some of the main factors that influence group effectiveness and highlights the role that group interaction processes can play in promoting better group performance. The second part of the chapter focuses on interaction processes, and presents an approach to develop a range of diagnostic and action skills that can be employed to improve group effectiveness

Determinants of group effectiveness

One of the most promising models of group effectiveness, in terms of offering a basis for diagnosing strengths and weaknesses in groups, is that advanced by Hackman (1987). He identifies three criteria for assessing group effectiveness. The first deals with the actual output of the group. He argues that group output should meet or exceed the performance standards of the people who receive and/or review it. He proposes this criterion rather than some more 'objective' index of performance because, in his opinion, what happens to a group tends to depend most on how its performance is viewed by these key people. The second criterion deals with the state of the group as a performing unit. The social processes used in carrying out the work of the group should maintain or enhance the capability of members to work together in the future. A group would not be very effective if, in the process of achieving an acceptable task output, members ended up fighting or not trusting each other and it destroyed itself. The third criterion deals with the impact of the group experience on individual members. He argues that the group experience, on balance, should satisfy rather than frustrate the personal needs of group members.

Hackman's model is attractive because it embraces this broadly based measure of effectiveness and because it focuses on variables which are powerful (that is, they make non-trivial differences to how a group performs), and which, at least potentially, can be managed. He attempts to explain why some groups perform better than others by proposing that effectiveness is a joint function of:

- the level of *effort* group members expend collectively on carrying out the task;
- the amount of *knowledge and skill* members bring to bear on the group task;
- the appropriateness to the task of the *performance strategies* used by the group in its work.

Asking questions about effort (are members working hard enough?), knowledge and skill (do members possess the required knowledge and skill and are they using it effectively?) and performance strategies (has the group developed appropriate ways of working on the task?) can provide valuable data about how well the group is performing. Hackman's model examines the various features of a group and its context which can lead to an improvement in its level of effort, its application of member knowledge and skill, and the appropriateness of its performance strategies. The framework adopted here to explore some of the main factors contributing to group effectiveness is based on Hackman's model.

Effort

A number of factors can influence the amount of effort group members expend on carrying out the task.

Task design

The design of the task can have an enormous impact on member motivation. Handy (1985) points to the importance of task salience and task clarity. Hackman (1987), extrapolating from the model of individual task motivation developed by Hackman and Oldham (1980), suggests that group norms encouraging high effort are likely to emerge when the task is challenging, important to the organisation or its clients, is 'owned' by the group and when it generates regular feedback on how group members are performing. Task design therefore provides an important part of the foundation upon which long-term group effectiveness can be built. It could even be argued that a well-designed task is a necessary (although probably not sufficient) condition for effective performance; so much so that improvements in the quality of group interaction processes are unlikely to do much to compensate for a very poorly designed task, except over the short term. Thus, although task design will not receive much attention in this chapter its implications for group effectiveness must not be underestimated.

Reward system

Closely linked with task design is the organisational reward system. Where the reward system provides groups with challenging performance objectives and reinforces their achievement, effort will be higher than where objectives are unclear, lack challenge or where the level of performance achieved by the group appears to have no consequence.

Group interaction processes

Group interaction processes can have an important influence on the level of effort members will expend on the task. People can develop process skills that will minimise what Hackman (following Steiner) labels the inevitable 'overhead costs' which must be paid when group members perform tasks. Coordinating member activities takes time and energy away from productive work. In some groups these overhead costs are much higher than in others because members lack the process skills to ensure that activities are coordinated efficiently.

As groups increase in size, the amount of effort invested by each member tends to decline. Latane *et al.* (1979) refer to this as 'social loafing'. In a larger group people may feel less responsible for the task outcome or feel that they can hide behind others and get away with less preparation than would be possible in a smaller group or if they were doing the task alone. Skilful management of the group process can limit certain kinds of motivational loss.

The quality of group interaction process can have other motivational consequences. For example, it can exaggerate or reduce considerably the motivational losses which tend to arise as a result of the way conflict is managed in the group. Deutsch (1960) emphasises the importance of those behaviours, such as mediating, which help to 'maintain' the group in good working order (see below).

Hackman also argues that where individuals do not value membership of the group their investment of effort is likely to be low, even if the task is well designed. On the other hand, where people identify themselves strongly with their team, this commitment will encourage them to work hard in order to make their team one of the best. The aim of many team-building exercises is to cultivate this sense of team spirit (see West 1994).

Knowledge and skill

Several factors will be considered under this heading: group composition, group size and group interaction processes. Group members need to be technically and functionally competent.

Group composition

A group will not be able to perform effectively if it does not have access to the resources it requires to complete its task. Knowledge and skill are key resources.

The availability of task-relevant expertise is largely determined by group composition. Unfortunately, all too often the composition of a group is determined by factors such as seniority or personal preference rather than ability or technical expertise. It may also be decided to assign certain people to a group because they represent the interests of various constituents, rather than because of their knowledge and skill. This kind of consideration has implications for group size.

Group size

Many groups in organisations are larger than they really need to be because additional members are recruited for 'political reasons'. Large groups composed in this way can be effective insofar as their representative membership helps ensure that their output will be well received; however, the quality of the output of large groups may be inferior to that of small groups. A number of factors may account for this. Large groups encourage social loafing (see above) and can adversely affect participation rates: some people find it much more difficult to contribute within a large group. This can be important for two reasons. First, because there is a tendency for those who make the biggest contribution to exercise most influence, and vice versa (Handy 1985), and second, because the people who do not contribute may deprive the group of relevant knowledge and skill.

Group interaction processes

Hackman (1987) draws attention to two other factors which, given the group's composition, can influence the availability of knowledge and skill to all members. The first concerns the *weighing of member contributions*. Hackman argues that the knowledge and skill of group members can be wasted if the group solicits and weighs contributions in a way that is incongruent with members' expertise. Sometimes group members give more credence to contributions from certain people, even if they do not possess the most task-relevant expertise, because of their age or status. The second factor he labels *collective learning*. There can be a synergetic effect when members of a group interact in a way that helps them learn from each other, thus increasing the total pool of talent available to the group.

The interpersonal skill of group members can influence the extent to which the task-relevant expertise, discussed above, is applied to the work of the group. Some people lack the interpersonal competence necessary to work with others on a common task and can seriously undermine the group's ability to perform effectively. It is within this context that the work of Belbin (1981) and Deutsch (1960), discussed later in this chapter, is of importance.

Performance strategies

Performance strategies are often taken for granted and are never questioned. As a result people sometimes work hard to little effect because the way their group has set about its task is not as productive as it might be. According to Hackman, the likelihood that a group will employ a task-appropriate performance strategy is increased when three conditions are satisfied. These three conditions are discussed under two headings: availability of information, and group interaction processes.

Availability of information

One of these conditions concerns the availability of information for group members to use when assessing their performance and evaluating alternative strategies. The organisational context within which some groups perform may offer easy access to relevant feedback. Other groups may have to operate in an environment where information is so limited that it may be difficult even to determine the criteria which will be used to assess the quality of their output. Faced with this kind of environment, groups may either react passively and accept this state of affairs as something which they cannot influence, or deliberately allocate resources to the task of changing the environment so as to increase the likelihood that it will yield the required data.

Group interaction processes

A second condition concerns the extent to which group interaction processes encourage the use of available information. Hackman argues that the performance strategy is more likely to be appropriate to the task when group norms exist which support both an explicit assessment of the performance situation and an active consideration of alternative ways of proceeding with the work. Before starting work, some groups always allow a little time to check out what the task is and how they should proceed. They may also, from time to time, take stock of how things are going and consider whether they should change the way they are working. Other groups, however, tend to plunge straight into the task and never give a second thought to performance strategy.

A third condition involves the existence of group interaction processes which, on the one hand, foster creativity, and on the other, help the group minimise slippage on strategy implementation. Greater creativity will increase the likelihood of members generating new ideas and improved ways of proceeding with the work. However, this is unlikely to occur in those groups where there are strong pressures for conformity and where the expression of deviant ideas is discouraged.

Many factors can contribute to 'slippage', but one variable which has much to do with both the appropriateness of the chosen strategy and the way in which the chosen strategy is implemented is the quality of decision making. One of the most widely discussed problems associated with group decision making has been described by Janis (1982) as 'groupthink'. Groupthink occurs when the pressure to reach a consensus interferes with critical thinking, thus inhibiting the appraisal of possible alternatives. Janis has identified eight symptoms of groupthink:

1 *Invulnerability*: Members become over-optimistic and assume that the group's past success will continue.
2 *Stereotyping*: Members ignore disconfirming data by forming negative stereotypes which discredit the sources of such information.
3 *Rationalisation*: Members find rationalisations which explain away evidence that threatens their emerging consensus.
4 *Illusion of morality*: Members believe that right is on their side and tend to be blind to the moral implications of their policy.
5 *Pressure*: Members are discouraged from expressing doubts too forcefully.
6 *Self-censorship*: Members keep quiet about misgivings and try to minimise their doubts.
7 *Mindguards*: Members protect the group from being exposed to disturbing ideas.
8 *Unanimity*: Members screen out the possibility of divergent views as soon as the most vocal members are in agreement.

Groups that experience problems with decision making, such as those described by Janis, are more likely than others to choose an inappropriate strategy in the first place. They are also likely to make poor decisions about how the chosen strategy should be implemented. The decision-making procedures adopted by a group are an important element in its overall performance strategy.

The importance of group interaction processes and interpersonal skills

The first part of this chapter has drawn attention to some of the main factors which influence group effectiveness and has highlighted the role group interaction processes can play in promoting better group performance. It has been shown that the quality of group interaction processes can influence the 'overhead costs' associated with coordinating group activity, the motivational losses that can occur through either 'social loafing' or conflict management and the synergetic gains that can be derived from high levels of commitment to the group. All these factors can have a direct effect on the amount of *effort* group members will expend on carrying out the task.

The amount of *knowledge and skill* members bring to bear on the task can also be influenced by the quality of group interaction processes. Attention was focused on participation rates, the weighting of member contributions and the benefits of collective learning. Furthermore, the process skills of group members were shown to affect the extent to which task-relevant skills are actually applied to the task.

It has also been shown that the quality of group interaction processes can have implications for the *appropriateness of the performance strategies* used by the group. Behaviours that support situation scanning and strategy planning, foster creativity, improve decision making and minimise slippage in strategy implementation can have an important impact on group effectiveness.

The second part of this chapter takes a closer look at group interaction processes and suggests ways in which either the group as a whole or individual group members can develop skills which will increase group effectiveness.

Improving group performance: diagnostic and action skills

One way to improve the effectiveness of a group is to improve the diagnostic and action skills of its members. A football analogy illustrates this point. Players use their diagnostic skills to understand what is going on and, at half time, share their diagnosis with other members of the team. They do this in an attempt to understand what, in the first half, they could have done differently to secure a better result and what, in the second half, they need to attend to if they are to improve their performance. Players also develop and use action skills such as marking, running with the ball, passing and shooting. These are the skills that, given their diagnosis of what needs to be done, enable them to intervene and take the action required to secure desired goals.

The development of diagnostic and action skills can improve the effectiveness of work groups. However, all too often the culture which characterises many work groups emphasises the *task* (what the group has to do) and ignores the *process* (how the group works together in order to accomplish the task). Consequently, in practice, little effort is invested in the development of process (diagnostic and action) skills.

Returning to the football analogy for a moment, while many players may engage eagerly in a post-match discussion of the process (how the game was played) their diagnosis may be far from accurate. The players may have poor diagnostic skills. They may be highly subjective in their review and attribute lack of success to their opponents' foul play, fail to recall many of their own shortcomings and only see themselves in an unrealistically favourable light. Even when they want to be objective when making their analysis, they may experience difficulty reaching a sound diagnosis because they lack an awareness of what kinds of behaviours and relationships are important and deserve attention.

The first part of this chapter addressed this issue and identified a number of problems which detract from group effectiveness. This second part offers some suggestions about those aspects of group behaviour which might deserve attention, presents a range of diagnostic tools which can be used to help determine what is going on in the group, and indicates the kind of action which may be necessary to improve matters.

The first step in making a diagnosis is to observe what is going on, to collect data. If we try to observe a group of people working together we quickly realise that so much is happening that it is impossible to pay attention to everything at the same time. The task can be made much easier if we focus our attention on certain aspects of how the group is working together. What follows is an introduction to several approaches to group observation that we can use as a basis for diagnosing what is going on in a group.

Frequency and duration of communication

In the discussion of different approaches to studying interpersonal interactions in Chapter 1, reference was made to one behavioural tradition that focuses attention on the patterns of interaction, without reference to verbal or emotional content.

We can measure the frequency of communication by simply placing a check-mark against each group member's name every time he or she says something. A crude measure of duration can be obtained by repeating the procedure every ten seconds until the speaker has stopped talking. We can summarise this data to show who spoke most often, who made long speeches and who tended to rely more on short contributions. For example, Figure 11.1 shows that David hardly spoke at all whereas, Victoria and Liz both made twelve separate contributions; however, Victoria made much longer speeches than Liz.

	0′	5′	10′
VICTORIA	/// //////// ////// ///	// ////// /// /////////	////// ///// /// //////
JAMES	/ / /// /	/ // //	
LIZ	/ // // / /	/ // / // /	/ /
TONY	////	/// /////	////// // ////// / /////
DAVID			/// // //

Figure 11.1 Frequency and duration of communication.

Recording participation rates for each five-minute period can provide us with data about how the pattern of participation changes over the course of the meeting. Figure 11.1 indicates that while James participated fairly frequently throughout the first ten minutes of the meeting he said nothing during the final period, whereas David made no contribution until the last five minutes.

Simple analyses of this kind can point to a number of important issues. For example, it may be found that some quiet members have relevant contributions that they wish to make but they are experiencing difficulty breaking into the conversation. A remedy may be for us (or some other member of the group) to assume a 'gatekeeper' role, checking from time to time whether the quiet members wish to contribute.

We may find, however, that quiet members do not contribute because they lack confidence or fear attack. This kind of problem can be overcome if we (and other members of the group) are more encouraging and accepting of member contributions.

It is possible, of course, that people who are seen to be quiet are not quiet at all. Observation may reveal that they actually do make contributions but they are ignored. Should this be the case, it may be useful to consider whether this is because past experience has taught us that what they have to say is not worth listening to or because the group is disinclined to give proper weight to 'deviant' opinions or to contributions, whatever their worth, from certain kinds of members: women, engineers, juniors in rank, young or new recruits.

Bearing in mind the research findings already reported (that those who talk most often exercise most influence), it may be helpful to enquire whether those who do most of the talking are those who have most to contribute in terms of knowledge, skill and experience. If not, it may be worth promoting norms and procedures within the group which will both lead to a more effective sharing of airtime and to the discovery of those who possess relevant knowledge, skill and experience.

Communication patterns

We may find it useful to observe who interacts with whom. We can record data in a number of ways but one relatively straightforward method is illustrated in Figure 11.2.

Draw a line from the speaker to the recipient with the arrow indicating the direction of communication. In practice this may not be as easy as it appears because it is not always clear to whom a remark is addressed. Body posture and direction of gaze can help determine this but on some occasions a remark may not be aimed at anybody in particular, but addressed to the group as a whole. We can record this by drawing a line which ends in the middle of the circle. Arrows at each end of a line can be used to indicate that

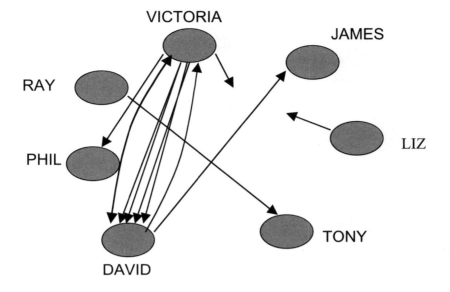

Figure 11.2 Communication patterns.

the initiator of a message received an immediate response from the recipient. Because observation charts of this kind soon become congested, it may be necessary for us to use several charts as the meeting progresses and then aggregate the results.

The interaction patterns revealed by this kind of analysis may provide many clues about how the group is working together. They may indicate whether the group is united in its efforts or whether various subgroups and cliques are operating to propagate particular views and influence decision making. They may also highlight the effectiveness or ineffectiveness of the group's performance strategy. For example, in situations where a quick decision is required and where the appropriate way forward will be fairly obvious once certain information has been shared, the interaction pattern often referred to as the 'wheel', shown in Figure 11.3, may be most appropriate.

We can sometimes observe this pattern in formal committees where the majority of all communications are addressed to the chairperson. Groups adopting this wheel pattern tend to reach decisions much more quickly than groups which adopt the 'all channel' pattern shown in Figure 11.4. If, however, the group needs to reach a creative solution to a complex problem it may find that the 'wheel' is considerably less effective than the 'all channel' pattern. Research evidence suggests that 'all channel' patterns are most likely to produce the best solution when the group is faced with a complex open-ended problem. All channel interaction patterns may also be more appropriate in those circumstances where it is necessary for the group to reach a consensus.

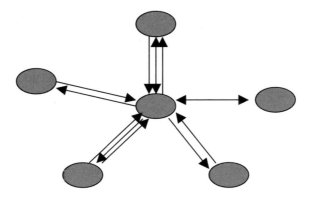

Figure 11.3 Wheel.

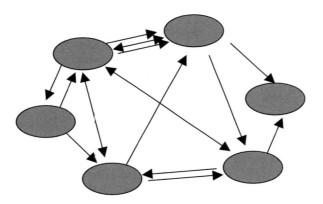

Figure 11.4 All channel.

It is important to stress, however, that interaction patterns only provide clues as to what may be going on in a group and great care must be exercised when interpreting findings. The interaction pattern, for example, between Victoria and David in Figure 11.2 shows that Victoria tends to address most of her communications to David. She may talk most with David because he tends to support her ideas and she identifies him as an ally. Alternatively she may address many of her messages to him because he is the person from whom she expects most opposition, and she therefore feels that the best way forward is to first confront him in order to judge the strength of the opposition she may face.

The apparent target of a communication is not the only aspect of interaction which deserves our attention. Eye movements that proceed and/or follow a communication can also be a rich source of data. Paying attention to such glances can help unearth important relationships. Ray may glance at James before talking to Tony and then again when he has finished. This may indicate that James is an important 'other' for Ray: a boss or informal leader, an opponent or possibly someone who may be hurt by what he has to say.

Speakers often look to leaders for permission to speak or for feedback on what was said. They may also look towards possible opponents for their reaction. Observing the pattern of such glances over a period can reveal alliances. If Ray, Victoria and Liz all glance at James, and Phil and Tony look towards David, this may signal the existence of two subgroups, at least when certain issues are being discussed.

Interaction patterns highlight the existence of relationships. However, we may require knowledge about the content of communications if we are to really understand the nature of these relationships.

Role functions

Another way we can analyse how a group is working is to examine member behaviour in terms of its purpose or function.

Morton Deutsch (1960), in conjunction with his research on cooperation and competition in groups, which he conducted in 1947, was one of the first to develop a system for categorising role functions. He argued that members of an effective group must perform two kinds of function: one concerned with completing the task, and the other with strengthening and maintaining the group.

TASK FUNCTIONS

If a group is to be successful in terms of completing its task, members must define the problem/task and suggest possible ways forward, share facts and opinions relevant to solving the problem or completing the task, elaborate and clarify ideas, challenge and evaluate proposals, make decisions, etc. Difficulties may arise if some members push their own views but fail to pay attention to those held by others, if vaguely stated proposals are left unclarified, if some members push for a decision before the problem has been explored fully or alternative solutions debated, or if the group loses its sense of direction and wastes time on irrelevant business.

MAINTENANCE FUNCTIONS

Just as a machine has to be maintained if it is to remain in good working order, so a group demands regular maintenance if it is to be effective when working on task issues. Quiet members may require encouragement if they are to make a proper contribution, those who have withdrawn and 'taken their bat home' after an argument may require help if they are to reintegrate with the group, and those who are unhappy with the way the group is being managed may find it difficult to continue working on the task until some of their concerns have been explored.

Based on the work of Deutsch, several methods for observing and categorising role functions have been developed. These methods have the advantage that they avoid self-report bias. An observer can categorise the behaviour of group members as it actually occurs rather than relying on members reporting, at some later date, how they thought they behaved.

The category set presented here draws on the work of Deutsch, and Benne and Sheets (1948), but it focuses attention on those role functions which the author has found most useful when observing groups. There are eleven task roles and five maintenance roles:

Task roles

1 *Initiator*. Defines a group problem; proposes tasks or immediate objectives; suggests a new procedure or a different approach to solving the problem.
2 *Information seeker*. Asks for information and facts relevant to the problem being discussed, seeks clarification of suggestions.
3 *Opinion seeker*. Asks for opinions, seeks clarification of values pertinent to what the group is undertaking or of values in a suggestion made.
4 *Information giver*. Offers facts or generalisations which are 'authoritative' or related to own experience.
5 *Opinion giver*. States opinions or beliefs.
6 *Elaborator*. Expands and explores ideas, offers examples or provides a rationale for suggestions made previously. Tries to envisage how an idea or suggestion would work out if adopted by the group.
7 *Evaluator/critic*. Evaluates or questions the 'practicality', logic, facts or the procedure of a suggestion or some aspect of the group's discussion.
8 *Coordinator*. Shows or clarifies the relationship among various ideas, tries to pull ideas and suggestions together or tries to coordinate the activities of members of the group.
9 *Decision manager*. Prods the group to a decision, sends up 'trial balloons' to test group opinions.
10 *Recorder*. Records the progress of the discussion, records decisions, acts as the 'group memory'.
11 *Supporter/follower*. Offers positive support for an argument or proposal, or signals a willingness to go along with an idea.

Maintenance roles

1 *Encourager*. Praises, agrees with and accepts the contribution of others in a way that encourages them to participate more fully in the group.

2 *Gatekeeper*. Attempts to keep communication channels open by inviting contributions or proposing procedures that will enable everyone to contribute.

3 *Mediator*. Attempts to reconcile disagreements or to relieve tension by jesting or pouring oil on troubled waters.

4 *Compromiser*. Operates from within a conflict in which his or her idea or position is involved. Offers to compromise or holds back from escalating a conflict.

5 *Standard setter*. Suggests and defends standards for the group to achieve in terms of output or procedures.

This category set is not exhaustive because it includes only behaviour that helps the group work effectively. Some behaviour is more concerned with the satisfaction of individual needs and is often dysfunctional from the point of view of group effectiveness. Benne and Sheates discuss a number of such roles. For example, the aggressor, a person who attacks others, jokes aggressively or shows envy towards another's contribution by trying to take credit for it, or the playboy, a person who makes a display of his lack of involvement in the

Role \ Name	Victoria	James	Liz	Tony	David
TASK ROLES					
INITIATOR	//	/	/		
INFORMATION SEEKER		//	//	//	
OPINION SEEKER	/		/////		
INFORMATION GIVER	///// ////				
OPINION GIVER	/////	///// ////			
ELABORATOR	/////		//		//
EVALUATOR/CRITIC		////			
CO-ORDINATOR	/		///		
DECISION MANAGER	//				
RECORDER			//	/	
SUPPORTER/FOLLOWER					////
MAINTENANCE ROLES					
ENCOURAGER			//		
GATEKEEPER			///		
MEDIATOR			//		
COMPROMISER			/		/
STANDARD SETTER	/				

Figure 11.5 Role functions record sheet.

group by trivialising the task and distracting others by fooling around. While it can be helpful to draw attention to these kinds of dysfunctional behaviour, the focus of attention of the category set presented here is functional group behaviour.

A necessary first step for diagnosing role behaviour in groups is the collection of data. We can record role functions using the matrix presented in Figure 11.5. We place a check mark in the appropriate cell each time a member of the group performs one of the functions listed. We can then use the data generated by this procedure in a number of ways.

We can review the overall performance of the group by noting the kinds of behaviour we observed for the group as a whole. An initial analysis may focus on the balance between task and maintenance behaviours. While task behaviour normally predominates, in some very task-oriented groups there may be no evidence of any maintenance functions being performed, a state of affairs which, over the longer term, could threaten the ability of the group to continue working effectively.

Within each of the broad task and maintenance categories the low incidence or complete absence of particular role functions may point to areas of group functioning which deserve attention. For example:

1   If nobody performs the evaluator/critic role there may be a danger of the group arriving at the kind of ill-considered solutions illustrated earlier when the phenomenon of groupthink was discussed.
2   If nobody performs the coordinator role the discussion might lack focus, related issues and underlying themes may go unrecognised, members may either duplicate or fail to undertake necessary preparatory or follow-up work and the group may fail to 'pull together'. Consequently, the overhead costs, discussed above, may be unnecessarily high.
3   If nobody acts as decision manager the group may miss decision points and the discussion may drift from topic to topic before any decisions have been made. Alternatively, the group may rush into decisions before all the relevant facts have been considered or alternative solutions examined. These kinds of behaviour can also create problems to do with coordination (thus increasing overhead costs), and can lead to the adoption of inappropriate performance strategies by the group.
4   If nobody acts as mediator conflicts may go unresolved. Members may withdraw psychologically from the group or – possibly more damaging – may pursue hidden agendas to get back at the other party. This may lead to motivational losses or the diversion of effort to activities which detract from group effectiveness.
5   If nobody performs the gatekeeper role people who have a contribution they wish to make may remain silent, and the group may be deprived of a potentially important contribution in terms of task-relevant expertise.

We can also audit an individual's behaviour and review the kind of contribution he or she normally makes to the work of the group. We can do this by focusing attention on the range of role functions an individual performs. Some people confine themselves to a narrow range of behaviours whereas other have a wide repertoire at their disposal. Another focus for analysis may be the appropriateness and/or timeliness of the behaviour in terms of its consequences for group effectiveness. Returning to the football analogy, there is little advantage in being expert at shooting the ball and scoring goals if you fail to recognise the difference between your own and your opponents' goal. A wide range of action skills can increase a person's effectiveness, but only if they are applied appropriately. A good mediator, for example, may have a low tolerance for any kind of conflict and, on some occasions, by intervening to smooth things over, may inhibit the exploration of important differences in the group. Similarly, a compromiser may be too ready to let go of a good idea if pressured by a more assertive member. If the person who is good at mediating had not mediated and the compromiser had not compromised, the group in the examples presented may have accomplished its task more successfully.

If a member is unhappy with his or her own performance an audit of the role functions performed may suggest alternative ways of behaving.

Dedicated devil's advocates – the people who always see the problems and pitfalls which others appear to overlook – may find that many of their contributions tend to be ignored by the rest of the group. While the evaluator/critic role is essential, if it is the only role a person performs it may be rendered ineffective. Performing other roles and making a wider range of contributions can help avoid the negative consequences sometimes associated with the label 'group critic'.

The person who is happy to offer the group information or opinions but never seeks ideas from others may find that they are less effective than they could be. Such a person may consider achieving a better balance between giving and seeking both information and opinion.

One of the most popular approaches to examining role functions has been developed by Belbin (1993b). He produced research evidence that identifies eight key team roles which need to be exercised in a group if it is to be effective. He later extended this to include a ninth role of 'specialist'. Belbin argues that people differ in their ability and inclination to play these different roles. The original eight roles are:

1 *Coordinator*, the person who is a good judge of people, who recognises where the team's strengths and weaknesses lie, and coordinates and controls the work of members, making the best use of the team's resources in order to achieve group goals. The coordinator tends to be the kind of person who is calm, self-confident and controlled.

2   *Shaper*, the person who offers dominant task-leadership and tries to galvanise the group into action. The shaper tends to be outgoing, impulsive and impatient when seeking to impose some shape or pattern on group discussions or the outcome of group activities.

3   *Plant*, the person who is the major source of original ideas and proposals: very intelligent, often introverted and usually more interested in fundamental principles than practical detail.

4   *Resource investigator*, the person who, rather than being the originator of ideas, is someone who picks up ideas and information from others, especially from outside the group, and develops them. This kind of person tends to be an extrovert, an enthusiast and a good communicator. The resource-investigator performs as the group's diplomat, salesperson or liaison officer.

5   *Monitor evaluator*, the person who is serious minded, prudent and, unlike the shaper or resource investigator, has a built-in immunity from enthusiasm. The monitor evaluator is able to stand back and evaluate ideas and suggestions so that the team is better placed to take balanced decisions.

6   *Implementer*, the person who turns concepts and plans into practical working procedures. The implementer is methodical, trustworthy, efficient and willing to do what has to be done, even if it is not intrinsically interesting or pleasant.

7   *Team worker*, the person who supports and builds on other people's strengths and underpins their weaknesses. The team worker tends to be skilled at listening to others, facilitating communications within the group and dealing with difficult interpersonal situations.

8   *Completer-finisher*, the person who is motivated to finalise anything which is started, and to do so with thoroughness. The completer-finisher's relentless follow-through is important but not always popular.

The Belbin Team Role Self-Perception Inventory (BTRSPI) provides a profile of the roles a person typically performs, based on responses to a set of questions that explore how the respondent normally behaves in certain situations. This inventory is widely used by trainers and consultants. It has, however, been the focus of critical debate (Belbin 1993b; Furnham *et al.* 1993a, 1993b; Senior 1997, 1998; Senior and Swailes 1998).

One of the main problems that has been highlighted is related to the fact that the BTRSPI is an ipsative (forced choice) rather than a normative measure. Respondents are required to rank order items which load on to a set of preferred group roles in order to produce a profile of preferred (strongest) and least preferred (weakest) roles. The rank ordering involves distributing a fixed total of points between the different roles. The effect of allocating a high ranking (more points) to one or more roles means that there are fewer points available to allocate to the other roles. This procedure can be very useful in highlighting the relative strengths and weaknesses of a given individual's profile, but it may not provide as good an indicator of how that individual compares with others. For example, one individual might have very high scores for resource investigator and team worker and low scores for a number of other roles. Somebody else may have only an average to high score for team worker (because s/he scored very high on some other roles) and yet may still be able to perform this role better than the first individual (who had a very high score for team worker). Another criticism (Furnham *et al.* 1993a) is that the wording of some items is too vague. Other studies using the BTRSPI, however, have found some support for the link Belbin makes between team role balance and team performance (Senior 1997).

While the *diagnostic* techniques outlined here are important, they are not sufficient if group members are to begin to work together more effectively. Members need to be able to *intervene*, to take the action required to improve matters. This involves the development of action as well as diagnostic skills. If quiet members need encouragement somebody needs to recognise this need and intervene to satisfy it. If members recognise a need for better coordination they should be able to either intervene and perform the coordinator role themselves or persuade somebody else to do so.

A group can be strengthened and can work more effectively if members:

1   Become more aware of the wide range of role functions that need to be performed.
2   Have the ability to observe which role functions are being over-used or neglected and identify what changes are necessary.
3   Possess the necessary skill to modify their own behaviour so as to provide needed role functions.

Practice can extend an individual's repertoire of group roles. One approach we can adopt to develop the skills necessary to perform a wider range of role functions is to identify those role functions most neglected (by us and others) and to deliberately seek out opportunities to practise them. Just as some people seek to widen their vocabulary by choosing a new word each day and finding at least five opportunities to use it, so group members can widen their repertoire of role functions by practising under-used behaviours until they become second nature.

An essential first step in developing behaviours that contribute to the achievement of group tasks and the maintenance of group performance is to practise observing and categorising role functions. This is the purpose of Exercise 11.1.

Exercise 11.1 Observing and categorising role functions

Aim: To practise observing and categorising role functions.

Procedure: Two or three people watch a video tape recording of a group meeting (e.g. an off-air recording of a panel discussion).

Stage 1: Everybody observes the behaviour of a single group member

- *Working independently*, use the role functions record form presented below to categorise the behaviours of the person singled out for observation. (*Note*: as mentioned earlier in this chapter, this is not an exhaustive category set of all behaviours, and therefore you may observe some behaviours that cannot be allocated to a category.)
- *Working as a group,* share your record of observations. Identify a

Role functions record form

ROLES \ NAMES					
TASK ROLES					
INITIATOR					
INFORMATION SEEKER					
OPINION SEEKER					
INFORMATION GIVER					
OPINION GIVER					
ELABORATOR					
EVALUATOR/CRITIC					
CO-ORDINATOR					
DECISION MANAGER					
RECORDER					
SUPPORTER/FOLLOWER					
MAINTENANCE ROLES					
ENCOURAGER					
GATEKEEPER					
MEDIATOR					
COMPROMISER					
STANDARD SETTER					

selection of behaviours that members of your group categorised differently.

View the tape a second time, pausing at each disputed behaviour. Discuss each disputed behaviour in the light of the role definitions presented in this chapter and try to reach agreement on how the behaviour should be categorised.

Stage 2: Everybody observes the behaviour of all members of the total group

This is very demanding because there is so much more information to attend to than in the first stage of the exercise. Use a second copy of the Role Functions Record Form.

Stage 3: Review the behaviour of members of the group you observed in terms of task and maintenance role functions

- Consider whether there was a low incidence or complete absence of some role functions/behaviours.
- What effect, if any, did this have on the way the group performed?
- What action could group members take to improve the way the group worked together?

Interpersonal style and group climate

Much of the above discussion reflects a role-oriented approach to team building where the focus of attention is on how members behave in relation to the role functions (behaviours) that are required in order to promote effective group performance. A complementary approach focuses more attention on the individual differences that affect how people typically behave in group settings.

In order to identify the underlying dimensions of interpersonal behaviour, Hare (1982) reviewed the development of different approaches to the observation of behaviour and the various studies which factor analysed the results of such observations. The four dimensions which emerged as important are presented in Figure 11.6. These are dominant versus submissive, positive versus negative, serious versus expressive and conforming versus non-conforming. We can use these dimensions to identify an individual's interpersonal style or to describe group climate.

Relating these dimensions to the role functions presented above, we might expect that dominant group members would engage most frequently in such behaviour as initiating, giving information and opinions, evaluating and decision managing, and less frequently in such behaviour as compromising and mediating. Positive members may be more sensitive to the need for maintenance functions than negative members. In particular we may expect the positive member to seek information and opinions in an encouraging way, to act as a gatekeeper when necessary, and to avoid unnecessary conflict and confrontation.

Serious members are more likely to engage in group-oriented functional behaviours rather than the individually oriented dysfunctional behaviours which can often be observed in groups (see Benne and Sheats 1948). While

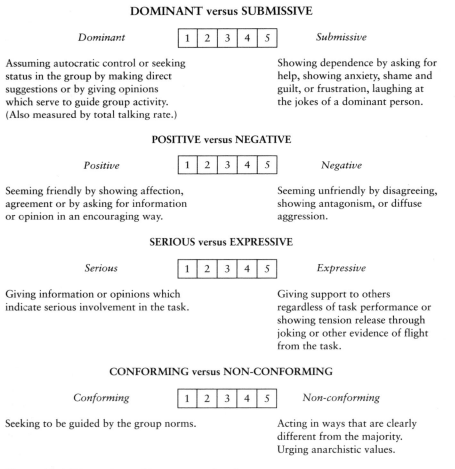

DOMINANT versus SUBMISSIVE

Dominant | 1 | 2 | 3 | 4 | 5 | *Submissive*

Assuming autocratic control or seeking status in the group by making direct suggestions or by giving opinions which serve to guide group activity. (Also measured by total talking rate.)

Showing dependence by asking for help, showing anxiety, shame and guilt, or frustration, laughing at the jokes of a dominant person.

POSITIVE versus NEGATIVE

Positive | 1 | 2 | 3 | 4 | 5 | *Negative*

Seeming friendly by showing affection, agreement or by asking for information or opinion in an encouraging way.

Seeming unfriendly by disagreeing, showing antagonism, or diffuse aggression.

SERIOUS versus EXPRESSIVE

Serious | 1 | 2 | 3 | 4 | 5 | *Expressive*

Giving information or opinions which indicate serious involvement in the task.

Giving support to others regardless of task performance or showing tension release through joking or other evidence of flight from the task.

CONFORMING versus NON-CONFORMING

Conforming | 1 | 2 | 3 | 4 | 5 | *Non-conforming*

Seeking to be guided by the group norms.

Acting in ways that are clearly different from the majority. Urging anarchistic values.

Figure 11.6 Dimensions of interpersonal style.

serious members are likely to be very task oriented, this will not prevent them from paying attention to group maintenance requirements if the failure to do so would impede task accomplishment. Expressive members, on the other hand, are likely to evidence much less concern for the task. They are likely to be more committed to the achievement of personal goals within the context of the group.

Conforming members are likely to be very aware of and guided by group norms and to engage in behaviour which will preserve traditional attitudes and practices within the group. However, should group opinion begin to move, conforming members may decide to go along with the change in order to protect their place in the group. Conforming members are less likely than non-conforming members to engage in evaluative or critical behaviour or to propose initiatives which are out of line with group thinking. Non-conforming members, on the other hand, are much less likely to compromise their views simply to preserve group solidarity or to protect their position as members.

Hare's four dimensions of interpersonal style provides us with a useful set of bench-marks that can be used to improve the way we behave in group settings. We can use these as a basis for experimentation and developing more effective interpersonal/communication styles. For example:

- If we are dissatisfied with the amount of influence we have, we may decide to experiment with new behaviours, observe the consequences and, if the desired outcome is achieved, modify our interpersonal style to incorporate the new behaviour.
- If we believe that we are too submissive (on the dominant versus submissive scale), we may attempt to exercise more influence by experimenting with more assertive behaviours. These may include taking initiatives, expressing opinions, talking more in the group and engaging in many of the behaviours discussed in Chapter 9 on asserting.
- If we see ourselves as too friendly and agreeable, we may decide to experiment with more negative behaviours, agreeing less and challenging more.
- Paying attention to the other two dimensions may also suggest ways of exercising more influence. We might behave in a more serious way, joking less and being more clearly involved in the task, or we might conform more by seeking to accomplish the task in ways which are acceptable to the group.

If the group as a whole is perceived to be ineffective, it may be worth considering whether this is because:

- too many people are trying to dominate, and power struggles get in the way of the task (dominant versus submissive);

281

- the atmosphere is overly negative and not conducive to cooperative effort (positive versus negative);
- members evidence little commitment to the task and are too flippant in their approach (serious versus expressive);
- the group lacks discipline and coordinated effort (conforming versus non-conforming).

In the final chapter of this book reference is made to transactional analysis and FIRO-B. Both are conceptual models that can be used to diagnose and manage the way people behave in group settings.

Performance strategies

How a group organises itself will have an important impact on how successful it will be in completing its task. Hackman (1987) argues that one of the key factors which will increase the likelihood of a group employing a task-appropriate performance strategy is the existence of a group norm which supports explicitly an assessment of alternative ways of proceeding with the task. Too often the possibility of adopting an alternative performance strategy is never considered. The routine is accepted as the inevitable. Even the purpose of the group can escape scrutiny, and in extreme cases some members may not know why they are there or may have completely different views to those held by their colleagues about the nature of the task confronting them.

When observing a group at work, is it worth asking ourselves whether the members have developed an approach to work which is fully appropriate for the task being performed? Note whether performance strategies are ever discussed explicitly or whether anyone ever initiates a review of how well the group is performing.

Many of the problems noted above can be avoided if members at least recognise the need to clarify group purpose and consider alternatives before selecting a performance strategy (a process which is likely to manifest itself through initiator, elaborator, evaluator and standard setter roles). At a fairly mechanistic level this may involve members of a board of directors deciding the kind of item to be included on the agenda (a reflection of purpose) and then, in terms of performance strategy, deciding about the information they should receive prior to a meeting, the preparatory work they should undertake, the procedures that should be employed during the meeting for exploring issues and making decisions and the steps to be taken to ensure that board members take the necessary action to implement decisions after the meeting.

More generally, the legitimacy of paying attention to such issues as clarifying purpose, identifying expertise, defining acceptable risk, promoting creativity and generating ideas, weighing alternatives, and gaining commitment to decisions needs to be established if the group is to be effective.

One aspect of performance strategy that deserves a more detailed discussion is decision making.

Decision making

Group decision making is often ineffective because group members do not possess the necessary information or task-relevant expertise and/or because they fail to behave rationally. These information deficits and irrational behaviours impair decision making by distorting the way problems are defined, influencing the nature and range of alternative solutions that are generated, and influencing the way the group evaluates and chooses between the available alternatives.

Reference has already been made to the way social pressures for conformity can result in irrational behaviour that leads to what Janis (1982) has described as 'groupthink'. The consequence is often poor decisions because little effort is given to the procurement of new information, only a handful of alternatives are considered, and those which are considered are evaluated inadequately. There is also a strong tendency for group members to maintain things as they are and to give little attention to contingency planning.

Harvey (1974) has identified a related process that he has labelled 'the Abilene Paradox'. This concerns the group's inability to manage agreement. He points to the tendency for some groups to take action which contradicts the desires of all of its members. The underlying dynamics of the paradox appear to be that while, individually, group members know what needs to be done to solve the problem, they are reluctant to take whatever action is required. This reluctance stems from the fear that their action will be disapproved of by others and that this disapproval will result in rejection. Consequently, each individual refrains from confronting others with their view of reality. It is each individual's failure to confront that results in the group making decisions which nobody agrees with. Each member goes along with and even actively contributes to bringing about a decision because they believe that everybody else agrees that this is the best way forward. The reality is that everybody agrees that it is not the best way forward but everybody behaves in a way that makes it impossible for this agreement to come to light.

Another phenomenon worthy of mention (referred to as risky-shift) is the tendency in some groups for members to make decisions which involve a higher level of risk than they would normally be inclined to accept if they were personally responsible for the decision. Stoner (1968) found that while individuals favoured relatively safe decisions which offered the prospect of moderate pay-offs, many groups tended to favour relatively risky decisions which offered the prospect of higher pay-offs. Several explanations have been advanced to account for this, including the possibility that the people who are inclined to take risks are more influential than conservative people

283

in group discussions; that risk taking is regarded as a desirable cultural characteristic, especially in some organisations, and that this characteristic is more likely to be expressed in group settings; and that responsibility for a group decision can more easily be attributed to others if something should go wrong.

Although non-assertive behaviour and a failure to confront can lead to problems in some groups, in others a major source of difficulty is overly aggressive behaviour and the attempt by some members to impose their view on others. This manifests itself in win-lose approaches to decision making, a consequence of which can be that members invest a great deal of their time and energy in promoting and defending their own, or their allies', preferred solution and attacking and undermining others. Ensuring that one's preferred solution is adopted can assume a much greater importance in the eyes of group members than ensuring that the best solution is chosen. This kind of approach to decision making can have enormous costs in terms of group cohesion, *esprit de corps* and member commitment to group decisions.

This brief review of some of the factors that can undermine the effectiveness of group decision-making procedures emphasises the importance of ensuring that the group adopts appropriate performance strategies, especially in relation to decision making. One of the factors we might consider when evaluating the efficacy of decision-making processes is the range of alternative solutions that the group typically generates: a feature of groupthink is that only one or a small handful of (often similar) alternatives are considered. Another is the way that the group weighs and evaluates alternative solutions. All four of the phenomena discussed above (groupthink, the Abilene Paradox, risky-shift and aggressive win–lose battles) evidence weaknesses that are associated with the way alternatives are evaluated. It is also worth paying attention to the availability and use made of relevant knowledge and expertise.

Taking action to improve group decision making

Diagnosing the appropriateness of current decision-making procedures involves observing how the group defines problems, generates ideas and evaluates alternatives. It also involves observing the effect these activities have on the quality of decisions, and on the feelings and behaviours of those involved in making and implementing them. Figure 11.7 offers a diagnostic check-list which we can use to help highlight some aspects of the decision-making processes that may require attention.

In some groups there is a reluctance to challenge the way problems are defined, whereas in others definitions are always discussed, clarified and elaborated. Sometimes it depends on who it is in the group who presents the problem. We should note whether members are reluctant to challenge the

Definition of problem understood by all	NO	☐☐☐	YES
Number of ideas generated	FEW	☐☐☐	MANY
Quality of ideas/creativity	LOW	☐☐☐	HIGH
Pressure for conformity	HIGH	☐☐☐	LOW
Willingness to listen to others	LOW	☐☐☐	HIGH
Openness to disconfirming data	CLOSED	☐☐☐	OPEN
Level of risk inherent in decision	LOW	☐☐☐	HIGH
Commitment of members to decision	LOW	☐☐☐	HIGH

Figure 11.7 Group decision-making check-list.

way problems are defined when they are presented by some members rather than by others, and consider how the decision-making process may be modified to reduce this tendency.

We should also pay attention to the quantity and quality of ideas and alternative solutions that are generated by the group. Some groups latch on to, develop and go on to implement the first solution they come up with, without ever considering whether alternative solutions might be better. If too few ideas are generated or if the group appears to lack creativity, think about how the decision-making procedure may be modified to overcome this. Look also for evidence of risky-shift factors influencing decision making and consider whether they help or hinder the quality of decisions.

Attempt to assess the impact of group norms and interpersonal conflict. Creativity may be low because of strong pressures to conform. Similar pressures may make it difficult for some members to confront the way solutions are defined, especially so for those who are non-assertive. Power plays between individuals and subgroups and attempts to dominate might also induce win–lose rather than win-win approaches to decision making. People may be closed to ideas other than their own and reject data which disconfirms their own view. Modifying the decision-making process, possibly by introducing more formality and restricting the opportunities for open discussion, may offer a way of minimising these problems.

Paying attention to such outcomes as feelings of accomplishment, group cohesiveness and members' commitment to decisions may also point to the need to modify the decision-making procedure.

Improving your ability to work with groups

This final section of the chapter contains two exercises that can be used to help you develop the skills necessary to work effectively with groups (Exercises 11.2 and 11.3). The format of these exercises is often referred to as a 'fishbowl' because one group is located in the centre of the room, surrounded by members of a second group who observe how members of the first group behave.

Exercise 11.2 Fishbowl: Group on group

Aims

1   To practise observing how people behave in group settings and identifying the effect this has on group performance (practise diagnostic skills).
2   To participate in a group discussion (practise action skills).
3   To practise giving and receiving feedback (see the guidelines presented in Chapter 8).

Procedure

Divide into two groups (suggested maximum number in each group about nine). If the class size is greater than eighteen, pairs of groups can engage in the exercise simultaneously. Times can be adjusted if required.

One group sits in a circle and discusses an assigned topic. The other group sits around the outside of the 'fishbowl' and observes members of the first group as they work on the assigned task.

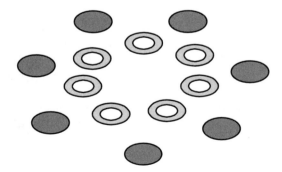

The group in the 'fishbowl' spends 15 to 20 minutes discussing an assigned topic.

At the end of this period, members of the observer group spend 10 to 15 minutes sharing (with members of the group in the fishbowl) their observations about how well they worked together on the assigned task.

When this procedure has been completed, the pairs of groups can exchange places and repeat the process.

Finally, members of both groups should review what they have learned from this exercise.

Discussion topics (select one)

1   Agree on the most and least useful aspects of this course on inter-personal skills.
2   Think about your experience on this course and about how people have behaved when working in groups. Agree a rank-ordered list of those behaviours that have made the *greatest contribution* to group effectiveness.
3   Think about your experience on this course and about how people have behaved when working in groups. Agree a rank-ordered list of those behaviours that have *done most to undermine* group effec-tiveness.

What to observe

1   *Clarity of group objectives*: Did everybody in the group have a shared understanding of the group's task?
2   *Effort and involvement*: Did all members of the group work hard on the task? Was everybody involved?
3   *Leadership and influence*: Were leadership functions shared by all members or concentrated in one or two persons? Was control imposed on group members or widely shared?
4   *Weighting of member contributions*: Were contributions welcomed and sought from everybody or only from a favoured few?
5   *Listening:* Did members listen to each other?
6   *Conflict management:* How were differences of opinion managed?
7   *Decision making:* How were decisions made? Did the group seek consensus, did a majority view prevail or did a minority impose their view on others?

Overall: What were the group's strong and weak points?

Exercise 11.3 involves one person focusing attention on a particular individual in the inner circle.

Exercise 11.3 Fishbowl: Individual on individual

The 'fishbowl format' can be adapted in a number of ways. Instead of asking participants in the outer group to observe everybody in the inner group, individuals may be assigned one particular person to observe and to give feedback to that person based on their observations.

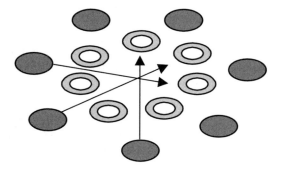

The advantage of this format is that the observer can devote more attention to observing a single person and can practise coding all aspects of that person's behaviour.

Observers may comment on any aspect of behaviour. If your observer focuses on role functions, for example, you might consider the feedback you receive and:

1　Reflect on the role functions you typically perform when working in a group and identify those that you tend to under- or over-use.
2　Seek out opportunities to change your behaviour. You might decide to make less use of one or more of the role functions you typically over-use, or make more use of those you under-use.
3　After you have practised these new ways of behaving, observe the consequences of the changes you have made.

Summary

This chapter provides a set of guidelines designed to help you work more effectively in groups. The underlying theme has been that, to achieve this end, you need to develop diagnostic skills that will help you identify the group's strengths and weaknesses, and action skills that will enable you to intervene to correct weaknesses and, where appropriate, build on strengths.

The first part of the chapter identified effort, knowledge and skill, and performance strategies as the key variables affecting group performance. The way in which group interaction processes affect each of these was explored in order to generate a range of indicators that could be used when interpreting data about behaviour in groups and when planning appropriate interventions to improve group performance.

The second part of the chapter introduced a number of ways of observing and recording behaviour in groups. Particular attention was paid to the frequency and duration of communication, communication patterns, role functions, interpersonal style and group climate, performance strategies and decision-making procedures. Suggestions about how these observations can be used to diagnose problems together with indications of how the diagnosis can be used to plan alternative ways of behaving were also offered.

References

Belbin, R.M. (1981) *Management Teams: Why They Succeed or Fail*, London: Heinemann.

Belbin, R.M. (1993a) 'A reply to the Belbin Team Role Self-Perception Inventory by Furnham, Steele and Pendleton', *Journal of Occupational and Organizational Psychology* 66: 411–424.

Belbin, R.M. (1993b) *Team Roles at Work*, London: Heinemann.

Benne, K.D. and Sheates, P. (1948) 'Functional roles of group members', *Journal of Social Issues* 2: 42–47.

Deutsch, M. (1949) 'A theory of co-operation and competition', *Human Relations* 2 (2): 129–159.

Deutsch, M. (1960) 'The effects of co-operation and competition on group processes', in D. Cartwright and A. Zander (eds) *Group Dynamics*, New York: Harper & Row, pp. 414–448.

Furnham, A., Steele, H. and Pendleton, D. (1993a) 'A psychometric assessment of the Belbin Team Role Self-Perception Inventory', *Journal of Occupational and Organizational Psychology* 66: 245–257.

Furnham, A., Steele, H. and Pendleton, D. (1993b) 'A response to Dr Belbin's reply', *Journal of Occupational and Organizational Psychology* 66: 261.

Hackman, J.R. (1987) 'The design of work teams', in J.W. Lorsch (ed.) *Handbook of Organizational Behaviour*, Englewood Cliffs, NJ: Prentice Hall.

Hackman, J.R. and Oldham, G.R. (1980) *Work Redesign*, Reading, MA: Addison-Wesley.

Handy, C.B. (1985) *Understanding Organizations*, Harmondsworth: Penguin Books.

Hare, A.P. (1982) *Creativity in Small Groups*, Beverly Hills, CA: Sage.

Harvey, J.B. (1974) 'The Abilene Paradox: the management of agreement', *Organizatiional Dynamics* summer: 63–80.

Hayes, N. (1997) *Successful Team Management*, London: International Thompson Business Press.

Janis, I.L. (1982) *Groupthink* (2nd edn), Boston, MA: Houghton Mifflin.

Katzenback, J.R. and Smith, D.K. (1993) *The Wisdom of Teams: Creating the High Performance Organisation*, Boston, MA: Harvard Business School Press.

Latane, B., Williams, K. and Hoskins, S. (1979) 'Many hands make light work: the causes and consequences of social loafing', *Journal of Personality and Social Psychology* 37: 822–832.

Senior, B. (1997) 'Team roles and team performance: is there "really" a link?', *Journal of Occupational and Organizational Psychology* 70: 241–258.

Senior, B. (1998) 'An empirically-based assessment of Belbin's team roles', *Human Resource Management Journal* 8 (3): 54–60.

Senior, B. and Swailes, S. (1998) 'A comparison of the Belbin Self-Perception Inventory and Observer's Assessment Sheet as measures of an individual's team roles', *International Journal of Selection and Assessment* 6 (1): 1–8.

Stoner, J. (1968) 'Risky and cautious shifts in group decisions: the influence of widely held values', *Journal of Experimental Social Psychology* 4: 442–459.

West, M.A. (1994) *Effective Teamwork*, Leicester: BPS Books.

12

MANAGING RELATIONSHIPS
MORE EFFECTIVELY

Learning objectives

To develop an awareness of conceptual models that can provide a holistic view of social interaction and facilitate the reading of behaviour and the constructing of courses of action that will bring about desired outcomes.

After reading this chapter you will:

- Be more aware of roles and role relationships.
- Recognise some of the signals that enable people to diagnose the roles that others are assuming.
- Be familiar with the basics of transactional analysis and understand how ego states can affect interpersonal transactions.
- Recognise how interpersonal needs can affect reciprocal compatibility and the quality of relationships.

Managing relationships more effectively

This book offers a series of conceptual frameworks which can be used for reading the behaviour of others and for constructing conduct that will increase the probability that desired outcomes will be achieved. Interpersonal skill refers to the nature of such conduct and is defined as goal-directed behaviours used in face-to-face interactions which are effective in bringing about a desired state of affairs.

While broad areas of interpersonal skill have been considered under a series of chapter headings such as listening, information getting, helping and negotiating, attention has also been focused on smaller units of behaviour such as attending, probing and giving feedback. It was noted in Chapter 2 that an effective approach to the development of interpersonal skills focuses, in the first instance, on these smaller units of behaviour. This is a micro-skills approach to skill development.

From micro skills to a more macro perspective

A recurring theme, introduced in Chapter 1 and developed in later chapters, is the need to pay attention to the ways in which the nature of relationships can affect outcomes. In Chapter 6, for example, it was argued that it would be naive to view the interview simply in terms of one person asking questions and getting information from another. The interview is a social encounter in which the willingness of one party to provide full, honest and accurate answers to the questions asked by another is influenced by a number of factors.

One of these factors is the way the respondent defines the situation and role of the interviewer. In the selection interview the job applicant is likely to accept the interviewer's right to ask questions and feel obliged to give appropriate answers. This may not be the case if the same questions were asked by a ticket collector on a railway train. However, the context of the interaction and the role of the person asking the questions is not the only factor that will determine the kind of answer the respondent will give. The respondent's perception of the interviewer's attitudes, feelings and behaviour will also be important.

We tend to weigh the costs and benefits of behaving in particular ways before deciding how to act.

- If job applicants in a selection interview feel that their interviewers are behaving like critical parents and evaluating all they say, they may distort their answers or provide only carefully selected information so that the interviewers will view them in the best possible light.
- In a performance appraisal interview, subordinates who feel a need for more direction and guidance may offer their appraiser/boss more information than subordinates who feel that they are being subjected to too much detailed supervision and who feel a need to maintain as much autonomy as possible.

The aim of this concluding chapter is to develop these themes and to point to further areas of study that will help the reader develop a more holistic view of social interaction.

Role theory

The way people interpret situations and perceive others will influence how they will behave towards the people they encounter. It will also influence how they expect others to behave towards them. For example, the way a new employee behaves towards somebody s/he meets for the first time will depend upon whether this other person is perceived to be a boss, colleague or subordinate. The other's role will also influence how s/he expects them to behave in return. Perhaps the new employee expects a subordinate to pay more attention to what s/he says than either a boss or a colleague.

Millar and Gallagher (1997) argue that the selection interview may be conceptualised in terms of a set of rules and roles. Tuller (1989), for example, notes that interviewers typically offer applicants the opportunity to ask questions at the end of the interview, and most applicants recognise that responding to this kind of invitation and asking some intelligent-sounding questions may not be an option they can afford to ignore if they are to impress. Interviewees from Asian cultures, however, may be taken completely by surprise by such an invitation. They might not conceive of the role of interviewee as one which allows the role occupant to ask questions. As Millar and Gallagher note, the potential for misunderstandings and miscommunication in this kind of situation is considerable and, in the case of this example, the Asian job applicant may create a poor impression by declining the offer to ask questions (see Sarangi 1994).

Handy (1985) illustrates the importance of roles in social interaction with reference to the way Charles Marlow behaves towards Mr Hardcastle in *She Stoops to Conquer*. Marlow is under the impression that Hardcastle is the innkeeper and therefore behaves towards him according to his stereotype of the role of innkeeper. However, Hardcastle is not the innkeeper. He is Marlow's prospective father-in-law and he behaves towards Marlow in a manner appropriate to a future son-in-law. As Handy reports, the ensuing bewilderment and frustration on the part of the two characters who both receive information that so vehemently conflicts with their stereotypes of the other's role is great entertainment for the audience who are party to the role confusion. Marlow and Hardcastle were bewildered because their behaviour towards the other did not produce the anticipated response. Their role expectations were not confirmed.

The example of Marlow and Hardcastle illustrates the point that people play many roles. Sometimes it is relatively easy for one person to identify the role being played by another. A man in a blue uniform in a car fitted with blue flashing lights is likely to be a police officer. Costume, terms of address, the words they use, body language and other cues provide the signs that designate roles. However, there are some occasions when it is difficult to determine another's role, particularly if that person is known to occupy a range of different roles and when the available role signs are ambiguous. Even within the course of a relatively short period of time the same person can play many roles. Before arriving at work in the morning a worker may have played the roles of spouse, parent, passenger, friend and customer. These roles are not necessarily tied to situations or relationships. Role relationships may change within the context of the same conversation. In the early stages of a conversation two negotiators may relate as friends before they eventually 'get down to business'. Two people may sometimes have the opportunity to conduct their interactions in terms of several different role relationships. The same two people may be husband and wife, subordinate and boss or political rivals. This kind of situation heightens the chance of the people involved experiencing role ambiguity and role conflict.

Role ambiguity arises whenever a person is unclear what role s/he should play in a situation or what role somebody else is playing. Role conflict arises when a person has the possibility of playing two incompatible roles at the same time. For example, a policewoman may observe her brother committing a crime and have to decide whether to play the role of police officer and apprehend the criminal or the role of sister and protect her brother from the force of the law. The offending brother may also be faced with a dilemma, especially if he is unclear what role his sister is likely to perform. Does he attack the police officer in an attempt to escape or appeal to his sister for help?

People use role signs (for example, speech and body language) to signal the role they have in mind for themselves. Others are sometimes happy to accept a person's definition of their own role but this need not always be the case. For example, when a sales executive and a product development engineer meet to consider their approach to an important customer they plan to visit later in the day, the marketing executive may see the customer visit as *his* meeting and signal to the product development engineer that she should follow his lead. The engineer, on the other hand, may be convinced that it should be *her* meeting because the profitability of the deal depends upon agreeing the right product specification. She may therefore reject the role the marketing executive proffers for himself and respond in an uncooperative manner to his assertive behaviours. Her lack of cooperation may force the marketing executive to redefine his role and persuade him to adopt a more conciliatory and egalitarian response to his colleague.

Developing a better awareness of role relationships and the ways others interpret roles can help a person construct conduct that has a greater probability of leading to desired outcomes.

Transactional analysis

Transactional analysis provides a useful model for understanding the nature of interpersonal relationships. It was pioneered by Eric Berne (1964: 72), and offers a theory of personality that can be used for analysing the nature of interpersonal relationships or 'transactions'. Personality is presented in terms of three ego states: parent, adult and child. When people initiate transactions with others they do so from one of these ego states. They also point their transaction towards a particular ego state of the others. In transactional analysis the structure of personality is presented diagrammatically as three circles (see Figure 12.1).

The balance of these ego states may vary from person to person and for the same person from time to time. According to Berne, it is the ego state that predominates which determines behaviour. On one occasion a person may behave as an adult and on another occasion the same person may behave as a critical parent.

294

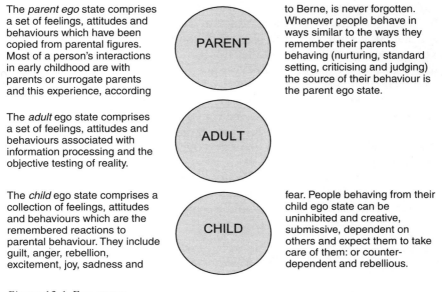

The *parent ego* state comprises a set of feelings, attitudes and behaviours which have been copied from parental figures. Most of a person's interactions in early childhood are with parents or surrogate parents and this experience, according to Berne, is never forgotten. Whenever people behave in ways similar to the ways they remember their parents behaving (nurturing, standard setting, criticising and judging) the source of their behaviour is the parent ego state.

The *adult* ego state comprises a set of feelings, attitudes and behaviours associated with information processing and the objective testing of reality.

The *child* ego state comprises a collection of feelings, attitudes and behaviours which are the remembered reactions to parental behaviour. They include guilt, anger, rebellion, excitement, joy, sadness and fear. People behaving from their child ego state can be uninhibited and creative, submissive, dependent on others and expect them to take care of them: or counter-dependent and rebellious.

Figure 12.1 Ego states.

This model can be usefully employed to improve people's awareness of their own personal style and how this can affect the quality of social interaction. As noted above, the basic unit of behaviour is referred to as a *transaction*. It involves one person doing or saying something to another and the other responding. By paying attention to the nature of a transaction it is possible to diagnose the ego state from which it originated. For example, transactions originating from the Critical Parent ego state are often spoken in a critical condescending way, and include the frequent use of words such as never, should, ought and don't. They are often accompanied by non-verbal behaviours such as frowning and pointing. The attitudes being expressed by such transactions tend to be judgemental and authoritarian.

Transactions originating from the adult ego state tend to be associated with a confident voice, thoughtful or interested expression and include words such as where? why? what? The attitude of the person behaving in an adult manner tends to be open and/or evaluative.

In contrast, the free child ego state tends to be the source of transactions which are spontaneous, uninhibited and expressed in an excited voice.

This structural analysis of personality provides a basis for analysing and understanding the nature of interactions. According to Berne, every interaction between people involves a transaction between their ego states. The originator of a transaction targets their behaviour at a particular ego state in the other person and assumes that the recipient will respond from the targeted ego state. When this happens the transaction is described as a parallel transaction. For example, when a manager asks a secretary where the telephone directory is the transaction may be originated from the adult ego state and targeted at the secretary's adult ego state (see Figure 12.2). The transaction will be a parallel transaction when the secretary replies with a response from the adult ego state that is targeted at the manager's adult ego state: 'You lent it to Bob' (see Figure 12.3). However, if the manager fails to hook the targeted ego state in the secretary, the transaction will be crossed. An example of a crossed transaction would be if the secretary replies from the parent ego state and targets the child ego state of the manager: 'How come you can never find things when you want them?' (see Figure 12.4).

In crossed transactions the originator of the messages receives a response from an unexpected ego state, whereas in parallel transactions the originator receives an expected response from the ego state that was targeted.

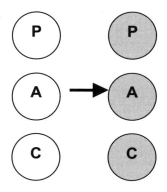

Figure 12.2 Manager to secretary: 'Where is the telephone directory?'

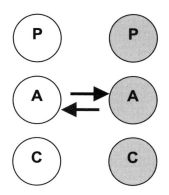

Figure 12.3 Secretary to manager (parallel transaction): 'You lent it to Bob.'

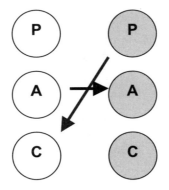

Figure 12.4 Secretary to manager (crossed transaction): 'How come you can never find things when you want them?'

Transactional analysis offers a useful model for understanding and improving interactions by helping people identify the ego states that tend to be the source of their transactions in particular situations or with certain individuals. If people decide, on reflection, that the source of some of their transactions adversely affects outcomes, they may attempt to modify the ego state from which they originate their transactions.

For example, a person who has taken a day off work to await the arrival of a telephone engineer to install a new telephone may feel let down when the engineer fails to turn up. The customer's normal response in such a situation may have been to phone the telephone company and issue a stern rebuke (i.e. to engage in a transaction originated from the critical parent ego state and targeted at the compliant child ego state of the company's customer service manager). However, the customer may remember that in the past such complaints have resulted in acrimonious arguments and little action. On this occasion, therefore, the customer may deliberately decide to originate the transaction from the child ego state and target it at the nurturing parent ego state of the customer service manager. S/he may explain that s/he lives alone in a large, isolated house and that s/he is afraid of intruders at night. This may motivate the customer service manager to do everything possible to help the customer feel more secure.

Thinking about interactions in terms of ego states can yield useful diagnostic information that can be used to manage relationships more effectively. Only a very brief review of some of the most basic ideas of transactional analysis is presented here, but it at least illustrates how important it is to pay attention to the personalities of those involved in social interactions.

Interpersonal needs

Schutz (1958) advanced the notion that the needs of people engaged in social interactions can be an important determinant of the quality of the relationship. He focuses attention on three basic interpersonal needs: inclusion, control and affection.

1   *Inclusion* refers to the need to be with people or to be alone, to have enough contact to avoid loneliness and enough aloneness to avoid enmeshment and enjoy solitude.
2   *Control* refers to decision-making processes between people and areas of power, influence and authority. It involves the need to achieve enough influence to be able to control important outcomes and to be able to relinquish enough control to be able to lean on others and allow them to take responsibility for outcomes.
3   *Affection* refers to close personal emotional feelings such as love and hate. It involves the need to avoid being engulfed in emotional entanglements and the need to avoid having too little affection and a life without love and warmth.

Schutz makes an interesting distinction between *expressed behaviour* – the behaviour we feel comfortable expressing towards other people – and *wanted behaviour* – the behaviour we want from others (i.e. the behaviour we want them to express towards us). He developed FIRO-B (Fundamental Interpersonal Relations Orientation-Behaviour), an instrument that explores the levels of behaviour that people are comfortable with in relation to these three needs. He argues that people have different levels of need. In terms of wanted behaviour, if they experience more than their preferred need for inclusion they will feel crowded, whereas if they experience less than their preferred need they will feel left out. If they experience more than their preferred need for control they will feel pushed, whereas if they experience less they will feel that they are not being offered sufficient direction. Similarly, if they experience more than their preferred need for affection they will feel smothered, whereas if they experience less they will feel unloved and rejected.

The success of a relationship is affected by the degree to which the parties to the relationship see the potential for satisfying their needs (reciprocal compatibility). For example, a person who has a high need for expressed control is likely to attempt to exert control and influence others. If s/he relates to others who have a high need for wanted control the relationship is more likely to be mutually satisfying than if s/he relates to others who have a low need for wanted control. People with a high need for wanted control are comfortable when somebody else tells them what to do, and are therefore likely to respond positively to those people who want to take charge. If, on the other hand, both parties to the relationship have a high need to control others and a low need to be controlled then the relationship is less likely to be satisfying for either party. They will both want to take control and tell the other what to do and they will both resist accepting directions from the other. In such circumstances there will be a high probability that their goal-directed behaviour will fail to produce desired outcomes.

Being aware of why a relationship is not as satisfying as it might be offers the possibility of managing the relationship more effectively. If the stakes are judged to be high enough to justify the effort, one of the parties involved may decide to modify their behaviour, adapt to the situation and, for example, allow the other person to take control. On the other hand they may both agree to modify their behaviour, and they may seek to identify areas where they are compatible and to build on these.

Managing relationships more effectively

The conceptual models presented in this final chapter provide a basis for understanding why some goal-directed behaviours may be less successful than others or why relationships with certain individuals may be more satisfactory than relationships with others. These models suggest a range of diagnostic questions and action strategies that offer a basis for managing relationships more effectively.

Role theory focuses attention on the roles people play and the ways they perceive the roles played by others. Sometimes it may be possible to improve a relationship if people signal more clearly the roles that they think are appropriate for themselves and others and if they challenge what they believe to be inappropriate role expectations and behaviours.

Transactional analysis may also offer an alternative perspective and suggest ways in which desired goals may be achieved more effectively. For example, a manager's lack of success in negotiations may be attributed to a tendency (when negotiating with people who originate transactions from their parent ego state) to allow others to hook the manager into responding from the compliant child ego state. The way forward may be for the manager to modify this response pattern and to respond from the adult ego state. Deliberately crossing transactions in this way can have the effect of forcing the other negotiator to follow the manager's lead, and to engage in a parallel transaction by also originating transactions from own and targeting them at the other's adult ego state.

An awareness of own and others' needs can enable people to assess what they should do to make their behaviour more effective. For example, if managers are aware that they have a high need to exert control they may be alert to the possibility that their helping/mentoring style may be too prescriptive.

Conclusion

Interpersonal competence involves the ability to understand the nature of social interactions, to be able to read behaviour, and to act in ways that will bring about desired outcomes. This book provides a clearly structured and comprehensive overview of the interpersonal skills essential for effective functioning in a business environment. Some broad conceptual frameworks that offer different ways of thinking about social interaction are presented in Chapter 1 and in this chapter. These conceptual frameworks point to a range of diagnostic questions that we can use to help us hone our interpersonal competence. The hierarchical model of interpersonal skill that underpins the micro-skills approach to skill development (which is the core theme of this book) is elaborated in Chapter 2. The ways in which an awareness of self and others affects interpersonal competence are discussed in Chapter 3.

Chapters 4 to 7 focus on core skills that are important in their own right (listening, listening to non-verbal messages, questioning and information getting, and presenting information to others). Each of these core skills involves many elements (micro skills) but they also form an important element of more complex skills. Some of these more complex skills (helping, asserting and influencing, negotiating and working with groups) are discussed in Chapters 8 to 11.

While the content of this book is grounded in theory and solid empirical data, it does not attempt to offer a searching critique of theories or a detailed exposition of empirical studies. The aim of the book is to facilitate the development of interpersonal competence. Selected theories and concepts that are widely regarded for their practical utility are presented as a vehicle for achieving this end. An important feature of the book is the wide range of exercises that have been designed to help us explore our interpersonal competence, and to practise and evaluate new ways of relating to others.

References

Berne, E. (1964) *Games People Play*, New York: Grove Press.

Berne, E. (1972) *What Do You Say After You Say Hello?*, London: Corgi.

Handy, C. (1985) *Understanding Organisations*, London: Penguin Business Books.

Millar, R. and Gallagher, M. (1997) 'The selection interview', in O.D.W. Hargie, *The Handbook of Communication Skills* (2nd edn), London: Routledge.

Sarangi, S. (1994) 'Accounting for mismatches in intercultural selection interviews', *Multilingua* 13: 163–194.

Schutz, W.C. (1958) *FIRO: A Three Dimensional Theory of Interpersonal Behaviour*, New York: Holt Rinehart. (Reprinted 1966 as *The Interpersonal Underworld*, Palo Alto, CA: Science and Behaviour Books.)

Tuller, W.L. (1989) 'The employment interview as a cognitive performing script', in R.W. Eder and G.R. Ferris (eds) *The Employment Interview: Theory Research and Practice*, Newbury Park, CA: Sage.

AUTHOR INDEX

Page numbers in brackets indicate where the full reference can be found. There are some entries that are only bracketed. This indicates that the entry refers to a co-author who was not cited in the text.

SUBJECT INDEX